OTHER BOOKS BY THOMAS KIERNAN

❊ ❊ ❊

The Secretariat Factor

Arafat

The Arabs

The Miracle of Coogan's Bluff

Shrinks, Etc.

Jane

Oh My Aching Back

Who's Who in the History of Philosophy

The Negro Impact on Western Civilization (Editor)

The History of Psychiatry and Psychology

THE
INTRICATE
MUSIC

THE INTRICATE MUSIC

A Biography of John Steinbeck

THOMAS KIERNAN

LITTLE, BROWN AND COMPANY   Boston ✳ Toronto

FIRST EDITION

LIBRARY OF CONGRESS CATALOGING IN PUBLICATION DATA

Kiernan, Thomas.
   The intricate music.

   Includes bibliographical references and index.
   1. Steinbeck, John, 1902–1968–Biography.
   2. Authors, American–20th century–Biography.
   I. Title.
PS3537.T3234Z716 813'.5'2 [B] 79–12595
ISBN 0–316–49202–7

The author is grateful to the following publishers and individuals for permission
to reprint material as noted below:

Chronicle Books for passages from *John Steinbeck: The Errant Knight* by
Nelson Valjean, 1975.

Farrar, Straus & Giroux, Inc. for passages from *The Acts of King Arthur and
His Noble Knights* by John Steinbeck, from the Winchester Mss. of Thomas
Malory and Other Sources, edited by Chase Horton.

The John Steinbeck Collection in the Department of Special Collections,
Cecil H. Green Library, Stanford University, Stanford, California.

The Viking Press for passages from *Travels with Charley* by John Steinbeck,
copyright © 1961, 1962 by the Curtis Publishing Co., Inc., copyright © 1962
by John Steinbeck, and from *Steinbeck: A Life in Letters,* ed. Elaine Steinbeck and Robert Wallsten, copyright © 1975 by Elaine A. Steinbeck and
Robert Wallsten. All rights reserved, reprinted by permission.

MV

Designed by Janis Capone

*Published simultaneously in Canada
by Little, Brown & Company (Canada) Limited*

PRINTED IN THE UNITED STATES OF AMERICA

For Padraic and Joshua

❋ ❋ ❋ ❋ ❋ ❋ ❋ INTRODUCTION

As *a literature student in college in the early 1920s, John* Steinbeck took a liking to the work of James Branch Cabell, a noted author of the period. As a struggling young writer not long after, Steinbeck was offered the chance to personally meet his literary hero. He declined, claiming that he did not want to risk disillusionment.

As a college literature student in the mid-1950s, I took a liking to the work of John Steinbeck. A few years later, given the opportunity to meet him, I jumped at it. I risked disillusionment. And I got it.

Part of my disillusionment derived from unrealistic expectations, to be sure. And part undoubtedly had to do with the fact that, unknown to me, Steinbeck was suffering at age fifty-seven from a dangerous physical ailment. Nevertheless, I found him to be a disagreeable man — politically pompous and literarily hostile, a person in whom vindictiveness and petty intolerance seemed to be the warp and woof of life. How, I wondered, could a man of such repugnant personality have written some of the most sensitive and expressive literature of our century?

However, I remained an ardent admirer of his work. As time went on, a curiosity grew in me about the disparity I perceived between Steinbeck the writer and Steinbeck the man I had met. I knew a lot about the writing. I wanted to know more about the person.

Fortunately, I had a second chance to meet him. During the mid-sixties I was an editor for a New York book publisher and was trying to put together an anthology of specially written short stories from the pens of a number of our major but aging writers. It was to be a commemorative volume that would celebrate the art these authors had given to our culture. I approached Steinbeck in the hope of persuading him to contribute.

He was older by eight years then and had only two years to live. During the course of a long discussion I found him considerably less disagreeable than at our first encounter. Yet there filtered through his speech and general demeanor the bile of a man profoundly unhappy with himself. His interest in contributing to my project was lukewarm at best, undoubtedly because, as he remarked to me, "It smacks of one of those Old Timers games you read about at Yankee Stadium. That kind of geriatric celebrity I don't need."

Recalling my curiosity about his life, I turned our talk to the question of biography. Had he ever thought of writing an autobiography? Yes, but he had decided against it. What about biography? He testily disclaimed interest in having his life studied by anyone else.

We talked further about it. It was an old literary axiom that a study of a notable writer's life can be the definitive clue to his art. Yet most of our important writers had gone to great pains to separate their personal lives from their work. Or at least to disabuse potential biographers of the idea that detailed examinations and analyses of their lives could yield significant insights into the origins and meanings of their art. I asked Steinbeck why he thought this was so. He held forth at length on the question. In the following, I do not quote him verbatim; rather,

I give the sense of what he said based on the notes I took afterward.

"There are two reasons," Steinbeck began. "One is that writers write out of recognition of their own personal failings. What I mean is that for them, the act of writing is an attempt to rectify what they see lacking in themselves. It's like a parent and child. The parent invariably brings up the child to be free of all those traits that he loathes in himself. It is when the child reveals through his behavior or personality that he possesses one of those traits, that the parent becomes most impatient with him. The parent wants the child to be all the things he's not. He wants him to be able to get all the approval, success, happiness he's never been able to. Since the parent can not receive satisfaction from the world directly because of his own personality failings, he seeks it vicariously through the child. The work of a writer is his child. The writer has not received, can not receive, the kind of personal satisfaction he wants from the world because of this, that, or the next personality quirk he is saddled with. So he seeks satisfaction vicariously, through his work. The work, the product, is the substitute for himself that he presents to the world. If he is lucky enough to have the world approve of it, applaud it, ask for more, then he becomes doubly insistent on shielding his real self from the world. Why? Because he is afraid that if the world is allowed to see his real self, it will no longer accept the idealized image presented through his work.

"Now I'm talking from my own experience. I've thought a lot about why I set out to write. Although I didn't know it at the time, I think I can say now that one of the big reasons was this: I instinctively recognized in writing an opportunity to transcend some of my personal failings — things about myself that I didn't particularly like and wanted to change but didn't know how. So it's my experience, but my experience isn't unique. Most writers I ever knew operated from the same motivation. It's not so much that serious writers are out to change the world — all that romantic crap you hear from the academics. It's that they're out to change the way the world perceives them as personalities, as people."

And what was the second reason Steinbeck had alluded to?

"The second thing is that writers are by their very nature private people, in many cases lonely, frightened, insecure, incapable of relating comfortably to other people. The entire act of writing is private and solitary. Writers themselves do not seek celebrity. Christ, when I walk down a street here in New York and some stranger recognizes me, I feel embarrassed, uncomfortable. I am a private person. Almost every good writer I know is. The ideal life for a writer is for his work to be celebrated and for himself to be unknown. That's not just coyness or false modesty. Writers thrive on privacy, many even on loneliness and despair. It's the writer's condition. Today, with television, you see writers who go out and get interviewed before millions of people to plug their books. Some of them are even becoming celebrities. I find the whole business ridiculous. Does it make them better writers? Worse writers? No, it has nothing to do with being writers. Except that by exposing their real selves to public scrutiny before that unforgiving camera eye, they run the risk of no longer being taken seriously. Take someone like Norman Mailer. The guy had a promising career as an important writer. Now he's no longer a writer, but a performer with a pen. Sure, television has revolutionized our life here. A lot of modern writers believe that to be 'with it' they have to go out and gain that kind of personal recognition, warts and all exposed for the entire country to see. But there's no way television can be compatible with what writing is all about. An accomplished writer writes ultimately for the sake of writing. Not in the art-for-art's-sake sense, for the writer will always be writing to be read by someone. But in the sense that it is a pure need, a compulsion based on what I described before — not to change the world but to change himself, or the way the world sees him. And because of this, no writer wants the world to see him in any other way than it sees him through his work."

What of the proposition, then, that a study of the writer's life can provide crucial insights into his works?

"I don't buy it," he answered. "In the first place, an auto-biography — forget it. Where's the challenge? I can't think of anything more boring than having to write about yourself. Any-way, anything I might have to say about myself, my observa-tions, my feelings about this or that, I have already said in a number of books.

"As for a biography — well, we go back to the proposition, and then to what I said about why writers write. Now it's fairly well known that I have had a long-standing fascination for marine life. Here comes a biographer, then, to write some 'in-depth' study of my life. The next thing you know he's saying that *Cannery Row* was written out of some deep-seated need to satisfy my curiosity about fish. I'm exaggerating, of course, but isn't that the net result of most biographies of people who have gained some degree of literary fame? Most of the time the biog-raphers are wrong, and in their silly psychoanalyzing they're wrong in the most ridiculous, laughable ways. What do I care if Mark Twain, according to some biographer, might have written 'Huck Finn' because his parents were stern puritans who deprived him of normal boyhood pleasures? What earthly clue is there to the frigid beauty of *The Red Badge of Courage* to know that Crane might have written it to expunge his guilt for his own cowardly behavior as a soldier? The fact that it was written, that it exists, is all that's really important. As a piece of writing it needs no motivational analysis. All the reasons for its existence lie in its essence. Sure, I'll read a biography of Crane. Not because I'm seeking clues to the meanings of what he wrote, but because I'm interested in learning what his problems as a writer might have been. That is, the problems between his estimate of his real self and his hopes for what he wanted his real self to be. Out of that process of problem resolution there develops in every writer a storytelling imagination — which is what I'd really be interested in when reading about the life of any writer. Not the why, but the how. How this particular imagination, this particular creative organism developed and expanded, set up ever-increasingly complex storytelling problems and overcame them or didn't overcome them. Of course, no writer can explain his technique. Nor should he be obliged to. And if *he* can't, why should someone else presume to.

"It gets back to the fact that writing is utterly personal, utterly private. Take a baseball analogy. You go out and watch Willie Mays play center field. You marvel at his gifts, are grateful for the fact that someone like him exists to lift you the way he does, and you feel that you really get something out of watching him play, some solid sense of truth and perfection and grace. So you rush out and buy a biography of Mr. Mays and you learn that he grew up underprivileged on some dusty sandlot in Alabama, that he didn't get very much of an education, that his syntax stinks as a result and he's timid with girls. Does that make you appreciate Mays the center fielder any more or less? Of course not. Willie Mays is an entity unto himself, and you take your joy from his performance.

"The same with a writer. I don't need a biography to enhance my work. Or detract from it. The work is understood and judged on its own. Clues? What outside clues are required if the work is worthwhile? If it is worthwhile, it will contain its own clues.

"However" — and here Steinbeck raised a finger in a mock-admonitory fashion — "if somebody wanted to write my biography with a view to showing me exactly how my storytelling imagination evolved, I might be interested in reading it. If they could take the yin and the yang of my personal development, the real self versus the idealized self, and show how the two interacted to form my impulse to write, and then how that impulse spawned a raw imagination and awkward technique that over the years gained the virtue of becoming only a little less raw and awkward, I would be very pleased to learn all this. Trouble is, by the time anyone was able to come up with a comprehendible formulation I would be long gone from this planet and it wouldn't do me a bit of good."

Of the major writers who arrived and flourished in what is often called the golden age of American literature — the 1920s and 1930s — John Steinbeck has largely been ignored by biographers. This is as he wanted it. As is evident from the above, he distrusted literary biography in general. And he was elsewhere outspoken on the question of potential biographies of himself, even at an early age. After the publication of Steinbeck's first book, *Cup of Gold*, in 1929, an acquaintance, Nelson Valjean, also a budding writer, suggested that someday he might want to write Steinbeck's biography.

"A shy person who valued personal privacy above all else," Valjean has said, "he asked me not to."[1] Steinbeck remained unwavering in his resistance to biographical treatment while he was alive, and was not very pleased about the prospect of one or more posthumous biographies.

When he dismissed the idea in his later years, he was not merely concerned with his personal privacy. According to Robert Wallsten, a close friend who co-edited a recently published volume of Steinbeck's selected letters, "John's animadversions on the matter of a biography emanated at least partly, I would guess, from his concern for the value of his estate. He was fairly secure in his position as a writer who was being 'studied' in the schools, which meant that his accumulation of books, especially the older ones, continued to sell, providing him with very nice royalties. He wanted that situation to continue so that after he died, the royalties would keep on flowing to Elaine [his widow]. He was afraid in the last few years that a biography after he was dead would somehow come out to make him look bad and therefore damage his reputation, thus compromising the interest in his books and causing the royalties to stop. That's the main reason he was against a biography. On the other hand, I think he recognized that a biography done by hands which he could trust might well serve to enhance his reputation and kindle even wider interest in his books. There were several potential biographers he trusted, but he also knew that they were almost too trustworthy. That is, they were so loyal and admiring that anything they wrote would be attacked for being too soft and uncritical. The net effect would be just as damaging as an 'unfriendly' biography. It was a Hobson's choice for John, and he resolved it finally by just rejecting the idea of a biography altogether and leaving it in Elaine's hands to deal with once he was gone."[2]

The book of letters that Wallsten edited in conjunction with Elaine Steinbeck certainly provides an insight into Steinbeck's life. It is immensely worth reading, even to someone with no prior interest in Steinbeck. Yet because it was culled from a much larger body of Steinbeck's correspondence, and was carefully edited by two people understandably acting in what they took to be Steinbeck's best interests, its effect is only equivalent to a glimpse into his life. This despite the fact that its publisher has promoted the book as obviating the need for a full-scale biography. I had a chance to examine the original typescript of the book prior to its abridgment, and I think it is safe to say that it provides us with a mere taste of John Steinbeck as a man. As Robert Wallsten conceded to me, "Even though I was heavily involved in the work on the book, and am proud of what Elaine and I accomplished, it is ridiculous for anyone to suppose that a heavily edited selection of a man's letters is a substitute for a good biography."

It is hard to disagree. Even had the letters contained in the book not been carefully selected and edited to form a particular image of Steinbeck the man, they would still be a poor substitute for an independent outsider's competent recounting of his life. The letters a man writes over the span of his life (and Steinbeck wrote thousands), whether or not he intends them for posthumous publication, are inevitably self-conscious and self-serving. We would get a much different view of Richard

Nixon, for instance, if we had to rely on a reading of his correspondence — or memoirs, for that matter — than that which history has provided us.

This is the first full-scale biography of John Steinbeck to be published. But not the first to be written. Shortly after her husband's death, Elaine Steinbeck agreed to cooperate with Professor Jackson Benson of San Diego State University in his desire to write a biography. Because of her commitment to Professor Benson, Mrs. Steinbeck felt that it would be a breach of etiquette and possibly of ethics to cooperate with me. Nevertheless she has indirectly done so, for which I extend to her my gratitude.

Many others who knew John Steinbeck, either intimately or casually, have also helped. A list of their names would be of no interest to the reader, but I would single out for thanks the aforementioned Robert Wallsten, who knew John Steinbeck well in his later years and was able to make me understand and sympathize with the reasons behind the disagreeable idiosyncrasies of his personality.

I set out to write this biography because of my admiration for Steinbeck's works as a writer and my desire to understand him as a man. Heretofore, there has been nothing in print, aside from his own books, that could give me that understanding. In writing this book, I have tried to follow his veiled prescription to me of many years ago about how he would have liked to see a biography of himself — a book that would convey an insight into the causative evolution of his art and craft, a book about how he worked out the conflict between his actual self and the self he yearned to be.

During that same conversation he told me that his goal as a writer of fiction had been "to cut up reality and make it more real. . . . This is the intricate music of the art of fiction. It's the music I have always tried to play."

This book, then, is about the intricate music of John Steinbeck.

❊ ❊ ❊ ❊ ❊ ❊ ❊ ❊ ❊ ❊ ❊ *Part One*

✤ ✤ ✤ ✤ ✤ ✤ ✤ ✤ CHAPTER ONE

*J*ohn Steinbeck was never "Johnny," never "Jack." Christened John Ernst Steinbeck III, he was born on the afternoon of February 27, 1902, in the main bedroom of his parents' house in Salinas, California. He was always known as John.

The fact that he never acquired the usual diminutives may may have stemmed from the fact that from the moment he entered the world his visage conveyed an intensity and seriousness of purpose that would later become the hallmark of his life. His infant features were, to put it kindly, not the ones found on the label of a Pablum box. A wisp of dark, wiry hair topped a long, narrow skull that had been further elongated by its trip through his mother's birth canal. Narrow-set eyes and a bent, sloping nose that ended in thick nostrils were the focus of his face. Below, a large but pursy mouth hovered over a thick, markedly receded chin. Two small jugged ears prominently bracketed the face, giving the hours-old child the look of a querulous rodent.

His parents, John Ernst Steinbeck II and Olive Hamilton Steinbeck, were disappointed. Having produced two daughters ten and eight years earlier, they had been struggling to have this baby for a long time. Once Olive became pregnant, their attention had turned to their hopes for its sex. True to the times, to his German heritage, and to his status as one of Salinas's respected businessmen, the senior Steinbeck had yearned for a son. Olive, a schoolteacher and a woman of independent thought and culture, was pleased to satisfy her husband's wish. But she had had her own reasons for wanting a son.

The Steinbeck family had its beginnings twelve years earlier in 1890. John Ernst Steinbeck was the son of Johannes Adolph Grosssteinbeck, a cabinetmaker from a region of Germany near Dortmund. In 1856, when he was seventeen, Johannes Adolph journeyed with his family on an Easter pilgrimage to Jerusalem, where he met an American girl from Massachusetts, Almira Ann Dickson, the daughter of a resident missionary family. A romance blossomed and the two were married in the Holy Land on June 1 of that year. A few years later Johannes Adolph and his wife came from Germany to the United States and settled in St. Augustine, Florida. Johannes Adolph Grosssteinbeck changed his name to John Adolph Steinbeck and found employment as a joiner and carpenter. In 1863, Almira Steinbeck gave birth to her third son, who was named John Ernst II. Shortly afterward her husband, John Adolph, was drafted into the Confederate Army and sent to fight in the Civil War. When the war was over John Adolph and Almira, along with their three sons, moved to Leominster, Massachusetts so that she could renew her ties with her family. Work for John Adolph in Massachusetts was scarce, however, and after a number of years of struggle he and Almira determined to look for a more productive life elsewhere. They had heard of the great westward migration and decided to chance it.

Traveling overland by himself with a modest stake from Almira's family, John Adolph arrived in California in the spring of 1874. After casting about for opportunities, he found himself in the small town of Hollister in the central part of the state, where he used his stake to open a grain and flour mill. By fall he had enough money to bring Almira and his sons from Massachusetts.

By 1877 John Adolph was prospering. He used his profits from the mill to buy ten acres of land near Hollister, which he planted in fruit, and he continued to add to his holdings over the next few years. The family was soon living in comfortable circumstances, and John Adolph became known around Hollister for his willingness to work hard and deal honestly.

In 1890, at the age of twenty-seven, John Ernst decided to strike out on his own. He moved to King City, sixty miles south, and acquired a job as a bookkeeper. There he met Olive Hamilton, a twenty-four-year-old schoolteacher who had begun her teaching career at the age of seventeen and had taught at one-room schoolhouses in the remotest reaches of Monterey County.

Olive Hamilton's parents were from the northern part of Ireland, near Londonderry. Her father, Samuel, from a farming family, had emigrated from Ireland to California in 1851, followed soon after by his wife Elizabeth. They eventually settled in San Jose, at the foot of San Francisco Bay, where Olive was born in 1866. Thereafter they moved to a ranch near King City, where Samuel took up farming again and worked as a blacksmith and well digger on the side. As time went on he gained a reputation as an inventor of sorts, a clever fabricator of farming implements which he sold to his neighbors. He also became celebrated locally as a spinner of tales. On more than one occasion in her later years, Olive Hamilton Steinbeck attributed her son John's narrative gifts to her father's "great gift of gab." Steinbeck himself, in *East of Eden,* acknowledged his maternal grandfather's reputation. "It was a very bad day," he wrote, "when three or four men were not standing around the forge, listening to Samuel's hammer and his talk."

Olive Hamilton and John Ernst Steinbeck were married in King City in 1891. The following year brought the birth of their first child, Esther. Shortly thereafter they moved to Paso Robles, where John Ernst took a job with a Southern Pacific flour mill. Following the birth of their second child in the spring of 1894, they moved to Salinas, where they decided to settle permanently. John Ernst became the manager of another large flour mill and then opened his own grain and feed store, which he was operating successfully at the time his son was born in 1902.

John Steinbeck inherited most of his physical features from his father. Which is why John Ernst may have been disappointed in the infant's appearance, despite his satisfaction at having been presented with a son. His two daughters, the nine-year-old Esther, a redhead, and the seven-year-old Elizabeth, a blonde, took after their mother, a short, plump, buxom woman with round, dollish features. John Ernst, also on the hefty side, had the coarse face of a German burgher — a fact about which he had always been self-conscious. When he saw his son, he must have dreaded the prospect of having to look at himself, as in a mirror, every day thenceforth.

Olive was disappointed for a different reason. She was one of the few cultured women in a town of three thousand that was for the most part agricultural in its character. Salinas had developed as the packing and shipping hub of the long, fertile river valley that stretched north and south from its center. The valley lay thirty miles inland from central California's rugged Pacific coast and the fishing ports of the Monterey Peninsula, with a completely different topography and climate. Its principal industries were the farming and shipping of lettuce, celery and other vegetables, which were distributed by rail from Salinas to the major markets of the West and Midwest, and the growing of sugar beet which was refined at local mills into sugar.

So, although a prosperous community, Salinas was a social and cultural byway — as John Steinbeck would later mockingly call it, "Lettuceberg." To the intellectually ambitious Olive Steinbeck, it was a community devoid of the kind of interesting stimuli needed to broaden a person's perspective. Only the prosperity of her husband's business and the comfortable life the family was able to enjoy softened her displeasure with her surroundings. She was already in the process of raising Esther and Elizabeth in the social and cultural niceties she believed all Steinbeck children should not be without.

Her desire for a son had not only been the manifestation of a dutiful wife's obligation to support her husband's wishes; it was also the expression of a need on her part to acquire a male offspring to whom she could impart her sense of the world. Daughters were one thing to rear in an intellectual tradition. But daughters would never be able to apply their training and devotion to learning beyond their own circumscribed circles as future mothers and possibly schoolteachers themselves.

With a male child it would be different. A boy possessed unlimited potential for adult endeavor. Olive had promised herself that if she were blessed with a son, she would mold him into a man of broad intellectual capacity, a man who might one day be a great university professor, scientist or scholar. Thus her disappointment when she first beheld her newborn child. "He has the looks of a businessman," she is said to have remarked sourly to a visitor a few days after John's birth. "Oh, well, if that's God's wish, the least I can do is make sure that he's a businessman with culture."

John Steinbeck, of course, did not grow up to be a businessman, although some who knew him well say that as a writer, unlike many, he had an acute sense of the business aspects of his vocation. This undoubtedly stemmed from the fact that both his parents were extremely money conscious and instilled in all their children a respect for the acquisition of money through hard work, as well as a sharp sense of anxiety over the prospect of its unavailability. Olive Steinbeck particularly, as fastidious about practical matters as she was about cultural concerns, was forever providing object lessons to her offspring about the value of money and the virtues of impeccable bookkeeping. In her view, money and culture went hand in glove: only those with a reasonable amount of money were capable of proper aesthetic and intellectual enjoyment; only those with a sufficient cultural overlay were capable of the proper disposition of their money.

As was the case in just about every middle-class but upwardly mobile American household at the time, Olive, the mother, was almost exclusively in charge of the children while John Ernst, the father, devoted most of his attention and energies to the task of providing. The family dwelling was a sizeable two-story mid-Victorian house at 130 Central Avenue, on the residential edge of Salinas's business district. The house was turreted, multigabled and many windowed, at once bulky and delicately filagreed on the outside, its style very much a reflection of the Steinbecks' dual and complementary preoccupation with substance and style. Although they were not Salinas's leading family, the Steinbecks were not far removed from that distinction, and the overstated majesty of their residence confirmed their status.

Such houses, built in the late nineteenth century throughout central and northern California, were designed to be giant badges of their owners' respectability, taste and, above all, financial circumstances. Today the house still stands on its original Central Avenue site. In the modern city of Salinas, its population grown to well over sixty thousand, the structure looks unremarkable. Ninety years ago, when Salinas was a flat, drab and dusty village, it and its neighboring houses must have been quite remarkable.

Within, the house provided a kaleidoscope of visual and aural stimuli that, to the small but growing John Steinbeck, was at once forbidding and delightful before it became merely familiar. The interior was a vast setting of cavernous paneled rooms, tall ceilings, dusted shafts of sunlight, creaking stairways, musty attic nooks, shadowed crannies, and the smell of oiled wood. It was a house that invited a small boy's wonder and demanded his exploration. Young John responded to the challenge. His later power of physical observation found their origins in the complex welter of sights, sounds and smells he was forced to assimilate as a three- and four-year-old who spent most of his time in this complex environment.

By the time he was three, John's features had recovered from the trauma of birth and reorganized themselves into a less homely configuration. His face still had a rodentlike aspect, however, one that was compounded by the unyieldingly sprung ears that jutted from his head at a sharp angle. Olive, with what was unintentional cruelty, had fallen into the habit of calling him "my little squirrel." His older sisters' taunting of his features was less unintentional; "muskrat" and "mouse" were only two of the jibes they habitually heaped on him when the sisterly urge to tease fell upon them. As a result, by the time he was four, John was hypersensitive about his looks and had developed an extreme case of shyness around strangers.

Not to discount the possibility of a natural childhood precocity, it was his timidity and increasing self-absorption that accounted for an early responsiveness to his mother's efforts to teach him to read. To Olive Steinbeck, the written word was the keystone of all cultural endeavor. Because of her plans for her son, and because as a mother and schoolmarm she wanted John to be well ahead of his peers once he started his formal education, she spent several hours a day with him, beginning on his third birthday, in the long and tedious process of teaching him to read.

John responded as willingly as his attention span permitted. By the age of four he was capable of reading aloud, if haltingly, from the primers his mother forced him to practice on. He later described the experience as the first solid block of memory he possessed from his childhood. Under his mother's stern discipline, and striving to please her, he had a painful, difficult time of it.

"Trying to make those simple words on the page leap into my mouth and then send them out as intelligible sounds, the sounds my mother mouthed to me, was so hard in the beginning," Steinbeck once said. "It seemed like aeons before I was able to catch on. But then, as always happens when one is learning a skill, the moment came. The magic moment when you suddenly have it. And after that it all begins to flow."

The dreary, repetitive lessons were only part of his early education in literacy. His mother also constantly read to him from more sophisticated books than the primers. First, at two, simple fairy tales. At three, passages from the Bible and English animal stories. At four, he graduated to listening to such as *Treasure Island, Robin Hood* and *Ivanhoe,* his mother, and sometimes his father, intoning, inflecting and play-reading the dialogue to heighten John's interest. By the time John was five he could read simple material easily and, although he resisted it, was becoming infused with an enthusiasm for the sounds and rhythms of words and sentences.

But there lurked in his enthusiasm a danger. As he became more caught up in his taste for language and his mounting compulsion to expand his reading horizons, he grew more introverted.

His second sharp memory of those earliest days of his life was of the great earthquake of 1906, which had left San Francisco, a hundred miles to the north, a fiery ruin and had raked the small business district of Salinas. Brought by his father to view the damage in town after the quake, the four-year-old John gazed in fearful fascination at the pile of rubble that had the day before been Salinas's leading department store. The experience simply added to his timidity. He compensated for his fears by burying his nose in the books of adventure and romance provided by his mother. And he began to muse on other and more distant things than the perplexing security of the Central Avenue house and his parents' stern but loving discipline.

When John was six he entered the local "baby school." As his mother had hoped, he was well ahead of his classmates in his reading and writing skills. But yoked by his timidity and by his awareness of his jug-eared homeliness, he was scarcely able to demonstrate his superiority. At that point he would gladly have traded the scholastic gifts his mother had bestowed on him for a bit more self-confidence and social ease. His mother coddled him, explaining away his introspectiveness by claiming that her son was "different," that he possessed a special intellectual sensitivity that his rougher-hewn peers were constitutionally incapable of appreciating. John half accepted this and took refuge in it. On the other hand he was embarrassed by it. He yearned to be out of his mother's protective but suffocating grasp and be one of the boys. He was caught in a trap between the need for his mother's tenderness and his need for his schoolmates' approval.

His father observed the development of John's personality with increasing annoyance. Three years earlier he and his wife had produced another daughter, John's younger sister Mary. With his two oldest daughters now in their teens, John Ernst chose to bestow most of his affection on his "baby girl." Son John had become so much of a "mama's boy" that he practically shut the lad out of his life, except for an occasional admonishment. By the time his son was seven, however, he felt he could no longer allow the situation between his wife and young John to continue. His admonishments increased, directed not only at his son but at Olive Steinbeck as well.

Tension between husband and wife over their respective convictions about what was best for John mounted. Olive clung to the position that John was something special, that in his specialness he was exceedingly vulnerable, and that his specialness should be nurtured and protected like a delicate plant. John Ernst heatedly demurred, insisting that his son's timidity and lack of backbone was purely the product of her overweening devotion to him, that John was no more special than any other boy in town, and that the sooner he learned this the better. Whereupon John Ernst decreed that henceforth he would take John under his wing. John was to spend half an hour alone with his father each night for father-son talks on the realities of life.

The talks lasted on a regular basis for only six months, thence dwindled to an occasional lecture. In his sternest tones John Ernst endeavored to put John wise to the ways of the world, to indoctrinate him into the virtues of amiability and fellowship and convince him of the crucial necessity of their development to his future as an adult. John listened partly awe-struck, partly fearful, and partly filled with a desire to please his father, whom he was sure he loved but uncertain he liked because of his recent treatment of his mother.

At the age of eight John passed out of baby school and was entered in the third grade of Salinas's West End Grammar School. It was at this time that he made his first tentative efforts to come out of himself. Unaccustomed to the techniques of natural congeniality, and still dominated by a burning shyness, he overdisported himself. In other words, he became an incorrigible in school, driving his teachers to angry distraction with his unexpected bursts of boisterous, irrational behavior. He was more successful with his schoolmates, however, who admired anyone capable of flustering their teachers. Nevertheless they were not hesitant to ridicule him when his antics appeared to be motivated by neither sense nor reason.

What followed was a year or so of such erratic behavior, with John growing markedly less agreeable to the school authorities and at the same time tentatively more acceptable to his male schoolmates. There were official letters to and conferences with Olive and John Ernst. Olive reddened in shame to learn of her son's high jinks. John Ernst, although he punished John on such occasions, was no doubt secretly pleased to know that his son was asserting himself.

By the time John was ten and in the fifth grade, he had worked out a behavioral *modus operandi* for himself that left all but him satisfied. Partly by instinct and partly as a result of his parents' pleadings, he learned to modify his behavior so that when he did assert himself he could do so without igniting the ire of his school superiors or provoking the jibes of his fellow students. Yet he remained, if no longer timid, still profoundly shy.

Moreover, he was utterly confused about himself as a social being. Wanting to mix, yearning for acceptance and approval, he was unable to seek these things gracefully or normally because of his shyness. Nevertheless, he valued some of the things his shyness brought him, not the least of which were the time and privacy to expand his nascent literary and scientific interests. In the end, however, he probably would have chosen a natural gregariousness over his habitual impulse to withdraw. As he noted some forty years later in his *Journal of a Novel,* "I remember the sorrow at not being part of things in my childhood. . . . Something cut me off always."[3]

❈ ❈ ❈ ❈ ❈ ❈ ❈ ❈ CHAPTER TWO

*The unhappy social impotence John Steinbeck experi*enced as a child was undoubtedly intensified by his budding intelligence. His intelligence remained largely unfocused until he was nine, when he made a singular discovery. Here is how he once described it:

> I remember that words — written or printed — were devils, and books, because they gave me pain, were my enemies. . . . Literature was in the air around me. The Bible I absorbed through my skin. My uncles exuded Shakespeare, and *Pilgrim's Progress* was mixed with my mother's milk. But these things came into my ears. They were sounds, rhythms, figures. Books were printed demons — the tongs and thumbscrews of outrageous persecution. And then, one day, an aunt gave me a book and fatuously ignored my resentment. I stared at the black print with hatred, and then, gradually, the pages opened and let me in. The magic happened. The Bible and Shakespeare and *Pilgrim's Progress* belonged to everyone. But this was mine — it was a cut version of the Caxton *Morte d'Arthur* of Thomas Malory. I loved the old spelling of the

words — and the words no longer used. Perhaps a passionate love of the English language opened to me from this one book.[4]

Seldom if ever in literary history has a youthful encounter with a single piece of literature so forcefully influenced an individual's career. Throughout his life Steinbeck credited Malory's *Morte d'Arthur* as being the force that shaped his eventual need to spend his life as a writer. Lest his recalled devotion to Malory's tales appear disingenuous, a familiarity with Steinbeck's works bears it out. In *Sweet Thursday*, for instance, a 1954 novel about some of the characters who peopled his ten-years-earlier *Cannery Row*, Steinbeck retold the story of the poor knight who made a wife out of flowers. In *Tortilla Flat*, his 1935 novel about California's Mexican *paisanos*, he likened his impoverished, illiterate characters to the knights of King Arthur's Round Table.

Arthurian overtones pervaded much of Steinbeck's fiction, both thematically and stylistically. Indeed, his fascination with the Malory legends would become a pursuit bordering on obsession. Later in his life, when he felt that his talents had turned stale and useless, he would devote several years and great amounts of money to the task of "translating" *Morte d'Arthur* from its archaic English into modern American vernacular — this despite discouragement from publishers and friends who saw little value in the pursuit.

The aunt who presented John with the copy of *Morte d'Arthur* was his mother's sister Molly. Aunt Molly, also known as Mrs. Edward Martin, lived with her husband on a picturesque ranch between Salinas and the Monterey Peninsula. Childless, she bestowed much of her affection on her nieces and nephew. John was her particular favorite and, if anything, she was even more adamant than his mother that he receive an early training in literature and music.

John was often sent to spend weekends at the Martin

ranch with his aunt. She would turn such occasions into non-stop cultural marathons, cranking out Caruso recordings on her gramophone, reading endless passages aloud from the classics, pouring Elizabethan verses into his barely comprehending six-and seven-year-old ears, leafing through picture books with him, and forcing him to invent and write down complete sentences in the style of the prose he had heard.

"It was education by osmosis," Steinbeck later said. "I couldn't stand it. I grew to hate it, grew to hate my aunt and dread those visits with her. I wanted to be out roaming the pastures and she had me trapped in a prison of words."

But his acquisition of *Morte d'Arthur* radically changed all that. What initially fascinated him about the Round Table tales was the language, which was totally foreign to the literary language he had been for so long drilled in. It was a language of mystery, paradox and strange meanings, a language filled with sonorous rhythms and thunderous cadences. "The very strangeness of the language dyd me enchante," he later wrote whimsically, "and vaulted me into an ancient scene."

And in that scene were all the vices that ever were — and courage and sadness and frustration, but particularly gallantry — perhaps the only single quality of man that the West has invented. I think my sense of right and wrong, my feeling of noblesse oblige, and any thought I might have against the oppressor and for the oppressed, came from this secret book. It did not outrage my sensibilities as nearly all the children's books did. It did not seem strange to me that Uther Pendragon wanted the wife of his vassal and took her by trickery. I was not frightened to find that there were evil knights, as well as noble ones. In my own town there were men who wore the clothes of virtue whom I knew to be bad. In pain or sorrow, or confusion, I went back to my magic book. Children are violent and cruel — and good — and I was all of these — and all of these were in the secret book. If I could not choose my way at the crossroads of love and loyalty, neither could Lancelot. I could understand the darkness of Mordred because he was in me too; and there was some Galahad in me, but perhaps not enough. The grail feeling was there, however, deep-planted, and perhaps always will be.[5]

Steinbeck wrote this some fifty years later, when he had the advantage of a finely developed adult perspective to describe a primitive childhood reaction. He could not have articulated his feelings with such precision then. But there can be no doubt that *Morte d'Arthur* provoked in him at the time a profound reaction, that it had an engaging and magical effect on his nine-year-old perception of the world and of himself. That it was a long-lasting reaction and had a signal influence on the shaping of his personality is attested to by the observations of two of his early childhood friends.

One of these was Glenn Graves, who lived in a house across Central Avenue from the Steinbecks. A year or so younger than John, Graves was if anything even shier and more homely. He once recalled that "somewhere around nine or ten John's personality began to change. He was still the silent type most of the time, or else he was doing something mischievous, but a new quality began to emerge. He began to tell me stories. He could sit for an hour spinning out a yarn of adventure on the high seas or a tale of ghosts in some old mansion somewhere or a story about knights chasing dragons in the Middle Ages. I knew that he'd got a lot of stories read to him by his mother and his aunt — I'd been around for some of them myself — so I figured it was just John doing what comes naturally. Little did I know that what he was doing was experimenting — experimenting in two ways. He'd started reading 'The Knights of the Round Table,' and I guess he was sort of testing his own ability to make up such stories. The other way was that he'd obviously come to see the effect other people's storytelling had on him — the reading from the books and so on. They made him listen to the person who was doing the telling. The person telling the story had a power over him. That was a new insight for him. And he thought, if he could be made to listen to someone else tell a story, what would happen if he was the one to tell the story? Wouldn't that give him a power over the person he was telling the story to? So he was experimenting with storytelling and using me as his guinea pig. He figured if it worked with me, he could capture other kids' interest in him with his stories."

Glenn Graves, a reticent youngster, proved to be a faithful listener to Steinbeck's tales. Almost as reticent, but not for the same reasons, was another boy who befriended John at about the age of ten. His name was Max Wagner and he had recently arrived in Salinas from Mexico, where he and his family had lived for several years. John took readily to Max, probably because the newcomer had a similar personality and felt himself a stranger in the unfamiliar environment of their Salinas neighborhood. John saw an opportunity to assert himself and, by playing the role of guide and leader, win the handsome, athletic Max's acceptance.

Max Wagner became John's second storytelling guinea pig. Max evidently functioned successfully, for fifty years later he recalled to Nelson Valjean that "John was good. . . . He was always interesting and dramatized everything. Storytelling was natural for him . . . not only the spooky stuff but other kinds too. And he made them all up."

Before venturing to experiment on Glenn and Max, John had honed his budding talents on his younger sister Mary, who was barely six when John received his copy of *Morte d'Arthur*. One can imagine him, after his initial revelations upon reading the knightly legends, cornering his sister and entertaining her with his first tentative tales. Her captive, wide-eyed wonder and gleeful responsiveness must have inspired in John the confidence to extend his storytelling beyond the household. Out of this filial interaction grew a devoted relationship between Mary and John that spanned their lifetimes — a relationship that neither had with their two older sisters.

With his immersion in the Arthurian legends and the subsequent cultivation of his own narrative powers, young John began to shed some of his demoralizing shyness and open himself up to the world. Although still haunted by a large measure of insecurity about himself and still capable of an occasional burst of errant behavior, as he matured during his eleventh and twelfth years John settled into a normal boyhood routine. He was not overburdened with friends, but neither was he without them. Those he did have were the Graves-Wagner types, boys much like himself in sensitivity and diffidence. And they tended to cling to him more than he did to them.

The rewards the young Steinbeck reaped through the cultivation of his storytelling skills were not limited to the improvement of his status among his peers. A more significant reward, albeit one that would not manifest itself for some time, was the concomitant development of a skill essential to any good novelist. This skill consists of the powers of visual and aural observation and of selective but detailed recall.

Almost all of John Steinbeck's finest fiction has his own experience as its matrix. Many of his most accomplished novels and stories are steeped in experiences he either underwent himself or witnessed or heard about in his youth. The characters who populate his work, the exterior landscapes and interior settings in which the action of his stories occurs, as well as the description and imagery he uses to chart and define his characters and places — almost invariably derived from his younger years.

It would not be farfetched to suppose that Steinbeck's success as a descriptive writer stemmed directly from his boyhood penchant for oral storytelling. One can imagine that as he rattled off his rudely improvised narratives — as his conscious mind nimbly invented the entertaining twists and turns that held his listeners in thrall — his unconscious mind, or at least that part of his conscious mind that was memory, fell into the habit of soaking up the sights and sounds of his environment and storing them away for use in future tales. Out of this habit, as his storytelling became more complex and sophisticated, there would have evolved a more deliberate impulse to observe and record until eventually a full-scale narrative dynamic was in the process of formation. Once fully formed, this dynamic — the power to selectively see, hear and reproduce in language — would fuse with Steinbeck's separately developing imagination to create one ingredient of the formula that produces significant writers.

Of course, Steinbeck's middle youth was by no means limited to puzzling out the Arthurian tales and making up stories for the entertainment of his friends. By the time he was ten he was accustomed to getting around Salinas freely. Not only did he have a neighborhood paper route which he negotiated each day on his bicycle, he also roamed farther afield in his spare time, sometimes with Glenn Graves and Max Wagner, but usually alone, in search of more varied experiences. In his later reminiscences, Steinbeck tended to render his boyhood in romantic, Tom Sawyer–like terms. It was not like that at all — Salinas, and his strict Episcopalian family, did not permit much in the way of Sawyeresque adventure.

Notwithstanding this, John did manage to soak up a wealth of youthful impressions. Without his parents' knowledge, he explored Salinas's Chinatown, its red-light district, its Mexican neighborhoods, the many backwaters and muddy lagoons created by the Salinas River. Later on he ventured into the countryside around Salinas and experienced the ranches and pastures and sere hills and the people of the region. Still later, on summer visits to his parents' vacation cottage in Pacific Grove, on Monterey's seaside, he immersed himself in the lives of the polyglot fishing-industry population.

Out of these boyhood experiences came some of his best and even lesser books and stories — *Cup of Gold, Tortilla Flat, The Long Valley, Cannery Row, East of Eden, Sweet Thursday, The Pastures of Heaven*. Probably the most illustrative of his boyhood-influenced works, however, was *The Red Pony*, a long short story or a brief novel, depending on one's interpretation of it.

In the summer of 1912, when John was ten, his father rewarded him for a stretch of tolerable behavior with a gift of a small chestnut pony named Jill. It was a momentous and happy event in John's young life, for he had always wanted a horse.[6]

The young John's reactions on receiving the pony can best be described by repeating what he wrote in 1936 about his youthful protagonist's similar experience in *The Red Pony*. "A red pony colt was looking at Jody out of the stall. . . . Jody's throat collapsed in on itself and cut his breath short. . . . Jody couldn't bear to look at the pony's eyes anymore. He gazed down at his hands for a moment, and he asked very shyly, 'Mine?' "

I don't mean to suggest by this that as a ten-year-old John Steinbeck was capable of analyzing and expressing his own emotions upon receiving *his* red pony. But he must have instinctively recorded the experience and, twenty-four years later, been compelled to release it.

The Red Pony, a minor American classic about a boy's discovery of the accidental but uncompromising cruelty of nature, was a tale that Steinbeck simply had to write, given his own boyhood perceptions. The story, as in all of Steinbeck's works, was nothing more than a vehicle for his larger theme, a theme that runs like a unifying thread through most of his literature: the eternal struggle between man as a unique deviation from mindless natural order, and man as a fated, helpless component of that order. Steinbeck in his art sought to do battle with universal philosophical questions. To mount his forces and prosecute his war, he invariably returned to the mundane scenes and characters and events of his youth. Between the two, as we shall further see, between the grand thematic metaphysical impulses in his writing and the ordinary characters and situations he focused on to express these impulses, lay the energy of Steinbeck's art.

❀ ❀ ❀ ❀ ❀ ❀ ❀ CHAPTER THREE

B y *the time John was ready to enter high school in 1915* he had, according to Glenn Graves, "settled down and come out of himself quite a bit." He was still withdrawn, and for the most part he let others take the initiative. But he was approachable, and when approached he usually responded.

"He had this very strong undercurrent about him," another boyhood friend has said. "He was sort of flip and brusque, and it ran through all his relationships. He seldom laughed, or even smiled. He was fairly . . . dour, I guess you'd call it. And he was defensive. I suppose that was part of his sensitivity, because he was easily hurt or insulted. He held the world at arm's length, even his good friends. Yet there was something very interesting about John. A lot of the kids found him interesting because he was smart and was given to making pithy comments about things. His comments were usually right on the mark, and it was as if he had a power to see right into the heart of things which the rest of us didn't. I think a lot of this may have been affectation on his part, his way of letting everyone else know he was different. The way he said things, too, with a kind of tired resignation tinged with bitterness or sarcasm — this caught people's eye, made them aware of him. The irony is that in high school, although a lot of the kids began to look up to him, he didn't seem to recognize it. He still felt somehow inferior in a lot of ways and kept himself wrapped in a shell. Maybe that's because he knew that the things the others admired him for — the things he said, the way he said them — was an act on his part. He probably didn't trust himself, so he could not trust the positive attitudes others showed him."

According to still others, the only person with whom the pre-adolescent Steinbeck felt completely comfortable was his younger sister Mary. By this time, his two older sisters had left home to attend college, his father was working with increased preoccupation at his business concerns, and his mother had become involved in a number of local cultural activities. The house was frequently empty during the afternoons after school, and John was assigned by his parents to look after his ten-year-old sister.

But it was as if storytelling were not enough. Just as his acquisition of *Morte d'Arthur* had triggered in John an impulse to invent his own stories, so did his own storytelling drive him back into the reading of books. His tales had begun to lose their inventiveness. He often lay in bed at night creating stories in his head, to be embellished and told the next day. During these sessions he came to realize that he had fallen into the habit of repeating himself to arrive at a good story, therefore making the tale, in his eyes, not so good. He grew conscious of a certain limitation on his imagination. It occurred to him that by scanning other books, not just *Morte d'Arthur,* he might perhaps find useful grist for his faltering imagination.

Motivated by this utilitarian purpose, he began to raid the family library. He was a slow reader though. The habit of moving his lips in silent pronunciation over each word, which his mother and aunt had instilled in him when teaching him to read, was still with him. It had become further entrenched by his efforts to wade through the strange Old English spellings and syntax of the Malory narratives. Thus he found rapid reading or scanning a constitutional impossibility. To make any sense of books, he had to read them slowly, his lips moving over each line in synchronization with his eyes. And as he read, he not only absorbed the narratives but became absorbed by them. Thus his utilitarian purpose was transformed into a purpose for its own sake.

His parents' library was stocked with a broad cross section of history, nineteenth-century fiction, and religious literature. Olive and John Ernst Steinbeck practiced the Episcopal faith. John and his sisters were regular Sunday school attendees, although John was known to have incurred his parents' wrath more than once by contriving ploys to avoid attendance. Despite his early exposure to the Bible through his parents' readings, his religious ardor had always been lukewarm at best. Now, approaching the age of thirteen, like countless other boys in the process of discovering themselves and their mental prowess, he had begun to quietly question the meaning of the concept of God and the value of religion in his life. His parents' religious literature began to hold little interest for him, therefore, except in its narrative aspects.

Neither did the many books on history that crammed the house's bookshelves. John decided at an early age that most historical writing lacked the pleasing rhythms and melodies and imagery that had so engaged his imagination when he read Malory's tales of Launcelot, Galahad, Merlin and Morgan le Fay. Where the prose of fiction pulsed and throbbed and vibrated with energy, historical narrative usually stuttered and stumbled into tensionless dormancy.

At his young age this was only an intuition on John's part, certainly not a conscious judgment. As he would say later in life, his initial attraction to fiction derived solely from the stories and characters and the wondrous worlds they created in his mind. Only when he was in the process of becoming a writer himself did he begin to analyze the stylistic and technical qualities that provide the understructure of fiction. Nevertheless, at thirteen, his senses were attuned to the dynamics of storytelling. It is therefore no wonder that he was drawn to the reading of fiction to the exclusion of almost anything else.

But it was not the fiction one would expect a thirteen-year-old to be attracted to. There were plenty of boys' adventure books lying about the house — books about cowboys in Texas and policemen in New York, spies in the Orient and safaris in Africa — all written to appeal to the pre-adolescent reader and designed to give him vicarious thrills, chills and a certain amount of education about faraway places and people. As we have seen, his discovery of the Arthurian tales had left the young Steinbeck with a disdain for the standard children's books of his youth.

Again, Steinbeck wrote of this disdain later in his life, when he might have had the temptation to revise certain aspects of his youth to make them more flattering to himself — a practice not uncommon among aging memoirists. But his claim is confirmed, at least partly independently, by what his sister Elizabeth once said about him. In a 1940 letter to a former college classmate, she remarked that John's success as an author was no surprise to her. She recalled returning home from college one year to find her parents complaining that John was spending too much time with his nose in books and magazines. Her brother was hiding out in his room, skipping meals, neglecting his house chores and "generally carrying on like a sloth." Her father asked Elizabeth to speak to John about his behavior. When she went to his room one afternoon, expecting to find him with his head buried "in naughty pulps," she was surprised to discover him intently reading *Madame Bovary*. Doubly surprised, in fact, for she had had trouble understanding *Madame Bovary* in a college literature course. She remonstrated with John, suggesting that if he had to read, he should at least tackle something he could comprehend. According to her, John ignored her remonstrances. Instead he read a few of Flaubert's sentence aloud to her. Then he looked up at her and confided that some day he would like to be able to write like Flaubert. "He said it with such intensity that it was hard to laugh at him," Elizabeth wrote. "And now he's done it."

John Steinbeck entered Salinas High School in August of 1915. By then his character and personality had begun to "set," which is to say that people responded to him much according to the way they perceived him. And there were basically two ways in which people perceived him: hostile or friendly. Whichever way he expressed himself, it was infused with a sense of there being something different about him. This quality was hard to narrow down, though. To some it was an innate brilliance, to others a powerful insecurity or lack of self-worth, to still others an inexplicable lassitude and indifference.

John remained a hardy introvert during his first two years in high school, at least in the view of his teachers. He was an above-average student in most of his subjects and a natural one in English composition and literature. Yet his ungainly features, also going through the process of "setting," gave him a slightly surly and moronic look that most of his teachers took for the real thing. In many ways, unthinking instructors reinforced his reticence by poking fun at John in front of his classmates. Too well reared and too timid to speak out in his own defense, he would burn with shame and save his reactions until he was released from the classroom. Then, often, he would unleash his stored-up resentment in some inane form of behavior that would serve only to confirm people's notions of him as an incorrigible.

By the time he was ready to enter his third year of high school, however, his facial features had completed the setting process and left him, surprisingly to many, with a reasonably unrepelling look. His nose was large and thick and his ears were still jugged, though not so prominent now that his head had filled out to fit them. He possessed a tall, broad, smooth forehead that seemed to indicate strength and confidence. But it only accentuated the narrowness of his eyes and the pinched wedge of his lower face. Yet, as if to balance his disproportioned features, his eyes exuded a compelling intelligence. A vivid blue, they might have truly been, as the saying goes, the windows of his soul. Capable of reflecting, by turns, fierceness, watchfulness, merriment and despair, they tended to divert people's attention from the dour, stony disarrangement of his face.

With the resolution of his features when he was about fifteen came a gradual outward relaxation of John's manner. Helping it along, perhaps, was the summer he spent at the cottage in Pacific Grove, a small religious community on the north end of the Monterey Peninsula, just above the fishing port of Monterey itself. The Steinbeck family had been repairing to the cottage to escape the baking summer heat of Salinas since shortly after John was born. The family would usually migrate *en masse* just before July fourth and spend at least six weeks in the tiny, one-bedroom cottage. During these visits John, close-quartered with his parents, his sisters and their friends, felt increasingly claustrophobic and bored. To relieve his boredom he took to escaping on his own into nearby Monterey. By the time he was fifteen he knew the quaint fishing and packing town well.

In the summer of 1917 the rest of the family was forced to put off its stay in Pacific Grove. But John, with nothing else to do, was given permission by his parents to spend two weeks on his own at the cottage with three of his classmates. John could not wait to go. He had regaled his schoolfriends with tall tales of his adventures during previous summers in the "fleshpots" of Monterey. Most of his tales revolved about his imagined sexual conquests. The other boys — whose only exposure to sexuality had come, like John's, from their brief, giggling, bicycle reconnoiterings of Salinas's Chinatown and its across-the-tracks red-light district — were impressed. John had been able to summon up the sights and sounds of the notorious Monterey to invest his boastings with convincing credibility. He was, of course, a virgin, which somewhat tempered his eagerness to take his friends to the cottage in Pacific Grove. They would expect him to arrange it so that they could duplicate his conquests. But arrive at the cottage they did.

By a stroke of luck, John's mother had arranged for a cleaning girl to come up from Monterey to spruce up the cottage and air it out in anticipation of their arrival. The girl was going about her chores when the four boys showed up. In her early twenties, she was a shapely, sultry creature of Portuguese extraction, the daughter of a Monterey cannery worker. The fact that her English was bad and her teeth worse detracted not a whit from her appeal; her bosom was ample and her hips swayed with ripely sensual arrogance.

John's schoolmates had previously heard him mention in one of his stories a "Maria." This girl announced that her name was Maria. The boys gazed upon John with salacious envy. He shrugged modestly, then decided to seize the time. Mustering up his courage, he sent his friends on an errand, then took the real Maria aside and explained his problem. He had brought his friends to the cottage to introduce them to the sexual variety of Monterey, he said. Did she perhaps know of any girls who might be willing to . . . ?

Yes, replied Marie, indicating herself.

John blanched. The girl held out her hand, palm up. Money.

Olive Steinbeck had given her son ten dollars for spending money during his two-week hiatus. Grudgingly he extracted it from his pocket and handed it to her. Whereupon she took his arm and, overpowering his trembling resistance, dragged him into the bedroom. Soon she was naked on the bed, her round dark breasts squeezing together like circus balloons as she extended her arms beckoningly.

Thus came John Steinbeck's introduction to sex. And that of his friends, for when they returned from the chore he had sent them on, they found the naked John wrapped in a quivering postcoital embrace with the equally naked cleaning girl. Maria made no attempt to recover her modesty. Instead she pried John off her and gazed invitingly at the other three. She evidently thought her ten-dollar fee included the whole group, for she uttered no protest when John, gathering his wits about him, jumped off the bed and said, "Who's next?"

The two-week stay in Pacific Grove turned into an unalloyed sexual marathon for the four fifteen-year-olds. Not only did Marie continue to make herself available with no further monetary demands, she also provided a few of her Monterey friends for the boys' delectation.

When the visit was over, John and his friends returned to their respective homes in Salinas sated and exhausted. But they wore on their faces the knowing glow of sexual mastery, a look, or leer, they carried with them through the remainder of the summer and into the beginning of their third year of high school. When they first returned from their idyll, they swore like blood brothers to keep their experience a secret. The impossibility of that soon proved itself, however, and by the time school reopened, John was looked upon by most of his male contemporaries with wonder and envy.

This went a long way toward further liberating him from his prison of shyness. And as he gained confidence in himself as a social being, he began to show signs of gregariousness. But it was always overlaid with his still-sober mien. Where before he'd shrink before his teachers, he now started to respond to them, challenge them, even engage them in classroom disputes over scholastic issues. His diffidence became mixed with a sardonic swagger that, if not endearing, was at least acceptable to most of the classmates whose approval he sought. Yet there continued to remain about him "something set apart," as his classmate Ignatius Cooper once recalled.

Ignatius Cooper and his two brothers were the school's only black students. He and his family, among the few blacks in Salinas, represented John Steinbeck's first exposure to black people. Steinbeck was to go on to espouse and write about a number of causes in his life. Many critics have wondered why a man of his commitment to the relief of oppression remained largely silent during the long struggle of blacks to achieve equal rights — a struggle which coincided with his own career.

Ignatius Cooper and his family may have had something to do with it. In the last major book he wrote, *Travels with Charley*, published in 1962, Steinbeck obliquely defended his lack of involvement in the civil rights movement by referring to Ignatius Cooper:

> I have many Southern friends, both Negro and white, many of them of superb minds and characters, and often, when not the problem but the mere suggestion of the Negro-white subject has come up, I have seen and felt them go into a room of experience which I cannot enter.
>
> Perhaps I, more than most people from the so-called North, am kept out of real and emotional understanding of the agony not because I, a white, have no experience with Negroes but because of the nature of my experience.
>
> In Salinas, where I was born and grew and went to school gathering the impressions that formed me, there was only one Negro family. The name was Cooper and the father and mother were there when I was born, but they had three sons, one a little older than I, one my age, and one a year younger, so that in grade school and high school there was always a Cooper in the grade ahead, one in my class, and one in the class below. . . . The father, universally called Mr. Cooper, ran a little trucking business — ran it well and made a good living. His wife was a warm and friendly woman who was good for a piece of gingerbread any time we wanted to put the hustle on her.
>
> If there was any color prejudice in Salinas I never knew or heard or felt a breath of it. The Coopers were respected and their self-respect was in no way forced. Ulysses, the oldest, was one of the best pole vaulters our town ever developed, a tall, quiet boy. I remember the lean grace of his movements in a track suit and I remember envying his smooth

and perfect timing. He died in his third year in high school and I was one of his pallbearers, and I think I was guilty of the sin of pride at being chosen. The second son, Ignatius, my classmate, was not my favorite, I discover now, because he was far and away the best student. In arithmetic and later in mathematics he topped our grades, and in Latin he not only was a better student but he didn't cheat. And who can like a classmate like that? . . . Beyond this giftedness, the Cooper boys were my friends.

Now, these were the only Negroes I knew or had contact with in the days of my flypaper childhood, and you can see how little I was prepared for the great world. . . . That was my Negro experience until I was full grown, perhaps too far grown to reform the inflexible habits of childhood. Oh, I have seen plenty since and have felt the shattering waves of violence and despair and confusion. . . . And, remembering the Coopers and how we felt about them, I think my main feeling [about the racial question] is sorrow at the curtain of fear and anger drawn down between us. . . .

Thus it remains that I am basically unfitted to take sides in the racial conflict.[7]

For his part, Ignatius Cooper remembered John years later as a usually quiet but sometimes pugnacious fellow who tended to speak his mind when something bothered him. He claimed that he was never close to John, and that Steinbeck's description of their relationship in *Travels with Charley* was inaccurate and probably self-serving. He felt that John disliked him and remembered that he was not very fond of John. He attributed the tension between them to boyhood personality and character differences. "Maybe he was jealous of my good grades, but I think it was more a matter of resenting my style. I was sort of cheerful and easygoing, whereas John was always sort of clenched up like a spring. I didn't care for him because of that — because you never knew where you stood with him. One time he'd be friendly, the next aloof, and the next he'd try to wound you with a wisecrack. . . . He was a smart kid, no doubt about it, but it was a different kind of 'smart' than the other smart kids had. He was too smart for his own good, because he seemed like an unhappy kid, mixed up, and it seemed like it was his intelligence that put him in that state. . . . He was the kind of boy who didn't like to compete. He wanted everything to come to him without having to work for it, and when he had to compete for something he'd usually shy away from it. And he was the kind of kid who could dish it out but couldn't take it. I mean he was very sensitive about his own feelings but was totally insensitive to other people's. He was selfish, self-centered, and not very courageous physically. He didn't work with people well. If he couldn't have things his way, he'd go off and sulk, or pretend he didn't care. I suppose that's why he became a writer. That way he could make the world conform to his wishes."

✳ ✳ ✳ ✳ ✳ ✳ ✳ CHAPTER FOUR

The setting of John Steinbeck's adolescent character was probably most accurately analyzed by his high school English teacher, Ora M. Cupp, in a 1940 letter to Nelson Valjean, who, as an editor of the *Salinas Index-Journal*, had been collecting biographical material on Steinbeck with the idea of doing a newspaper feature on him and eventually a biography. This was after *The Grapes of Wrath* had been published.

In her letter, Mrs. Cupp pictured John as having a "run of the mill college-material" IQ of about 120. She attributed the fact that he had later failed to make good in college not to any lack of brain power but to his "character traits." She remarked that John had the ability to do good work in school "when he felt inclined," but left the clear impression that he was seldom so inclined. "No argument in the world would have made John hand in . . . work if he decided not to." It was as if, once he made up his mind not to do something, he could not bring himself to do it. "I sometimes thought John would have been glad to have someone help him unmake-up his mind, but of course no one could."

John was lazy, then, indifferent, probably bored by curriculum learning, perhaps fearful of failing and therefore unwilling to try. Mrs. Cupp described him as being subject to vacillating moods and suggested that there was a strong streak of petulance in his character, an even stronger one of argumentativeness. "He didn't mind being loud or rude" when disagreeing with someone, even a teacher. He was likely to side with anyone he thought was not getting a square deal, and to be noisy in delivering his views. Yet Mrs. Cupp didn't quite trust his sincerity. "I felt I sometimes caught him with his tongue in his cheek," she said. She wondered if the books he later wrote — the ones that became celebrated for their defense of the poor, the exploited, the downtrodden — might not have been written insincerely. "These people were good copy," she remarked in her letter to Valjean. "Let the reader cry over them." Could John Steinbeck have been so cynical? "I'm willing to wager there were times when [he was writing that] he stood off and grinned at his own indignation."

"What was tendency in the boy may have become set, like plaster of Paris, in the man," said Steinbeck's former teacher. In her view, the most memorable aspect of his personality, aside from his shyness, was his capacity for bitterness. Whence it derived she could not divine. But she was sure of it. "I think one could feel his power to hate even while he was still in short pants, and in the 'grubby' state of boyhood."[8]

With all of that, did John ever evidence in his high school years an ambition to become a writer? Mrs. Cupp failed to mention it, which indicates that she never thought of John as a boy who would one day become an acclaimed author, no less an ordinary writer. The consensus among his contemporaries accorded with this. Few saw in John, an interesting verbal storyteller, either an aptitude or an ambition for writing. His mother, now somewhat of a social and cultural butterfly in Salinas, was projecting for him a college education and then a return to Salinas, where he would enter his father's feed-and-grain business, marry, and expand the family's roots in the town. His father was like-minded in his ambition for his son, nuturing the hope that after a financial education in college John would join forces with him to branch his business into other areas of Monterey County.

The pressures he received at home might have been one source of the young Steinbeck's personality problems in school. For the most part he was unhappy in Salinas and was beginning to yearn for the day when he could depart for greener and more interesting pastures — to do what, he could not know. On the other hand, he was attached to his mother by a bond that had been made strong by seventeen years of her solicitude. Although distant from his stern and humorless father in the way that unexpressive males always keep their distance, he loved and respected John Ernst and feared his wrath.

John had been raised with a powerful sense of Christian guilt over questions of loyalty and devotion to family and of obedience to the dictates of parents. He had violated these strictures in small ways many times in the previous years, earning his parents' rebukes and punishments. But these were minor, almost technical violations of the filial contract, behavioral errors of the kind that any child commits. To consciously ponder leaving the family hearth, or to consider going against his parents' larger career ambitions for him, was another matter altogether. Such thoughts carried with them the implication of much profounder punishments — if not administered by his family, then by some higher force that would forever mark him with shame.

Acting out of a need to suppress the foreboding created by his sense of guilt, John was reluctant to cultivate his intensifying desire to find another world. At the same time he was powerless to restrain it as it turned from instinct into conscious thought. He was thus thrust into a deep but indistinct moral dilemma — his obligation to his family and its principles versus his compulsion to find and define himself. The dilemma, although the source of confusion and unhappiness, served to awaken him for the first time to an awareness of the contradictions that ruled his life and of his own complexity as a human being. He would brood over this insight for a number of years to come. He would then synthesize it into a personal view of man — of man trapped between his animal impulses and the rules imposed on him by his mind — which would haunt him throughout his life and constitute the central, recurring thematic understructure of his literature.

At this time, however, John was not thinking in such terms — that is, of transforming his moral malaise into a world view that would manifest itself in literary expression. He was merely, though increasingly, searching for a way to detach himself from the horns of his immediate dilemma.

Those who ascribed to him no ambition, however vague or unrealistic, to become a writer were wrong. For by the time John was midway through his junior year in high school he was spending many a late night in his cramped attic room penning short stories and essays. He later recalled sending them "out to magazines under a false name and I never put a return address on them. I wonder what I was thinking of? I was scared to death to get a rejection slip, but more, to get an acceptance."

Although his parents were aware of his secret endeavor, only his sister Mary was permitted to know the contents of his manuscripts. He often tested them by reading excerpts to her. According to her, these first writing efforts represented John's transition from the invention of wild, macabre tales of previous years to the composition of more realistic stories — stories that had intelligible plots, characters and logic. She attributed his shift to writing to his boredom with vocal storytelling. He was a natural storyteller, she once said, and it was natural that once he grew tired of the vocal form he would seek another outlet in writing. He was growing up as well. He had been reading a lot of magazines, had seen what was being written, and had decided to try his hand at it.

His parents were not as sanguine about his literary activities. They were not so much afraid that he would create false hopes for himself by his nocturnal scribblings as they were concerned that his late hours were draining his health. John would often work in his room until two or three in the morning and then get up bleary eyed at seven to prepare for school. They were also worried about the effects his compulsive writing habit was having on his schoolwork. They had begun to talk about sending John to Stanford University once he completed high school a year hence, and they dreaded the prospect of his being rejected by Stanford because of poor marks.

Their first concern was borne out in May of 1918 as John was approaching the end of his junior year at Salinas High. Exhausted by his writing labors, he caught a cold that almost overnight turned into pneumonia and then pleurisy. What few drugs existed in those days offered faint hope for the control or cure of his disease, and he was soon near death. "I went down and down," he recalls in *East of Eden,* "until the wingtips of the angels brushed my eyes."

Finally his doctors decided that only emergency surgery could save him. In an operation performed at home, his chest was incised, a rib was removed, and the suffocating pleural pus was drained from his lung cavity. The verdict of the operation hung in the balance for several days while the Steinbeck family fearfully prayed over his wasted, comatose form. Then, almost imperceptibly, he began to improve. A brief relapse ensued, which he successfully overcame, and then he was on the long, slow road to recovery.

His recuperation confined him to bed through the remainder of the school year and into the summer vacation. He had much schoolwork to make up during the summer in order to move with the rest of his class into the final year of high school. His parents used his illness as an object lesson on the folly of squandering his health and future prospects in idle, amateurish writing. His father had read through some of his story manuscripts while John lay ill and had assured himself that his son's literary endeavors were merely that. Chastened, John agreed to forgo further writing and to apply himself completely during the coming year to his studies and to the extracurricular activities that would help him get into Stanford.

When school reconvened in the fall of 1918, John had satisfactorily made up his junior work and entered his senior year. True to his promise, he immersed himself in his studies and plunged into a broad round of after-school projects. Unable to go out for the football team because of his still-fragile condition, he managed to get himself elected president of the senior class, worked in the school's drama society, joined the science club, and became an editor of *El Gabilan*, the class yearbook.

The only writing of John Steinbeck's school years that has survived is that which was printed in *El Gabilan*. One example appeared in the 1918 edition, John's junior year:

> When the Student Body of a school runs smoothly, it is a good sign that the school is in good order. The Student Body is really the center of school life. All amusements and all obligations swing upon it, and our Student Body *is* running smoothly. This does not mean with lack of interest for there is always interest. . . . Truly, ours is a Student Body to be proud of because it does things. . . .

The piece goes on in this vein, didactic and dull and awkward in style. Perhaps the lonely nights in his attic room writing stories and essays for anonymous magazine publication had taught him something, however. For the yearbook of the following year contained a considerably more sophisticated piece endowed with a conscious sense of rhythm and sound, and even humor. It read in part:

> The English room, which is just down the hall from the office, is the sanctuary of Shakespeare, the temple of Milton and Byron, and the terror of Freshmen. English is a kind of

high brow idea of the American language. A hard job is made
of nothing at all and nothing at all is made of a hard job. . . .

Derivative, admittedly. Indeed, John may have copied it
directly, with only a few alterations, from something he had
read. It is true also that it is the kind of prose that any competent high school senior could write. It voices nevertheless a
hard-edged cynicism softened by an ironic sensitivity that very
accurately reflected John's outlook. Coupled with its sharp imagery and sense of pace, the piece in its entirety just barely hints
that the seventeen-year-old might have had an aptitude for
writing. Assuming that he did not lift it from an uncredited
source, it suggests imagination, inventiveness, selectivity and
unity. And it is a measure of the progress he had made from
the previous year.

The 1919 yearbook piece notwithstanding, few if any of
John Steinbeck's contemporaries perceived in him a wish or
potential to be a writer. Doubtlessly resorting to another image
of him, they evidently acknowledged his wanderlust and tendency to moralize, and foresaw a career in the pulpit. In the
yearbook's "Class Prognostications," it was prophesied of him:

> *The church of a far off city*
> *Came towering into view,*
> *Where John was preaching in solemn tones*
> *To many a well-filled pew.*

❀ ❀ ❀ ❀ ❀ ❀ ❀ ❀　CHAPTER FIVE

Nor did Steinbeck himself at this time harbor even a secret wish to pursue a career as a writer. During his later high school years he developed, along with his general interest in literature, an increasing fascination with natural science. It began with a school friend, Edward Silliman, whose father was by avocation an ornithologist. On his first visit to the Silliman house in Salinas, John took note of Silliman senior's extensive collection of materials relating to bird life. Included were dozens of stuffed birds, hundreds of bird skins, feather clusters and egg samples, all catalogued in detail, together with a large library of books about ornithology and other animal sciences. John took to visiting the Silliman home regularly to gaze at the collection and leaf through the books. Mr. Silliman, disappointed by his own son's lack of interest in his hobby, was glad to answer John's increasingly complex questions and lend him books to read.

Concurrently, during his summer stays in Pacific Grove, John was exposed to the nearby Hopkins Marine Station, a seaside biological laboratory run by Stanford University and devoted to the study of marine life. There he watched professors and summer students from the Stanford science departments pursue their field studies, embarking each day in glass-bottomed boats to retrieve fish, plant life and other marine specimens from the waters of Monterey Bay and the Pacific beyond. Initially attracted by the fact that the student life at Hopkins was at once carefree and serious, he took to visiting the lab complex and cadging rides on the boats.

Possibly his initial attraction to Hopkins derived from a personal need that had nothing to do with marine science. At about this time John was victimized by an eruption of teenage acne. It increasingly ravaged his face and compounded his self-consciousness. He learned, however, that long days in the sun and salt air of Monterey Bay tended to have a healing effect. By the end of the summer the tan he had acquired served to mask his condition and enabled him to return to school relatively clear faced. Once the tan faded, of course, the condition would return, and John would spend the rest of the school year vainly trying to resist picking at the ugly boils that once again erupted all over his face and neck.

No matter what his initial motivation for hanging about the Hopkins Marine Station, he quickly acquired a fascination for the work being done there. By his senior year in high school — having abandoned his story writing in the wake of his severe illness — he had begun to spend most of his spare time reading books on zoology, ornithology and other life sciences. And when he learned that his application to Stanford had been accepted, he began to answer questions about what he intended to do with his life by saying that he wanted to study science and become a scientist, preferably a marine biologist.

During the summer between his high school graduation and his matriculation at Stanford, however, Steinbeck went through a change of mind. Instead of passing the summer at Pacific Grove and loitering about the Hopkins lab, John decided to earn some money to augment the small monthly allowance his father would be sending to him at Stanford. Through his father he managed to get a summer job working as a laborer for a company that had a contract to dredge a network of canals that fed agricultural transport into the Salinas River and thence to Castroville on Monterey Bay.

Had it been a few years earlier, John's parents would have looked with disfavor on such a menial occupation. But times and fortunes had changed for the Steinbeck family. Moreover, John's wealthy Aunt Molly had died. While alive, she had insisted to Olive and John Ernst that she wished to contribute substantially to the children's college educations, since she had no children of her own. Even if she were to die, she promised, she had instructed her husband to carry out her wishes.

After her death, her husband remarried and thereafter indicated an unwillingness to part with funds he had received from Molly's estate to finance Olive and John Ernst's children's educations. The Steinbecks were too proud to make an issue of the matter. Instead, John Ernst sold his feed-and-grain business and put away the proceeds to finance first his two older daughters' educations, then John's and Mary's. He then took a position as a warehouse supervisor with the giant Spreckels sugar company, which operated the country's largest beet-sugar refining plant on the outskirts of Salinas. On his Spreckels salary, John Ernst and Olive were forced to modify their lifestyle. Although hardly in dire circumstances, they had to live more frugally in order to maintain the big home and the cottage in Pacific Grove. John would feel the pinch when he went to Stanford. His parents had the money to pay his board and tuition expenses, but, they cautioned him, there would be little left over for his weekly spending money, particularly if his sister Mary followed him at the university in a few years, as she professed to want to do.

So, with his parents' reluctant approval, John spent the

summer as a laborer. It was his first close-hand exposure to the roustabout life led by so much of Monterey County's polyglot populace. Mexicans, Chinese and thousands of unskilled immigrants from the eastern and midwestern states made up most of the county's common labor force, and representatives of each constituted the work gang to which John was assigned. His job was for the most part pick-and-shovel toil, restoring collapsed canal banks and leveling towpaths. Later in the summer he was transferred to one of the dredging barges as an oiler and wiper, but both jobs were tedious and boring and afforded John a good deal of time to observe the men he was working with.

Most struck him as an entirely new class of human being, one that he had never experienced before. He was at once repelled and fascinated by them. Many were illiterate, though colorfully and profanely articulate. Others were mentally retarded or moronic. All were without any gainful skills and tended to squander their earnings on payday drinking binges or card games. Their values were transitory and their ambitions limited.

Steinbeck, with his rough-hewn face and sturdy broad-shouldered body, appeared to fit in among his fellow workers. They called him "Johnny boy" and treated him to wild, profane tales of their pasts. They introduced him to liquor and marijuana and plotted, usually in vain, to separate him from his wages during their after-hours gambling ventures. John kept his distance from them, often blushing at their needling obscenities. But at the same time he developed a sympathetic feeling for them that grew out of an admiration for their animal recklessness and irresponsibility, combined with a pity for their lack of human sensibility and intelligence.

During the summer he took to reading about the kind of people he was working with in newspaper and magazine articles that professed to accurately portray California's poor and transient field-workers. He was disturbed to find that the portrayals were all wrong. Most of the articles drew cautionary pictures of an army of semicriminal dullards who were descending on California like swarms of locusts to pillage the state of its civility and resources. The articles, clearly prejudiced, were written to appeal to central California's rural old-guard population, which, for economic reasons, welcomed the expanding settlement of the state but not the backward form it was taking.

His reading jogged in John his first concrete perceptions of the divisions between the classes in Monterey County, and of the power of the written word to influence public opinion. He would often go home during the summer to find his parents and others expressing concern for his safety as a worker within this criminal element. John protested that the men with whom he worked wouldn't know how to go about being criminals; they were merely dumb, but picturesque.

But his parents ignored his protests, and the newspapers continued to slander the men he worked with. Finally, he took pen in hand and dashed off an angry letter to a San Francisco newspaper decrying what he took to be its deliberate falsification of the labor scene in the Salinas Valley in an article written to appeal to readers' fears and sell newspapers.

"I have worked with the men your article described for well over a month now," he wrote, "and I can tell you that the fellow who wrote it is living in a fairyland. . . . These men are outgoing and generous and surly and fractious, often happy with their lot, sometimes ill-tempered and nasty . . . all in all just like a lot of people I know who work in white collars and green eyeshades. . . . Your malinable [sic] article was obviously meant to stir up all those businessmen whose success depends on the willingness of these men to carry out their thankless backbreaking labor at slave's wages. . . . Isn't it ironic that among the very people who read your article and nodded approvingly over its conclusions are those who employ these poor creatures and prosper by the sweat of their brow?"

Steinbeck's indignation went unpublished by the news-paper. Because of that he began to spend his spare time writing brief sketches and observations about the men he worked with, possibly in an effort to isolate and define the humanity he perceived in them, or simply in an attempt to justify the defensiveness he felt about them, and therefore about himself, in the face of the concern voiced by his parents and others in Salinas.

What is more likely, given Ora Cupp's later assessment of John's "tongue-in-cheek" approach to things, is that he de-cided that he had stumbled on a good thing in his fellow workers. Although younger than most of them, he was able to feel vastly superior to them, and his sense of superiority gave him a taste of the self-confidence he had for so long lacked. Most of his sketches turned out to be caricatures of the men he worked with, their traits, both amusing and un-pleasant, drawn with a broad sardonic brush. They were also self-conscious and effect-ridden, as though Steinbeck cared more about the impression he wanted to make as their author than about the reader's impressions of the characters them-selves.

He would soon realize that his sketches were no good, that they lacked truth and even interest. Yet the very act of writing them awakened in Steinbeck an awareness of the challenge of writing out of one's own experience. His previous literary efforts had been modeled on the example of the many novels, legends and short stories on which he had been raised. That is, he had tried to invent his stories solely out of his imagination — an imagination molded by his exposure to the densely plotted and richly charactered fiction he was accustomed to reading — fiction that portrayed faraway events, foreign cultures and characters totally beyond his experience. Although he was obviously sensitive to this fiction and his imagination was responsive to its wonders, he had made the mistake of try-ing in his own way to duplicate it in his earlier attic-room writing efforts. Having learned, concurrent with his illness of the year before, that he couldn't convincingly convey the thoughts of an American soldier lying wounded in a trench in France in 1917, and that he couldn't truthfully realize the character of a European nobleman in conflict with the church over a bastard son in 1730 (both subjects of his previous short-story writing), John might have been grateful that his pneumonia had the effect of putting an end to his adolescent literary efforts.

Yet it clearly did not kill his still hidden and barely understood impulse to write. The impulse flowed undoubtedly from his many years of reading and his growing comprehension of the power that books and their authors had over him. Once he recognized and analyzed this power, he gradually found that he desired it for himself. The desire came partly, or in the long view, because a life lived in the imagination must have seemed to John a very good life indeed. But it developed mostly because he saw that writing had the potential of providing more immediate rewards — the self-respect, self-confidence and sense of self-worth that inspired the attention, respect, and admiration of others.

So the adolescent impulse to write had lain dormant for a year while Steinbeck cultivated other interests and decided that he might try science as a course of study in college. But then during his summer vacation came his experiences with the migrant pick-and-shovel laborers. In his recognition of how easily and cynically they were misunderstood by the region's middle-class gentry, and in his attempts to use the written word to rectify the situation, the impulse was refired. This time the impulse was secured in the harder cement of his experience. Trying for the first time to fictionalize from his own experience, John came to a crucial recognition of how difficult it was and, at the same time, how necessary. He had heard and read in high school the axiom that all good writing is based on what the writer knows at first hand. But John had never given it much consideration, feeling as a growing boy that his own experience was unremarkable and in no way comparable to that of the endlessly fascinating authors he had been nurtured on. Now, however, having more or less come to terms with his inability to invent credible fiction purely out of an imagination formed by the novels of notable writers of another age, he began to find material in his own life. And although his first attempts were awkward and self-conscious — most probably because in truth he cared less for the characters than for the effects he wanted to create — they did succeed in impressing on him the value of the axiom. As a potential writer, Steinbeck was on the verge of being reborn.

But merely the recognition of the axiom and the compelling awareness of its truth were not enough to complete the rebirth. It would take several years of college, a great deal more in the way of practice writing, and several long spells of reflective idleness before the rebirth of Steinbeck's potential was complete. And it would take longer still before the potential achieved actuality.

❋ ❋ ❋ ❋ ❋ ❋ ❋ ❋ CHAPTER SIX

Steinbeck went off to Stanford in the fall of 1919 with his springtime determination to study science on the wane. His summer on the Salinas canals had not only turned him into a fit and robust young man, it had also drawn his writing impulse to the surface of his ambition. In so doing, it had rooted the impulse in the solid soil of realistic possibility rather than in the sand of romantic dream. Steinbeck fully realized by now that to be a writer meant an intimate acquaintance with self-doubt, self-torture, hard and disciplined work, and, most likely, financial deprivation. With the first he already had some experience. In regard to the other three he was an innocent. On the possibility of poverty, however, his parents had exhaustively cautioned him just before he left for school. His father had warned him of the economic perils of a writer's life, and advised him that he could expect no financial support should he be so foolhardy as to press such an irrational ambition beyond college. John's parents had not made the financial sacrifices they had to subsidize such a frivolous pursuit as a writing career, John Ernst lectured.

John struck a bargain with his parents. He would speak no more of a writing career so long as they agreed to permit him to take a general liberal arts course at college rather than a science curriculum. It was for this reason, then, that he registered in liberal arts when he arrived at Stanford. On the line of his registration form that asked him to state his career preferences, he wrote, in order, teaching, journalism, and law.

Stanford University was only seventy miles from Salinas, but for the effect his removal to Palo Alto had on Steinbeck it might just as well have been seven thousand miles away. Yet with what was turning out to be typical Steinbeckian paradox, John, despite his oft-stated longing to get away from Salinas, soon became achingly homesick.

Upon his arrival at Stanford, he moved into his assigned dormitory quarters on the first floor of Encina Hall. Like most of the other buildings on the pastoral campus, Encina Hall had been constructed in the Spanish-mission style of architecture so prevalent in California. It was a five-story structure of buff colored stucco topped with a red tile roof. Stucco walls and tiled floors were the motif within as well, lending the interior, with its bare light bulbs suspended from ceilings, a cold, harsh, antiseptic look. John's room had a radically different atmosphere from the soft woods, muted wallpapers and seductive, calming shadows of the family house in Salinas. The ambience of Stanford was instantly foreign to him.

The summer had been good to John physically, and he showed up at Stanford in the bloom of health. Tanned and lean, his six-foot frame suggested a superior athlete, although his classmates would soon learn that his athletic prowess was minimal, due largely to his distaste for the physical violence of most collegiate sports. His acne had abated, and the effects of his summer in the sun had masked the residual pockmarks on his face. He wore his wiry brown hair cropped practically down to the scalp on the sides and back and only a little longer on top, unparted, a style which accentuated his jug ears and gave him the look of a slightly dim-witted country boy. The look was abetted by his large, bottom-heavy nose and fleshy mouth. Only his recently developed habit of emphatically arching his right eyebrow when making a point, and the capacity for mental absorption reflected in his sharp blue eyes, betrayed his native intelligence. When he was viewed as something of a rural rube during his first few weeks at Stanford, he began to let his hair grow out in the style of his more cosmopolitan classmates, eventually slicking it down with pomade and parting it in the middle.

One of these cosmopolites was George Mors of nearby Los Gatos, who became John's freshman roommate. Mors had entered Stanford with the idea of eventually making a military career for himself. Precise and meticulous, and with a sense of personal self-discipline that was unusual in a young man his age, he was also outgoing and friendly — all qualities that were in direct contrast to John's personality. After arriving at Stanford John reverted, almost despite himself, to the introversion of his earlier years. He was awkward and uncomfortable in this new environment of confident and sophisticated fellowship, and all the insecurities he had succeeded in at least partly modulating in his last year of high school returned.

Mors immediately liked him, however, or so he has recalled. Mors had somewhat of a practiced eye in sizing up people, and he saw in John's extremely reticent and withdrawn nature, which others took for surly unfriendliness, merely shyness and social discomfort. Mors was fair, handsome, athletic, graceful and eager to please. To John he was somewhat of a phenomenon — the first such contemporary with whom he had ever been in such close quarters. He was fascinated by Mors and yearned to be like him. Yet he secretly resented him for the ease with which he made his way in the freshman world of Stanford.

John was enrolled in the standard first-year liberal arts course. George, anticipating a military career, was registered in the engineering school, so the two attended few classes together and had little in common academically. Another thing that nettled John was Mors's certainty about the direction he wanted his life to take. Mors seemed in charge of his life and responded confidently when asked about his career ambitions. John on the other hand was vague and uncertain in his responses, finally settling on "teacher" to avoid possible ridicule should he indicate the more exotic preference of "writer." Indeed, so paralyzed was he by the self-induced demons of loneliness and alienation during his first months at Stanford that he thought little about writing. His powerful sense of inadequacy invaded even his vague hope of a literary career, and he made no attempt to write during this period.

What he did, mostly, was read. His increasingly compulsive reading habit was not for self-education, however, but for escape from the unhappy vicissitudes of campus life. Many of the boys in Encina Hall were athletes and had gone out for Stanford's freshman football team. Hoping for a measure of acceptance, John had tried out for the team but failed to make it. Thereafter he turned further into himself and took his solace in reading. Most of what he read, George Mors later recalled, "was junk — pulps, cheap magazines, girly books, that sort of thing."

If John got off on the wrong foot socially, his academic beginning was even worse. After a few weeks he began to lose interest in his courses. Soon he was cutting classes and failing to turn in assignments. Needing a scapegoat to justify his scholastic boredom, to make it appear legitimate rather than the fruit of his insecurities, he blamed it on the quality of the teaching at Stanford. "Idiots, all of them!" he was known to proclaim. "I can learn more studying on my own."

His attitude undoubtedly provided him with at least one sense of superiority in his life. But it was basically a self-delusion, since he made little or no effort to study on his own. As his indifference mounted, so did his lassitude. When he did attend classes he tended to be disruptive, whispering and giggling manically with one or two classmates who, for their own reasons, were given to pranks. The consensus of his professors on Steinbeck the freshman was that he was of average mentality but woefully immature emotionally. Whether any of them went to the trouble to explore the reasons for his behavior — loud and cocky one moment, difficult or surly the next — is unknown. What is known is that despite the professorial axiom that some first-year students take longer to adjust to college than others, they saw little promise in Steinbeck of a successful university career. They supported their opinion by giving him universally bad marks for the first quarter.

The second quarter of Steinbeck's freshman year was only a few weeks old when his disgruntlement and loneliness collided like two toxic amoebas and exploded into another episode of pneumonia. This was not as serious as before, but it was enough to win John a reprieve from Stanford. When he was granted permission to temporarily drop out of school in order to recuperate at home, he immediately returned to Salinas and the solicitous bosom of his family.

John remained at home throughout the rest of the school quarter and tried to screw up the courage to ask his parents to allow him not to return. Correctly anticipating their anguish over such a request, however, he remained silent. Recovered from his illness, he dutifully returned to Palo Alto in the spring of 1920 to resume his education.

Now behind in his studies, John spent the next two months in a serious effort to catch up. His resolve was tempered by the beginning of spring weather, however, and the rapid return of his restlessness. The Stanford campus, the former farm-estate of millionaire Senator Leland Stanford, was a mass of bucolic acreage lying between the Camino Real, the main road to San Francisco, and the tall hills that bordered the Pacific Ocean. John again took to skipping whole days of classes to roam the steep nether regions of the property.

The relationship between John and George Mors gradually ripened into a friendship. When John returned for the spring quarter, he moved back into their room in Encina Hall and proclaimed his determination to turn himself into a serious student. When Mors saw his determination start to flag, he went out of his way to encourage John to stick to his promise. Under Mors's prodding, John barely struggled along, at once resenting his roommate's interference and valuing it.

The only other friendship of any note that Steinbeck developed in his first year was with another freshman, Carlton Sheffield, who was from Long Beach, south of Los Angeles. Sheffield and Steinbeck shared classes, and he was John's principal cohort in classroom misbehavior. The difference between them was that Sheffield would go only so far in their joint miscreancy and then fade into the woodwork, leaving Steinbeck to carry on by himself. The result was that John ended up suffering most of the blame. What they had in common, aside from their immaturity, was their secret ambitions to become writers. Neither of them knew how to go about it except to act eccentric and moody. As they became closer they fed off each other. Where Sheffield possessed a semblance of self-discipline, however, John possessed none. Sheffield, who went by the nickname of "Duke," attended classes and got his assignments in on time. Steinbeck increasingly did neither.

A sudden appendicitis attack in early May sent Steinbeck to the hospital for surgery and put an end to whatever hopes he had for salvaging the third quarter. He returned home for the summer with credit for only three courses during the entire year. In these, two of which were in English composition, his grades were barely average. They represented an inauspicious beginning for a budding writer, a point his parents reminded him of when they received his school report.

His parents, nevertheless, were reasonably forgiving of his freshman effort at Stanford, chalking his sorry performance up to the bad luck of his illnesses. They were still willing to bear the financial burden of John's college education, even if it took five years instead of four, as it now appeared it would. They only wanted to be sure that John had abandoned his writing ambition — supporting their argument with his poor marks in English — and that he was prepared to pursue a more practical course of study, such as business or accounting.

John was pleased to be home once again, but he also bore a burden of guilt for having squandered his parents' resources. He did not look forward to returning to Stanford the following fall, much less to studying business, but he feared confrontation with his parents over his misery. Instead he went off with George Mors to spend the summer working as a surveyor's helper in a camp near the Pacific coast at Big Sur, fifty miles to the south, where the right of way for the scenic Pacific Coast Highway was being mapped.

The two eighteen-year-olds soon soured on their jobs. Both thrived on outdoor life, but they found the unremitting labor and paltry food that went with the survey jobs unbearable. In short order, on John's insistence, they quit and returned to Salinas. John's father got them maintenance jobs at the Spreckels sugar factory and they spent the rest of the summer there, with Mors living at the Steinbeck house.

During their time together that summer, John confided to Mors his dread of returning to Stanford. George, the shape of whose future was solidly etched in his mind and whose industry in pursuing his ambition was the envy of Steinbeck's parents, found it difficult to understand his friend's malaise. John said he wanted to be a writer and found college a waste of time. Mors reminded him that he had failed to turn the wasted time into productive time by writing, and had instead further squandered it by reading junk. John countered by arguing that he had to accumulate a certain amount of worldly experience before he could begin to write seriously. George asked him, with unassailable logic, whether going to college was not a form of experience; why didn't John begin writing about college life? Steinbeck shrugged. Who would want to read about a bunch of college boys, he demanded? College boys, Mors replied.

Steinbeck received a good deal of camaraderie from George Mors, but little sympathy. Since he admired George, though, he determined to take his advice to heart, or try to. Thus when the two returned to Stanford to begin their second year, still as roommates, John began to spend his spare time writing short stories about college life instead of reading pulps and wandering the campus. He was placed in a make-up program at the beginning of the school year, so that he was neither sophomore nor freshman but a combination of both. As a gesture to Mors he signed up for ROTC; the two had talked idly during the summer of jointly pursuing military careers, and George, who was already in ROTC, took the military training seriously.

Hardly a month had passed after his return before John fell into the previous year's pattern of skipping classes and postponing study assignments. True to his resolve, however, he continued to churn out stories about life on campus and present them to George to critique. And true to his promise, George rendered his opinions, all the while urging Steinbeck not to abandon his studies. (At the end of the summer John's mother, who had grown to be an unabashed admirer of George for his academic industriousness, had secretly extracted from him a promise to ride herd on her son when they returned to Palo Alto.)

George's comments on John's new literary efforts, however well meaning, were basically naive and often, John thought, patronizing. George Mors was not a fancier of fiction; his reading preferences lay in the area of science texts and military manuals, and it is doubtful that even a short-story writer of the artistry of a de Maupassant or O. Henry would have impressed him. He certainly was not impressed with Steinbeck's college-life stories, which he correctly surmised to be self-conscious exercises in character portrayal that strained credulity. He avoided stating his impressions outright, however. Rather, he remarked on the stories in a faintly praising or critical way. To John, his comments betrayed a lack of understanding of what Steinbeck was trying to accomplish.

"Too many words here," Mors would say, or "How can you compare a girl's leg to the silky smoothness of an eel? An eel isn't silky, it's slimy." In many respects Mors was intuitively right in his criticisms, for Steinbeck was still tied to the habit of writing almost solely for the effect he thought his conceits and images would have on the reader — in other words, overwriting, not trusting the reader to comprehend, seeking to gain power over the reader not through the interior logic of his stories but through the supposedly dazzling brilliance of his language and images.

In answer to Mors's criticisms, John would complain that his subject matter — college life and college students — was inherently uninteresting and could only be made interesting by linguistic "jazzing up." The point escaped Mors, or else he saw it merely as a weak rationalization on his roommate's part. All he knew was that much of what John was writing rang false, and he wasn't sure that it was the subject matter's fault. All the while he was expressing his reservations, Mors took pains to encourage Steinbeck to persevere. But John viewed George's positive expressions as emanating solely from his guilt at having had to criticize a friend, and he dismissed them.

After the fifth or sixth story, John threw up his hands in frustration and foreswore any further attempts to write out of his college experience. His decision only made him wish more for the kind of real-world experience he heard writers had to have before they could hope to write effectively. But he was unable to satisfy that hunger, partly due to lack of funds but mostly to his fear of his parents' reactions should he set out to do so, and he grew morose.

By now he was unable to return to his studies. In his six-week fling at writing he had all but ignored his courses and was on the verge of failure in every one. He ignored George Mors's reminders of his perilous academic position. As John grew more irritable he returned to his compulsive reading habits, burying his nose in magazines during most of his waking hours. Normally uncommunicative, he became more so, brusquely fending off anyone's friendly or sympathetic approach to him. To make some extra money he took a job as a busboy in an off-campus cafeteria in Palo Alto. But that lasted only a few days; he soon quit in sour boredom.

Finally, later in November of 1920, the breaking point came. In an effort to fulfill the responsibility thrust on him by Olive Steinbeck, George Mors sent her a note warning her of John's emotional paralysis. Mors explained that John had passed beyond his power to help and was on the verge of flunking out of school. He advised that she and her husband come to Stanford to have a talk with him. And he hoped that she would not reveal to John that he had taken the liberty of writing to her.

The anxious Olive Steinbeck showed up at Stanford by herself two days after receiving Mors's note. Confronting John in his room, she marched him off to a conference with the dean. There she learned that John's future at Stanford was indeed in extreme jeopardy. She pleaded with the dean for another chance for her son. He gravely granted John a two-week probationary period in which he would be required to attend every class and make up the examinations and assignments he had missed. Should he indicate by the end of the two weeks that he was serious about remaining at the university, his case would be reviewed and he would be given every possible consideration. Should he not, then he would be officially dismissed at the end of the term.

Olive Steinbeck thereupon closeted John in his room for a stern dressing down. From her point of view it was the worst thing she could have done; from John's, the best. Now that the problem was out in the open, John could match his mother in speaking his mind. After she tearfully elaborated the usual arguments about his responsibility to the family, John, also succumbing to tears, poured out a jumbled rationale for his irresponsibility, voicing his desire to leave school and embark on a life as a writer. She reminded him that his father would refuse to subsidize such folly. After much more at-odds discussion, she extracted from him a promise to follow the dean's imperative and make a concerted effort to salvage his university career.

As she returned to Salinas, Olive Steinbeck realized that John's determination to become a writer was not the idle wish she and her husband had hoped, but an apparently deep-seated compulsion. She seriously doubted that his pledge to reform would amount to anything, and she trembled to think what John Ernst's reaction would be when he learned of his only son's situation. She had disguised the real reason for her visit to Palo Alto. She knew that when she arrived back in Salinas, however, John Ernst would ask her how John was getting along. She could not lie to her husband. Despite John's promise, she would have to prepare his father for the worst. John Ernst, having become involved in local politics, was seeking the office of Monterey County treasurer. It would not do for him at this time to be distracted or unexpectedly embarrassed by John's college deportment.

John was embattled by conflicting emotions as he watched his mother leave. He had finally declared himself, which gave him some relief. But Olive had overridden his declaration with telling points of her own about responsibility and family loyalty that dissipated the relief with a further burden of guilt and confusion. And his pledge to make a full-out effort to avoid dismissal from the university, drawn from him under the duress of his warring needs, only tightened the jaws of his emotional vise.

He gave his pledge a brief try. For three or four days he attended every class and contemplated the missed assignments he was required to redeem. But his sensibilities were swamped by the enormity of the task and the brief time in which he had to carry it out. On a day in the beginning of December, George Mors returned to their room to find his roommate's clothes missing and a cryptic note from John saying that he had "gone to China."

❊ ❊ ❊ ❊ ❊ ❊ ❊ CHAPTER SEVEN

John had also sent a letter to his parents. In it he explained his reasons for quitting Stanford and begged their forgiveness "for the disappointment my selfish actions are sure to bring you." He said that he intended to go to San Francisco, find work on a ship, and spend his time at sea trying to sort out his problems and come to terms with his future. He promised to keep in touch by mail.

After his arrival in San Francisco, Steinbeck's sense of exhilaration at his liberation was short-lived. His mother had taken him to the city on occasion in his younger years and he had more recently made two or three weekend forays with George Mors and Duke Sheffield, but he didn't really know the city. With only a few dollars remaining from his school allowance, he found a cheap furnished room on the honky-tonk fringes of Market Street and spent the next few days wandering the waterfront hiring halls in search of a seagoing job. With no experience as a seaman, he was turned away at every place he applied. He moved across the bay and tried hiring halls there with equal lack of success. He thereupon took a temporary Christmas job in an Oakland department store and went from that to a brief stint as a stock boy in a haberdashery shop. But as the New Year passed and the prospects of going to sea further dimmed, John swallowed his pride and anxiety and headed home, spending a few days here and there on the way working as a pick-up laborer.

When he arrived in Salinas, expecting a heated show-down with his father, he was pleasantly surprised. John Ernst seemed to have accepted his son's quixotic actions, or perhaps Olive had prevailed upon him to refrain from pillorying John. In any event, he was welcomed home with a certain amount of relief, if not optimism, about his future. John took responsi-bility for his Stanford failure and repeated his wish to have some time on his own to work out his problems. While he was in San Francisco, his parents had received an official notice from Stanford dismissing John from the university because of his poor record. Appended to the notice, however, was the advice that the school would consider his reapplication to the university at a future date, provided that he could satisfactorily demonstrate that he was ready to take college seriously. With this glimmer of hope, John's parents agreed to indulge his wish for breathing space.

His father again used his influence as an employee of the Spreckels company to get John a job — a condition of his being allowed to remain out of college. In accord with his wish to be on his own, the job this time was as a hired hand on the huge, isolated Spreckels sugar-beet ranch some distance from Salinas, where John would live in a bunkhouse and eat in a common mess hall with the other hands.

When his mother went with him to the Salinas bus depot to see him off for Chualar, the nearest town to the ranch, he cadged enough money from her to buy a notebook and a packet of pencils. He told her that he was going to use his free time at the ranch to "finally determine" whether he "had it in him to become a writer." If he learned that he didn't — after all, he said, he would have nothing else to do at the ranch but prove to himself that he could or couldn't write — he promised that he would return to Stanford in the fall, become a dutiful student, and complete his college education.

As it turned out, during his stay of almost four months at the Spreckels ranch, John wrote hardly at all. He had arrived with the best of intentions, and during the first couple of weeks made sporadic attempts at the beginnings of stories. But the daily ranch work proved so physically exhausting that he had little energy left at night to move pen across paper, no less crank up his imagination. What little he did write, and what greater amounts he hoped to write, still derived from his imaginings of people and places and situations of which he had little or no direct knowledge or experience. Influenced perhaps by the few literary dicta he had absorbed from his English courses at Stanford, he conceived of what he wanted to write first in terms of thematic content. Settling on a theme, be it his perception of the inequality of justice or of the conflict between man's human and animal nature, he would then seek to contrive plots and characters that would illustrate it.

"Contrive" is the operative word for Steinbeck's conceptual approach to writing during this period. To be sure, he felt very strongly the storytelling impulse in himself. This impulse, plus the potential for ego gratification he saw in being a writer, were clearly the origins of his literary ambition. But Steinbeck at this time was also a budding philosopher, a thinker. Impelled by the religious conflict that simmered in his mind, the residue of his early religious upbringing versus his later independent perceptions of divinity, and by the countless moral and social paradoxes he observed in life, he was in the midst of making a number of important philosophical self-discoveries that would eventually become the dynamo of his artistic energy and the benchmark of his literary vision. His primary intellectual conception of writing, then — as opposed to his emotional and intuitive conception of it — was as a vehicle to advance the philosophical "truths" he was in the process of discovering. To use storytelling or the device of fiction to advance his views meant in his inexperienced mind the contriving of stories to serve the larger purpose of his philosophical insights. The situations and characters he tried to invent in his ongoing writing efforts were meant to serve mainly, if not exclusively, as frames for his philosophical canvases. It had not yet occurred to him that whatever philosophical truths he had to impart would be better served by allowing them to filter through his fictional situations and characters. He did not yet realize that the art of fiction was not frame and canvas but a form of unified expression in which all the elements — situation, character, action, theme and philosophy — are interdependent. Many years later, in a letter to George Mors in which he reflected on the months he spent after leaving Stanford, Steinbeck wrote that he remembered "all the foolish lies I told." He was referring to the dissembling he did with friends and family to ease the shame and discomfort he felt upon quitting school. His allusion might also have been to his writing efforts.

Nevertheless, Steinbeck did begin to sense during his stay at the Spreckels ranch that his conception of writing was all wrong. He sensed it undoubtedly through his aborted attempts to write complete stories. Facilely able to begin a work, as he proceeded he found it more and more difficult to credibly sustain it, to develop the action and characters believably within the grandiose thematic scope that had inspired his story. Most of the time he would get halfway through a piece of writing and then throw down his pencil and tear up the pages in despair, knowing that it didn't work but not knowing why.

If his writing had any discernible virtue at all, it was in his skill at physical description. His technique was usually to open a story with a description of the locale, be it the area around the White House in Washington (he had never been

to Washington), a Civil War battlefield in Georgia (nor
there), or a prostitute's bedroom in San Francisco (not there
either). All of his descriptions were distilled by imagination
out of the many books and magazines he had read, and were
mistaken in much of their extensive factual detail. But that
was not the point. The point was the amount of detail he
lavished on his descriptions. Even more important to him were
the flashes of skill he revealed in relating the detail. Although
wholly imagined, his painting of story-opening pictures was
sometimes brilliant in its imagery, at once concise in verbiage
and elaborate in implication. Consciously striving for poetic
effect, something he had learned from his extensive reading,
he often went overboard, probably because he did not trust
his own imagination or that of his intended reader. But at other
times he caught an object or a feature just right, so that the
reader, had there been one, might have said that there could
be no other possible way to describe what Steinbeck had
described.

Notwithstanding this talent, which Steinbeck may or
may not have recognized in himself (the likelihood is that he
thought of the descriptive function of the writer as merely a
device to open a story and jog a plot into action), he remained
far from solving the problem of his lifeless literary inventions.
Discouraged, he again abandoned his writing efforts and sank
all his energy into the job to which he had been promoted
at the Spreckels ranch. He was now a crew foreman.

As a foreman, he was in charge of a gang of half a dozen
laborers whose task was to load railroad cars with great burlap
bags of beets being transported to the Spreckels sugar plant.
In order to maintain the respect of his older coworkers, all of
whom were coarse, uneducated, hard-drinking roustabouts of
only marginal intelligence, he had to set the example by working harder than any of them. He soon exhausted himself.
Gaining no satisfaction from his supervisory responsibilities,
and fast growing bored with the monotony of the job and life

at the steaming, dusty ranch, John abruptly quit and returned
to Salinas. He took up residence again in his attic room in the
house on Central Avenue. His anxious parents waited to hear
his decision about his future, but he had none to convey. He
merely complained that working at the Spreckels ranch had
consumed too much of his energy, and that he'd not had
enough left to put his writing ambition to the test.

With the Steinbecks' stoic acceptance, John spent the
early weeks of summer lazing about and renewing his acquaintance with Salinas and its valley. During another long
and sometimes cantankerous discussion with his parents about
the practicality of his writing ambition, his father said something he hadn't expected to hear. In complaining of the vicious
circle of his aspiring writer's plight — of the frustration of trying to write out of his experience when all his experience consisted of was his exposure to college boys and *paisano* laborers
— John had exclaimed that it was impossible for him to
convey what he wanted to convey through such pedestrian
characters.

What was it that he was so anxious to convey through
his writing, his father sternly inquired?

This caught Steinbeck up short. Up to then he had
thought about the subject only in philosophical abstractions. He
began to answer, but stammered into a confused mélange of
nonsense. And then, as in a revelation, he realized that he
had no concrete idea of what he wanted to convey, or even
why he wanted so avidly to write. Although he managed to
rephrase his answer so that it appeared to make some sense, he
knew it was as empty and meritless as before. He crawled off
to bed that night to think long and hard about his revelation.

He carried the disturbing thought with him the next day
to the cottage in Pacific Grove, where he was to spend the
rest of the summer. It began to haunt him as he spent long
days wandering the streets of Monterey and the piney woods
of the peninsula, trying to find the answer. When an answer

didn't come, he fell into a profound depression that paralyzed his spirit and aspirations for months to come.

He started to drink, hanging out for hours on end in the sleazy bars of the Monterey waterfront, picking up an occasional dollar by taking an odd job here and there. He carried his anomie back to Salinas in the fall. Under his perplexed parents' prodding he sought work in town but was rejected for all the nonlaboring jobs he applied for, principally because of his surly, indifferent attitude and his eccentric appearance — he had taken to wearing shabby, surplus-purchased clothes and went days between bathing and shaving. His mother tried to excuse his behavior by describing it as a stage he was going through. His father, coming to the end of his patience, saw it as role playing: John had read of the Bohemian life of writers in Europe and New York and was emulating his image of them, in the hope of at least looking like a writer if he couldn't actually be one.

A further source of anguish was the fact that John began to seek out the company of Salinas's low-life types — men and women both. He was seen more than once staggering out of one of the combination saloon–pool halls along Salinas's infamous "Whorehouse Row" on California Street. And although no one actually saw him enter one, his parents feared that he was frequenting the brothels in the same neighborhood.

When he was sober, John spent his days on long treks out of town, often camping overnight along the banks of the Salinas River. He usually had a book with him, that of a celebrated modern writer, which he would study not for its entertainment value but as if he were searching for a key that would unlock the depression and confusion caused by the disappearance of his undefined literary purpose.

In February of 1922, Steinbeck's father forced him to visit a doctor for a complete checkup. Psychiatry was just a whisper in California at that time, and most of the whispers were dark and forbidding, overlaid with rumors of hypnotism and sexual abuse. Besides, there were no "head doctors" in Salinas, so John was put in the hands of the family's all-purpose physician. In a few weeks the report came back that except for a low-grade virus infection, brought about by his neglect of himself, there was nothing wrong with the Steinbecks' twenty-year-old son.

With no medical reason to account for John's increasingly intolerable behavior, John Ernst laid down the law. It was time for John to pull himself together and make something of himself. Or else. The argument that ensued drove John back to the cottage in Pacific Grove, where for a month or so he continued his intensive reading by day and his immersion in the back-street life of Monterey by night.

But then, gradually, a change came over him. As if by osmosis, the accumulation of subliminal impressions he had gained by his endless reading seeped into his awareness. He divined that the fiction that most forcefully stirred him was the kind in which the action flowed from the characters. Or better yet, from the logic, habits and perceptions of the characters as developed by their creators. He discovered that fiction in which the characters merely existed to serve the plot was invariably dull and wooden and false — exactly the kind of fiction he had been trying to write in high school, at Stanford, and at the Spreckels ranch. That fiction in which the story evolved directly out of the tensions and conflicts between the characters had credibility and completeness, and tended to be more satisfying to read. It mattered not at all that the characters might be ordinary and unremarkable in their social, cultural and mental dimensions; it was the human emotions invoked in them by their authors that seemed to be the important thing.

It was a second important revelation for Steinbeck. He quickly realized that brought up as he was on the Bible, on the classics, on Shakespeare, his entire literary orientation had been twisted. He had been instilled with the notion that to be great or important, literature had to be about great or important people — kings, princes, knights and geniuses; that sweeping themes could only be communicated through grandiose plots, characters and speech.

What he had more recently been reading suddenly convinced him otherwise. Not only was the art of effective characterization the key to the modern mode of writing, but characters (thus stories and their underlying themes) could come from anywhere as well — so long as they were consistent and truly drawn. An illiterate beggar could be as engaging a protagonist as could a nobleman.

Steinbeck's realization was revolutionary only to himself. What he was discovering had been a long-established literary rule of thumb. He had read the prescription in English textbooks and heard it from teachers: "Build your stories and books around people you know, create your characters from people whose values, attitudes and behavior you are familiar with." In other words, "write from your experience, no matter how limited or mundane you think it is." He had acknowledged but had failed to understand it.

The discovery sent Steinbeck back to his writing pads with a new outlook. At first he merely tested the waters, writing unconnected passages of description based on visual impressions of his surroundings. Since he was still at the cottage, his initial subjects were the cottage itself, the town of Pacific Grove, and then beyond to Monterey and the smells and sounds of its fish canneries and wharfside life.

His latent descriptive talent stood him in good stead in these endeavors. Although much of what he sketched was overstated and needlessly embellished, the result of his former writing habits, there shone through these first jottings a hard gleam of perceptivity, of a further talent for seeing the most important details of things and relating them in a way that gave them a visual and emotional impact, an identifiable immediacy.

Steinbeck was not yet sure of what he was about, and he had not yet developed the editorial instinct so essential to effective writing — that is, the sense of knowing what to include as vital, and what to exclude as mere decoration, in his writing. Yet he pressed on, now going farther afield to test his powers of observation and recording. He trekked across the Monterey Peninsula to the picturesque village of Carmel, then explored the Carmel River to its source in the steep mountains that crowded down on the peninsula from the southeast. He drifted farther south to the feral region of Big Sur and tried to see it in different perspectives than when he had earlier worked there in the survey camp. He came back up the coast and traced the rocky, majestic shoreline of the peninsula back to Monterey and Pacific Grove.

Throughout this journey Steinbeck carried pad and pencil and constantly jotted down his impressions, trying to transform his literal perceptions into literary ones. The way a wet rock jutting out of the Carmel River bed glistened in the misted winter sunlight, the way an old weathered fence rail lay askew at the entrance to an upland ranch, the way a cypress tree had been perversely contorted by decades of wind beating against the shore — these were just a few of the countless sights the essence of which Steinbeck tried to capture.

When he got back to the cottage, he sat down and slaved unremittingly for a week or so in an attempt to write an essay about his journey. Out tumbled a long catalogue of his impressions, some rich in imagery, others merely trite or overwrought. When he was finished, he timidly presented it to a Monterey newspaper in the expectation that the paper might want to publish it. His principal hope was that his by-line on a piece in the local paper would increase his importance among the few acquaintances he had made in Monterey, particularly the girls he had been vainly trying to impress by presenting himself as a practicing writer. A subsidiary hope derived from the growing need to be able to say, for his own sake, that he was a published writer.

The paper's editor returned the piece with a cryptic comment scrawled across the first page: "Not for us — it'll turn away the tourists." John's disappointment was so deep that he was unable to comprehend that the editor's damning assessment was in fact an inadvertent form of praise and encouragement. There was much wrong with the piece, of course — it was overwritten, self-consciously poetic and at places convoluted in its syntax. But in its more comely passages it spoke in a voice of lean, muscular authority that accurately, almost ruthlessly, reflected the scenic but unforgiving power of the topography Steinbeck had described. The editor might have said that John's essay was too darkly lyrical for a newspaper that sought to entice the tourist trade to the Monterey Peninsula (in it Steinbeck had castigated the tourist population for its mindless desecrations of the land), but that it showed literary promise.

He didn't, of course. And Steinbeck, mired in his disappointment, was incapable of seeing the positive implications of the editor's rejection. He remained undaunted, nevertheless. He instinctively sensed that in embracing the imperative to write out of his own experience, he had put himself onto something. He had gained at least spiritual satisfaction from his attempts to transform what to most people would be commonplace into the uncommon, indeed the unique. A rock, a wagon, a building — people saw these objects merely as objects, he thought, noticing only their outlines and duly registering the shapes in their consciousness. People only perceived the forest, never the individual trees. In his essay he had experienced the power of focusing on commonplace objects and particularizing their unique details and qualities. It was an experience of searching for the essence of a thing and, by transposing his vision of it into written images, capturing it.

Steinbeck did not put this to himself in so many words. But he had a growing sense of it as a result of his experience in writing the rejected essay. He was disappointed by the editor's rejection, yes. But for once, propelled by the power of his intuition, he refused to let rejection discourage him. As a prospective writer, he was beginning to grow up.

❊ ❊ ❊ ❊ ❊ ❊ ❊ CHAPTER EIGHT

S teinbeck was still on shaky terms with his family. He had gone home for a few days at Easter in the spring of 1922, shortly after he began his new writing experiments in Pacific Grove, but he was careful to say nothing of his most recent insights for fear of again arousing his father's ire. His parents were equally careful to avoid the subject of writing. For all they knew he was still in the process of finding himself. His sister Mary had been accepted at Stanford for the following fall, however, and she begged him to return so that they could be together. John shrugged off her pleas. If he returned, he said, he would practically have to start over again as a freshman. Although he was almost three years older than Mary, they would be classmates! The idea struck Steinbeck as intolerable; her presence would be a constant reminder of his failure. It would not be long before he changed his mind, however.

When he returned to Pacific Grove he resumed his writing experiments. This time he decided to expand them beyond his physical surroundings and apply them to people. In the same way as the month before, he started with brief sketches. Selecting people he knew from the bars and piers of Monterey, he set out to capture their unique qualities and traits in words — to make "these ordinary citizens of the town colorful and interesting, at least to me," as he once said. Then he invented a useful exercise. He would stroll the streets of Monterey and watch people he didn't know. He would focus on one or two salient characteristics, record them in his mind, and then return to the cottage and write long, detailed descriptions of them, trying to probe through his imagination into the centers of the characters that emerged.

Following that, he turned to sketches of people from his past — boyhood and college acquaintances; the Mexican, Chinese and Portuguese laborers with whom he had worked at Big Sur, Castroville, the Spreckels sugar-beet ranch, and so on; his grandfather Hamilton, his sisters, his Aunt Molly, his father. He found that realistic, identifiable characters emerged from these sketches. Particularly compelling were the laborers and ranchers he had encountered. The falsest characterizations were those of the people he knew best or felt closest to. He wondered about this. He distinguished between them by calling them the "rough hands" and the "smooth hands." The rough hands were basically the uneducated, uncultured people in his life whose tastes and appetites were on the lower end of the human spectrum. The smooth hands were the opposite — his family, his teachers, most of his school contemporaries. Not only were the rough hands somehow more truthfully realized in his sketches, they were easier to write about. Perhaps it was because he knew less about them and therefore was forced to invest more imagination in them.

Whatever the reason, Steinbeck's sketches began to turn into tentative stories. Finally, he resolved to write a complete short story based on some of the characters he had partially developed. He worked for days on it, and the result was a tale of an illiterate sardine fisherman who imagines that his wife is having a secret love affair with another man; it is not true, but his primitive imagination runs away with him until finally, in despair, he kills himself.

Steinbeck's purpose in the story was to depict the drudgery of the lives of Monterey's lower working class. For the first time in his writing endeavors, he edited himself as he composed the story, deleting words and phrases that compromised the realism of the characters and the action. It was not a bad beginning, he thought.

He was afraid that he had failed to establish a believable motivation for the fisherman's self-delusion and suicide, however. So he tore the story up and started again. This time he hit upon the device of having the man's wife taunt him with hints that she was having an affair. By doing so, she punished her husband for an insult he had thrown at her and at the same time was able to enrich her own impoverished, dreary life. Now the husband's actions made sense. An imaginary cuckold, he became a real one in his own mind as he slaved away at his boring labors at sea and imagined his wife in the arms of another man. Since he came from an ethnic heritage in which the physical harming of the mother of one's children was taboo, no matter the justification, he let his shame drive him to self-destruction.

With this version of the story, Steinbeck was able to expand upon his original point. The wife's imagination too became a victim of the dreariness of their lives, triggering the husband's, until tragedy followed. The existence of underpaid laborers and their families led to tragedy, Steinbeck was saying, because the quality of their lives was so dehumanizing that they had no place to turn for relief but to their imaginations. And when they did they were doomed, because the very same dreariness of their lives gave their imaginations too free a rein and let them get out of control.

The finished story had a symmetry and completeness that Steinbeck had never before been able to achieve. It still had glaring faults, mostly ones of grammar and syntax. But for the first time John felt that he had written a piece of fiction that was worthwhile. And he thought he recognized the reason. For once, he hadn't started out with a moral and then tried to invent a story to convey his message. Instead, he had started with two characters and nothing else in mind but to let them engage in a course of action based on their logic. As he set them down, they did indeed begin to interact in a way that led to a specific action. Once the action of the story began, he had only to minimally shape and control it. And it was out of the action that the story's theme evolved, almost magically. With the theme surfaced, he was able to bring the action to a logical, believable and moving conclusion. Once finished with the first draft, he could go back to fill in the gaps in logic and strengthen other weak spots. But he never had to utter or point to the theme. Nor did he have to disturb it or embellish it. The theme grew out of the characters and action and floated like an invisible soul throughout the tale.

John Steinbeck had learned a new way to write. He couldn't explain what it was. But he could and did marvel at it. More important, he had the good sense to trust and pursue it. He was destined to wander away from it in the years to come and try other approaches. But when the chips were down, he would return to it.

He showed the story to no one. Instead, he started another — this a Huck Finn type of yarn based on an experience from his childhood in 1914 when he and Glenn Graves formed their own personal militia to scout the hills east of Salinas for the invading "Hun." Here, mock warfare turned into real combat when the two youthful "soldiers" got lost in the hills and were confronted by the evil forces of nature in the form of a violent thunderstorm and a stalking mountain lion. And again a meaningful theme grew out of the story: the brutal contradictions between play warfare and real warfare. (At that time, the American populace was "playing" at war, the United

States not yet having joined in the hostilities of World War I.)

While Steinbeck worked on his stories, he also wrote another, less "literary," essay on the natural wonders of the Monterey Peninsula. Only three pages long, it was an attempt to lyrically but realistically describe the centuries-old life of a mammoth rock perched on a promontory of the Monterey coast, near Point Lobos. He delivered the manuscript to the same newspaper editor who had rejected his earlier piece. This time the editor called him into his office. In explaining why he had decided to decline the second essay, he told Steinbeck that he had a gift for capturing the kind of detail that breathed life into facts and actualities. He was not going to publish John's piece because, despite its occasional descriptive brilliance, it was inauthentic — semantically sloppy and naively senti-mental. Anticipating a literary rule that would be articulated a few years later — the "categorical imperative" — he advised Steinbeck that it was folly to ascribe thoughts and emotions that were unique to the human species to inanimate things. No matter how figuratively appealing it might seem to a novice writer, rocks (and for that matter trees and rivers and other components of the natural order) simply did not possess the sensibilities of humans. The effect of having to read that Steinbeck's Point Lobos rock "felt" this, "thought" that and "wondered" at a third thing, he said, was annoying. As a reader, he knew that John's conceits were false; as an editor he was even more irritated by the literary pretense of the piece.

The editor softened his criticism by returning to the question of Steinbeck's potential. "If you really want to learn to write," he said, "get into the newspaper business. What you've got to know is how to lay out the facts without projecting your imagination into them. Lay out the facts and let the reader draw his own impressions, instead of trying to force impressions on him with phony literary tricks."

Steinbeck asked the editor for a job. "Nothing doing. I can't afford to have you learn this trade on my time." He knew that

John had dropped out of college. He told him to go back to Stanford and study literature and journalism. "You've got the instincts of a good reporter, but you've got a long way to go before you're ready to start writing for a newspaper. Go back to school and learn what journalism is all about. Learn the principles. Get involved with the student newspaper. Then, when you graduate, come back and see me and we'll talk about a job."

The editor knew Steinbeck's father. John was not aware of it at the time, but the editor had mentioned to John Ernst his receipt of John's first article, the one about his trek across the peninsula. When John Ernst had asked what he thought of it, the editor had told him that it was amateurishly ambitious. Did he detect any talent, the senior Steinbeck had inquired? Sure, there was talent, the editor had replied. But thousands of kids had a talent for writing. There was talent and there was Talent. He didn't think John had the latter. One day, if he stuck to it and overcame all of his amateur's habits, he might turn himself into a competent journeyman writer. But he did not foresee John fulfilling the ambition, as described by his father, of becoming an important writer.

John Ernst had agreed and proceeded to tell the editor of the problems he and his wife had had with John over his ambition, including the fact that John had dropped out of Stanford. He had asked the editor as a favor to be blunt with his son in his assessment of John's talents. He himself had been unable to communicate with John on this question, and he was afraid that his son would waste his life in pursuit of an impossible dream. Perhaps receiving the word from the experienced newspaper editor would bring John to his senses and motivate him to return to college. The editor had agreed. It was his desire to accommodate the senior Steinbeck that had brought about his talk with John.

John was both dismayed and heartened by what he had been told. Dismayed because he believed he had been making progress with his new approach to writing. Heartened because in talking about journalism, the editor had talked about a form of writing John had little interest in. He wanted to write fiction and essays, and the editor's insistence on interpreting the pieces he had submitted in terms of journalism was, he thought, wrong. He briefly pondered showing the editor his two finished stories, but decided against it. He still had faith in what he was doing, and he was not going to let this cantankerous old newspaper hack discourage him.

What heartened him most, though, was an idea the editor had unwittingly put in his mind. Despite his increasingly exuberant devotion to his new writing experiments, John had been growing more and more anxious about his relations with his parents, especially his mother. On his trip home at Easter, his anxiety had changed to shame when he detected his mother fibbing to friends and relatives when asked what he was doing. His inexplicable idleness was obviously a deep embarrassment to her, and he once even overheard her tearfully castigate herself for having "to lie to protect John." Everyone, innocently or not, wanted to know what he was up to. She couldn't bring herself to tell them that she didn't know.

John had returned to Pacific Grove burdened by his guilt and strung taut by the tension of his indecision. He knew that he could not live much longer at the cottage on his parents' handouts. Besides, summer was approaching and he did not want to be there when his family came for their vacation; they would then see the full extent of his idleness and aimlessness. The time had come for him to make a hard decision on what he was going to do with himself.

A weekend visit to the cottage by Duke Sheffield from Stanford was the first step in Steinbeck's move to resolve his situation. Sheffield was approaching the end of his junior year and John, who had not seen him in over a year, was surprised at the way he had matured. Sheffield was a cheerfully intelligent fellow, shorter than John but sharing a similar shyness that in previous years had tended to manifest itself in the same kind of manic behavior John occasionally indulged in. But now, instead of the immature partner in classroom pranks Steinbeck remembered, Sheffield exuded an air of manly sobriety and sophistication.

He was majoring in English at Stanford and had his own ambitions to be a writer. Whatever lingering envy he might have had toward John's departure from Stanford two years before to "become a writer" was dissipated upon visiting him in Pacific Grove. All his friend had to show for the two years were a pair of short stories and two impressionistic essays about the Monterey Peninsula.

In a tone that was somewhat defensively superior, Steinbeck outlined to Sheffield his recently-arrived-at theory of writing and then showed him the two stories he had composed in accordance with the theory. Sheffield later recalled them as moderately impressive but lacking polish. "And yet they contained the seeds of what was eventually to make John famous." The overall effect, however, was satirical rather than serious, thought Sheffield, as if Steinbeck had not yet decided to take his characters seriously.

During the weekend, as the two young men talked, Steinbeck was at first sarcastic about Stanford and Sheffield's continuing attendance there. Sheffield later took this for defensiveness. As the weekend progressed, John began to listen to Duke's anecdotes about campus life and the interesting courses he was taking in the English department. Sheffield spoke confidently of literary theories and prose styles, alluding to books and writers John had heard of but never read. By Sunday afternoon, as Sheffield was preparing to return to Stanford, John's confidence in the uniqueness of his own writing theory was shattered. He realized, if only instinctively, that his knowledge of literature was at best limited, and that he still had a great deal to learn if he seriously intended to make a living as a writer. When Sheffield left, John was jealous of him. A desire to return to Stanford began to grow in him. It was the only alternative to settling down in some thankless job that would drain his literary energy and ambition.

But how could he overcome his misgivings? If he returned — provided the university were willing to have him back — he would have to adapt to a whole new group of classmates. He had already told his sister how uncomfortable he would feel as a twenty-year-old in a student body two and three years younger than himself. Finally, a return to college would be an admission of his mistake in leaving in the first place, an admission of his failure to accomplish what he had told everyone he had set out to accomplish. And wouldn't his parents insist that as a condition of financing his return he concede that his urge to become a writer had been a misguided one?

It was at this time that he had his talk with the newspaper editor. Though disappointed at the editor's refusal to print his article, he got an idea about how he might reconcile his problem. He would use the editor's counsel that he study journalism as his rationale for returning to college.

Steinbeck went back to Salinas late in May and announced to his parents that he was ready to resume college if Stanford would take him back. He declared that he had come to the realization that he lacked the talent to make a go of it as a writer. He had, however, found a realistic alternative, one that would afford him a chance to spend his life writing and still make a living: journalism. With their and Stanford's consent, he would return to the university and apply himself to the pursuit of a journalistic career. If that failed, he could always become a teacher.

To John Ernst and Olive Steinbeck, that was a reasonable compromise. John Ernst approved his son's proposal, consented to renew his financial support, and set out to use his influence as one of Monterey County's more distinguished citizens to get John readmitted to Stanford. He also sent a note of thanks to his friend the Monterey newspaper editor and solicited from him a letter of recommendation to Stanford on behalf of his son. As for Olive, she was less impressed by John's new vocational aspirations than by the apparent fact that he had finally "found" himself.

John Ernst placed a condition on his agreement to subsidize John's return to college. This was that until the fall, when he would return to Palo Alto, he must take a job. He would not have John lazing about the house, or about the Pacific Grove cottage, any longer. John agreed, and his father managed to secure him a job as an assistant in one of the testing laboratories at the Spreckels sugar plant. John started work there in mid-June.

It was early August before Stanford responded favorably to Steinbeck's application for readmission. The only hitch was that he would not be able to start with the fall quarter. Because he would technically still be part of the freshman class, and because that class had already been filled to its quota, he would have to wait until January when dismissals and dropouts provided an opening. He would be able at that time to make up his previous freshman course deficiencies and then move the following fall with the rest of the class into its sophomore year.

Steinbeck did not mind waiting, for it gave him an opportunity to earn and save extra money by extending his job at the Spreckels factory. He remained at the lab, growing to enjoy the precise work with test tubes, beakers and measures, until just before Christmas of 1922, when he left to prepare for his return to Stanford.

What pleased him about the job was the procedural correlation he saw between what chemists do and what writers do. The Spreckels chemists mixed countless substances in countless variations in their endeavors to arrive at desired results. Steinbeck had previously thought of the techniques of scientific experimentation and testing as the dullest work imaginable. But as he got into it himself, he realized that it was dynamic and satisfying. He became impressed by the way the lab's chemists handled their substances and implements to produce numerous other substances and combinations of substances, and by the ease with which they transposed chemical equations and formulations into tangible fluids and powders that had real-life uses. He likened their procedures to the writer's task of translating images and thoughts into characters and stories, of economically measuring and mixing and testing words to create impressions and feelings. Throughout the fall of 1922, while he waited to go back to college, he added this perception to his continuing literary endeavors. He composed two stories about the chemists at Spreckels, and in these and a few others he consciously wrote in what he imagined was the style of a chemist experimenting. That is, he strove to use as few words as possible, always paring and mixing, to achieve the visual and interior effects he sought in his descriptions.

Christmas was the occasion for a family reunion, with all the Steinbecks at home save sister Beth, who had married and moved to New York. Most of the interest at the feast table centered on Mary, back from her first semester at Stanford and bubbling with anecdotes about campus life. John sat and listened ruefully, almost sheepishly. He was still devoted to his younger sister, but her enthusiasm for Stanford seemed — well, childish. He dreaded the thought of having such innocents as his fellow students. Luckily, he mused, he had arranged to room with Duke Sheffield, who was in the middle of his final year. When Duke graduated, John would go into a single room on his own. At least he would not have to live with a freshman.

His musings were interrupted by his father, who rose to offer a Christmas toast. Raising his glass to Mary, he toasted her obvious delight with college. When he came around the table to John, he wished his son equal happiness on his return to Stanford and suggested that he say a prayer of thanks for having gotten a second chance. "Maybe," he said as he turned to the rest of the family, "our frustrated writer will apply himself this time around. I can assure you, son, that if you do, any career in the world will be open to you."

John was indeed grateful for the second chance. But his face flushed with a tinge of shame, for he knew that he was returning to Stanford only because he had no alternative. And for all his false starts and hapless efforts over the previous two years, and despite his more recent representations to his parents to the contrary, his dream was still to be a writer. Journalism was only a device to buy time.

W*hen Steinbeck arrived back at Stanford in January of* 1923, he took up residence with Duke Sheffield in a basement room in Encina Hall. Sheffield, an English major, viewed the last semester of his senior year as a milk run, the traditional view of all college seniors impatient to graduate. He was required to take only a few wrap-up courses and intended to spend most of his time in his own writing endeavors.

Steinbeck, on the other hand, was assigned a heavy course load. He was once again registered in the liberal arts program, where he wrote down "journalism" as his prospective major. If he were to make up the ground he had lost, he would have no time to indulge in independent writing. Infused with a resolve to restore his parents' faith and trust, he set out to excel in his studies.

If he didn't excel, he at least completed and passed all his courses. In June, when his grades were released, he was able to boast of three A's, a number of B's and only two C's. In accord with his subsidiary interest in the life sciences, one of his favorite and most successful courses was zoology, although he did well in French, history and poetry too.

Steinbeck renewed many of his acquaintances in the class of 1923 that spring, and almost all found a sharp change in him. Physically, his features had synchronized and smoothed out somewhat, softening the coarse angularity of his face. A particular broadness of shoulder distinguished his physique. Temperamentally, he was considerably less introspective than they remembered, but at the same time less prone to juvenile prankishness.

Steinbeck still kept his distance from most of his schoolmates, however. Only to Duke Sheffield did he abandon his reticence, and in six months the two became close friends. Indeed, in the sense of sharing intimate confidences, dreams and worries, Sheffield would turn out to be Steinbeck's closest friend for many years. With one exception, the two were much alike. The exception was that Steinbeck was much more intense, whereas Sheffield was placid and unflappable. Steinbeck's intensity would still drive him to extremes of behavior. Sheffield's phlegmatism usually kept him on an even, almost bland, keel. Where John fought the world, Duke accepted it.

Although Steinbeck did little or no writing that spring, most of his discussions with Sheffield revolved around the subject, with John using his roommate to test his theories of literary technique and style. By the same token, Sheffield used Steinbeck as a sounding board for the stories he was writing. After reading Duke's accumulated material, John rather mercilessly concluded that his friend talked about literature with more authority than he wrote it. He found Sheffield's writing style prolix, derivative and reflective, lacking in bite and tension and originality — the result, he thought, of Duke's four-year immersion in academics. He wondered whether the same thing would happen to him, if another three years at Stanford would dilute the individuality and inventiveness he hoped to achieve in his own writing.

When not studying and talking, the two young men spent much of their time in pursuit of the campus's coeds and on trips to San Francisco in Sheffield's car to sample the city's nightlife. Steinbeck was singularly unsuccessful in his encounters with the opposite sex. He inwardly lusted after a number of the more attractive girls on campus. But they, finding him outwardly timid and physically unappealing, gave him short shrift. Less attractive girls — ones who were inclined to be more responsive to his approaches — he was bored by. In limiting his pursuits exclusively to pretty girls, he manifested the universal need of the insecure and immature male to bolster his self-esteem through association with desirable and desired females. He knew, as every young man of his time knew, that much of his male peers' estimation of him would be shaped by the girls in whose company he was seen and about whom he could boast of sexual intimacies. Unfortunately for Steinbeck, he had to be content to influence his fellows' estimation of him in other ways, at least at this point in his life.

By June, John was able to demonstrate to his parents that he was capable of academic accomplishment. But he was at the same time falling into another state of restless impatience with his life. He just plain did not like college, no matter how well he did at it. His attitude was sharpened by the fact that his original class would be graduating, and that Duke Sheffield would no longer be around. He had made no friends in the freshman and sophomore classes. His fears of feeling out of place among his younger classmates during the following school year mounted. And his compulsive urge to write, grudgingly smothered for the previous six months, resurfaced with more force than ever.

He signed up for a zoology course at the Hopkins lab in Pacific Grove for the summer, along with his sister Mary. Mary and John lived at the family cottage and were joined for a while by Sheffield, who stopped for a postgraduation visit before returning to his home near Los Angeles. The longer

John was exposed to Duke the graduate, the more envious he became — and the less willing again to carry on with college. When Sheffield left for home, John went into another depression. When his parents arrived to spend a few weeks at the cottage, they immediately noticed it. Without John's having to tell them, they knew what it was about. Their pride in his performance the previous spring was shattered.

But John managed to avoid crushing them completely. It was not so much that he was depressed by having to go back to Stanford, he said, as by his knowledge that they were being forced to stretch their financial resources by keeping both Mary and himself at Stanford. He claimed that he felt an overwhelming guilt at being the cause of their financial sacrifice and said that he could not bear to return to college with that burden on him. The only way he could get anything out of Stanford thenceforth would be if he paid his own way — after all, he would soon be twenty-two years old, an age when his contemporaries would be earning their own ways in the world.

This took some of the edge off his parents' disappointment. John said that he would like not to drop out of Stanford, but to skip the fall semester so that he could earn enough money to resume in the spring. Reluctantly, his parents agreed. Arrangements were thereupon made with the university to grant him a financial leave of absence, and with the Spreckels sugar factory to give him another job as a lab technician.

Steinbeck spent the remainder of 1923 at the refinery. During these months he devoted much of his spare time to the resumption of his writing. Continuing in the framework of the work he had done the year before when he was on his own in Pacific Grove, he completed four or five brief stories. One, called "Fingers of Cloud," was a satire about a backward girl and her Filipino husband. Another, an even more satirical and somewhat obscure takeoff on life at Stanford, he titled "Adventures in Arcademy." His literary point of view was developing a strained but hard-edged sardonicism. Only an occasional lyrical flash saved it from outright parody and sarcasm.

When he was not working in the lab or writing, Steinbeck kept himself busy on his observation exercises. The poor Mexican laborers at the refinery particularly interested him in this respect. He spent much time watching them, cultivating their comradeship, then writing down tight descriptive vignettes in which he tried to reproduce their mannerisms and speech and the way they interacted. He also began a weekly correspondence with Duke Sheffield in southern California, one in which each penned long letters filled with philosophical musings on life and their application to the literature they both yearned to create. In one letter, Steinbeck wrote: "It's amazing how the very act of writing to you gives birth to ideas that never occurred to me before. Do you find this? I'll be going along, and then in the middle of a thought something totally unconnected will pop into my head. And it will open up a whole new field of thought that I've just got to follow. That's why I like these letters. I feel I'm learning more by putting my thoughts down than I could learn anywhere else. Some of them turn out to be useless, but some are very good and worth following."

With the need of only a little financial help from his father, Steinbeck returned to Stanford at the beginning of the January term in 1924. He signed up again for pre-journalism courses and moved into a tiny single room on the top floor of Encina Hall. His return marked the beginning of a rapid change in his life, particularly in his personality.

He was soon to be twenty-three. With his original classmates gone, he found himself less burdened by the inferiority that had previously haunted him. He was now a member of no specific class, although most of his courses were still at the sophomore level. But he was two and three years older than most of his schoolmates. This fact gave him a social confidence that he had never before experienced. His comparative physical maturity set him apart from his fellow students; moreover, his intelligence operated at a more serious and intense level than theirs. The deference they tended to show as a result provided him with a need to demonstrate a mental and emotional maturity that he had never before aspired to. Even his professors treated him differently from the other students, affording him a level of respect and attention that reinforced his newfound confidence. He was no longer John Steinbeck the class prankster and inscrutable introvert. Now he was Steinbeck the diligent student and intelligent young man.

Steinbeck eased into the new role with a certain amount of grace and a great amount of gratitude. He did not lose his natural reticence, however. He simply overlaid it with a conscious outgoingness — not gregariousness, certainly, but an expanding amiability that opened him up to friendship with and interest in others. Much of this new facet of Steinbeck's personality was surely the result of the acceptance he received from his fellow students because of his higher age and richer experience. Warming to his unaccustomed status, he seized upon it and began to shape his personality to further expand it. Part of his technique in doing so consisted of cultivating his more pleasant eccentricities and suppressing his less attractive ones. To his usual scruffy and tattered mode of dress he added a black beret, which provided the immediate Bohemian look he strove for. He moved about the campus carrying his books in an old cloth shoulder satchel, puffing on a newly acquired pipe and gazing ruminatively into the middle distance. He participated with more and more frequency in classroom discussion. As he lost his self-conscious tentativeness and grew more confident with himself in these public forums, he began to hold forth at length with imposing articulateness and wry, incisive humor. Often he would spontaneously introduce an idea simply to get an adversarial discussion under way, or he would pointedly differ with a teacher's viewpoint and then press his own interpretation (although he did not really believe in it) for the sake of challenge and argument. Within a period of a few months that spring, Steinbeck became a well-known character on the Stanford campus, liked and admired by most, envied by others. Much in this new manner was mere role-playing, a role that he had invented for himself, but part of it was genuine. The two elements gradually fused, however, to form a permanent aspect of his personality. It soon became impossible for anyone, including his sister Mary, to distinguish between the real John and the playacting John. When he affected an expression of pained, remote brilliance or soft-spoken contentiousness or intellectual condescension, his right eyebrow arching steeply, no one knew exactly how to respond. Steinbeck had learned to keep people off balance, and they respected him for it.

His new mien was reinforced by the publication in the Stanford *Spectator* (his first "published" writing) of one of the short stories he had written while out of school the previous fall. Almost immediately upon his return he had become friendly with a student named Frank Fenton, who lived a few doors down the corridor in Encina Hall. Fenton, who was aiming at a career in education, was on the editorial staff of the *Spectator*, the monthly campus newspaper. He had met Steinbeck the previous spring and was well acquainted with his writing ambitions. When John had failed to return for the fall term, Fenton assumed that he had once again dropped out for good to write. Surprised to see him back in January, he asked Steinbeck what he had accomplished. John said, "Oh, I got a few stories done." Fenton asked to see them. John showed him "Fingers of Cloud," the story about the backward ranch girl and her Filipino husband, which he had heavily revised. Fenton liked it and recommended it for publication in the *Spectator*. It appeared in the February 1924 issue and attracted considerable campus attention. A story about a couple of "weird" characters, sardonically told and bitingly satiric in effect, albeit bordering on caricature, it raised a number of eyebrows as well. So this is what Steinbeck is interested in, went the general reaction. Most did not know what to make of it. But they were impressed by the style and hard-bitten outlook of the story.

Almost everyone who ever went to college has come out with tales of at least one teacher who had a greater influence on his or her life than any other. In Steinbeck's case the teacher was Edith Mirrielees, whose courses in short-story writing were already legendary at Stanford. In those days of countless national magazines and "pulps," the short story was the country's most popular fictional genre. Anyone who had the remotest ambition to write usually cut his teeth on the short story. Short-story-writing courses were the mainstay of numerous college liberal arts programs, and the professors who taught them were often considered the cream of the liberal arts faculties.

Edith Mirrielees was a tall, aging, bespectacled woman who possessed a rare talent for communicating with students. She was an academic through and through, slightly disorganized, and she could spend weeks on a detailed analysis of a single story — a de Maupassant, a Melville — wringing every last drop of meaning and technique from it. Steinbeck had signed up for her course at the beginning of 1924. She read his *Spectator* story and commented favorably on it before the class, not failing, however, to point out its weaknesses. Steinbeck thereupon became her devoted pupil, and as the spring semester progressed he showed her some of his other stories and explained his theories about writing of the ordinary people of his experience. She encouraged him but asked him to try something completely different. Her course was really a course in experimental writing. She was the first to caution her students to write from their experience, but at the same time she encouraged them to experiment with inventing totally out of their imaginations for the purpose of broadening their technical horizons and getting a sense of their limitations. After reading several of Steinbeck's other stories, she suggested that he apply his definite narrative skills to a subject and environment foreign to his personal experience.

At first this went against his grain. He thought that it was his experience — the sights and sounds and characters of his observations — that had polished his prose style, which Professor Mirrielees obviously admired. She did not deny it, but tried to convince Steinbeck that exercises of the imagination could help stretch his style, which, though commendably direct, tended to be monotonous and flat in its sardonicism. His one major fault was that in achieving his style, he remained too much an outsider to his characters, too much an observer, so that he caught their form but not their substance. In other words, because he conceived of his characters more as descriptive objects than as people, they tended to be wooden and alike. A try at more imaginative characters and situations might add breadth and depth to his characterizations. Perhaps his striving for satire propelled him to a superior point of view, to a patronizing conception of his characters. This was clever and superficially *au courant*, she told him, but she doubted that he had the true lightning wit that sustained good satire. She didn't want to see him become bogged down in chasing a literary form to which he was temperamentally unsuited.

After mulling over her suggestions, Steinbeck was stumped. He started several stories out of his imagination but each time became so lost in the intricacies of manufacturing lively characters that he had to stop, convinced that his portrayals were counterfeit and clearly perceivable as such. He felt it natural to write in a satirical style, he complained to Mirrielees, and found the same objections to inventing plots and characters out of his imagination as he had a few years earlier in Pacific Grove. Professor Mirrielees responded by insisting that although his satire was fleetingly amusing, it would never get him anywhere as a writer. Having gotten to know Steinbeck a bit, she told him that in her view his penchant for satire was not a true writer's impulse but an expression of his personal defensiveness, that his avuncular tone shed less light on his characters than it did on him. She urged him to keep trying and suggested some experiments in allegory, since he had told her of his appreciation of the allegorical literature he had read in his youth.

Steinbeck found Mirrielees's comments at once edifying and embarrassing. No one had ever talked so candidly to him before, and with such authority and insight into his character. Although he at first resisted her assessment of him, he gradually began to accept the possibility of its truth. Since he had declared to her his intention of becoming a writer, and she had indicated that she thought his dream was a possible one, he grew more and more willing to put himself under her direction and to trust in her. He renewed his efforts to follow her prescription.

Steinbeck and his sister Mary were seeing a lot of each other by then — she had caught up to him and was his academic contemporary, taking several of the courses in which he was enrolled. They had developed between them what today would be called, in show-business, a "schtick." Harking back to their earlier years when John used to recite long passages to her from the King Arthur tales, in his approximation of their medieval English pronunciations, they took to conversing in the same medieval dialect to amuse their friends and give the impression that they were trading secrets that only they could understand. Out of this game-playing, the thought surfaced in Steinbeck's mind of writing a short story drawn from the Arthurian legends. When he proposed the idea to Edith Mirrielees, she approved.

John made several attempts to form a modern allegorical story based on *Morte d'Arthur*. In his discussions about it with Mirrielees, she remarked that in her view the Arthurian tales had served as the inspiration for the development of all Western literature. The modern novel, in her judgment, found its thematic roots in Malory's knightly narratives. Even the popular American Western, with its concern with the conflict between good and evil, and the hero's striving for moral rectitude, came out of the Arthurian tradition. The courage, chivalry, violence and questing after moral absolutes — all features of the Western genre — were not much different from the values expressed by Malory. Mirrielees suggested that John try to write a story, preferably something in the Western vein, that would incorporate these themes.

Excited by Mirrielees's insights, he went back to his notebook and made yet another stab at a story, inventing a Launcelotian character in cowboy garb on a ranch in Texas. Halfway through, he again gave up. The character emerged naive and false, a romanticized cowpoke whose natural insights into life and whose philosophical musings, as he tracked down an outlaw who had killed his father, made him totally unreal.

John's failure to follow through on the idea provoked him to raise in Mirrielees's class the question of whether it were really possible to transpose ancient themes and characters into modern literature. Mirrielees contended that it was not only possible but inevitable. "There are no new ideas in literature," she said, "just new characters who in their fictional interactions express old ideas differently." As a result of the discussion, she assigned each of her students to take a character in ancient literature or history and write a story around him in modern terms.

Steinbeck, who had also read a lot of tales about pirates and buccaneers in his childhood, for some reason decided to write his story around the character of the legendary pirate Henry Morgan. He researched the subject and produced a tale, called "A Lady in Infra-Red," which combined elements of eighteenth-century Caribbean buccaneering with medieval Arthuriana. The story, although it received only an average grade, would be the seed from which his first novel, to be written five years later, grew.

In the meantime, John busied himself in other activities.

He continued to make new friends, mostly students who, like himself, aspired to be writers. Moreover, somewhat to his surprise, he began to attract the kinds of girls to whom he was attracted. His persona was now almost unremittingly serious and shrewdly sensitive, and his newfound confidence in himself gave him the courage to pursue his own holy grails. His one athletic endeavor was to try out for the Stanford polo team. He was an experienced rider, having learned on his childhood pony and having polished his skills during his later years on various ranches. He derived great satisfaction from handling a spirited, flashy horse; most of it centered on his ego and his need to look good. He certainly looked good on a horse, but he was an indifferent polo player. He still lacked physical recklessness and shied away from the collisions and flying mallets that no avid polo player would fear. When he hurt a knee in a fall from a horse during a practice scrimmage, he gave up polo. But in order to earn some extra money he got a job at the Stanford stables exercising the green polo ponies and acclimatizing them to the sport.

He also kept up his letter writing, most of which was directed to Duke Sheffield, George Mors, and one or two other Stanford graduates he had known during his first stay at the university. Professor Mirrielees had recommended letter writing to her students as a form of literary discipline. The letters most people wrote, she said, were rambling and styleless forms of communication. She pointed to some of the great English and French authors who had devoted as much craft to their letters as they had to their novels and stories. She urged her students to treat each letter they wrote with as much seriousness and discipline as they devoted to their "creative" writing. She convinced them that the letter form provided an excellent opportunity to experiment with prose style and at the same time refine it. "Every time without exception that you take pen to paper," she was fond of saying, "be sure that you make the most of the opportunity." Another of her dicta was: "The best way to write a story is not to write to some imagined audience of readers. This promotes needless cleverness and self-consciousness. Nor should you try to fool yourself into thinking that you are writing for no reader at all, that you are writing simply for your own sake. This leads to obscurity and obtuseness. The best way to write is to imagine that you are writing a letter to an individual you know. Pick someone out in your mind, and then imagine that the story you are writing is really a letter to that person. In that way, you will make every effort to communicate clearly and succinctly. Which is why care and deliberation in writing real letters is so important. If you write good letters, if you write letters in which your points are well ordered and set down in simple clarity, you will write good stories."

Out of this, Steinbeck's intensive, lifelong habit of writing carefully crafted (although often sloppily presented) letters was born. Thereafter his letters took on a much improved prose quality. In his letters to Sheffield, Mors and others who had graduated, written in a crabbed, minuscule and sometimes indecipherable script, Steinbeck tested sentence constructions, word usages, cadences and rhythms. He had little patience with grammatical niceties, even less with spelling, claiming that he was more interested in the interior "sounds," unities, and meanings his words conveyed than the exterior appearances. He would often insist that grammatical preoccupation in writing, in both his fiction and his letters, was not the ally of clarity but its enemy. In his early years this may well have been simply a rationalization to excuse the fact that he had failed to develop grammatical skills, mostly out of laziness and inattentiveness. Later, however, it would become an integral part of his writing philosophy. As he gained writing experience, his knowledge of correct grammar and spelling improved, yet he deliberately continued to ignore much of it with the justification that it fettered his imagination.

With Edith Mirrielees's increasing attention and encouragement, particularly after he wrote "A Lady in Infra-Red," whatever doubts Steinbeck had about devoting his life to writing vanished. And as his confidence in his talents was reinforced, his social self-confidence blossomed apace. He became more genial and expansive, widened his circle of friends among the university's English and journalism majors, and grew more daring sexually. In this last regard he developed a series of ploys to win the attention of girls. They consisted mostly of putting on alternating faces of pained vulnerability, savage wit, and carefree humor. These seeming contradictions in his character, he found, appealed to girls. Coupled with his natural shyness and his opinionated mind, they produced a young man of mysterious dimensions compared to most of the other male students. Suddenly Steinbeck could say in truth that he had a sex life rather than boast of a nonexistent one, as he had in previous years. It began in February of 1924 with one or two Stanford coeds and the usual necking and petting in movie houses and hallways. When that became routine, Steinbeck sought more rewarding encounters with nonstudent girls in Palo Alto and other nearby communities. He finally "scored," as the saying went, on a frigid night in May on a sand dune near Half Moon Bay, where he had gone with a secretary from Redwood City to a beach party. It was his first complete sexual experience since the summer of 1917 with the Portuguese cleaning girl at the family cottage in Pacific Grove.

Although pleased to have attracted the attention of one of the Stanford faculty's leading lights, Edith Mirrielees, Steinbeck's relations with most of his other instructors were not so pleasant. Mirrielees's favorable criticisms of his writing imbued him with an arrogance that several other teachers found insufferable. One in particular was the woman who taught his course in news writing. In a letter to one of his other graduated Stanford friends, Carl Wilhelmson, in April of 1924, Steinbeck complained of having written a compelling mood piece for the teacher's journalism class only to have her refuse to accept it on the claim that it was unreal, that the things he had written simply did not happen. It was not so much her criticism that infuriated Steinbeck as it was the apparent condescension with which she offered it. Steinbeck said that he cursed her, and that as a result he was sure the instructor intended to flunk him in the course. He cared little, however, "since real writing and not journalism" was his destiny.

By this time, Steinbeck was once again confused over his continuing presence in college. On the one hand, his friends from the earlier years were out trying to make careers as writers, and he began to feel that time was passing him by. On the other, he enjoyed his new eminence at Stanford. Moreover, he felt secure in its cloistered atmosphere and gained spiritual nourishment from the approbation he received from Mirrielees and a few other teachers, as well as from his new friends — younger fellows such as Frank Fenton, Webster "Toby" Street and Robert Cathcart. He remained torn between leaving for good and continuing.

Several problems complicated his indecision. One, of course, was his parents. Although they had gone along with his intermittent approach to college, particularly since he was now bearing much of the financial burden, he continued to labor under anxieties at the prospect of totally disappointing them. He knew that to drop out of college for good would constitute in their minds an utter rejection of their hopes for him, and probably cause a permanent rift.

Another was Professor Mirrielees. She encouraged his writing, mixing her criticisms with gentle understanding. She even assured him that a few of the stories he had done were commercially publishable if further worked on, particularly "A Lady in Infra-Red." Yet when Steinbeck expressed his nagging desire to quit college for good and embark full-time on a writing career, she discouraged it, counseling him to complete his Stanford career and take seriously his journalism studies so that he would have something practical to sustain him once he graduated. She had no doubt, she said, that John had a chance to succeed as a writer. But it might take years before he was recognized, and she had seen how such years of struggle and poverty had broken the spirit of other talented would-be authors.

Steinbeck was able to acknowledge the wisdom of her advice, but he had no patience for the "years" it would take him to be recognized and able to make a living. In the inner recesses of his mind he was sure that he could achieve a moderate success, which was all he wanted, in a matter of months — once he was able to devote all his time and energy to writing. And yet, at the same time, he wondered if he were deceiving himself. He would never know unless he tried. But to try — to quit school and plunge into the real world — might give him an undesirable answer. At least he was safe with his dream at Stanford.

❋ ❋ ❋ ❋ ❋ ❋ ❋ ❋ CHAPTER TEN

So he did not quit college for good. Instead he again decided to skip the coming fall semester in order to earn sufficient money to return in January of 1925.

When he returned to Salinas in June he was able to boast of two achievements. One concerned his grades; except in military science, his marks for the 1924 spring term were above average and he brought home an A in Edith Mirrielees's short-story course. The second consisted of the publication of another story in the *Spectator* – the satirical piece he had written the year before, entitled "Adventures in Arcademy," which lampooned campus life at Stanford and especially certain administration and faculty members. He was not very proud of the story. The one he had hoped would be published, but which was not, was a piece he had written for Miss Mirrielees's class. It was another sardonic tale about a machinist who derives an overwhelming sense of power from operating his machine until the machine maims him. He curses God for his bad fortune, then, after a further mishap, imagines that God has punished him.

Steinbeck's determination to earn enough money during the coming months to finance his return to Stanford the following January rapidly dissolved during the summer of 1924. At first he looked for work in Monterey so that he could live at the cottage in Pacific Grove. Joined by Duke Sheffield, he was unsuccessful. The two young men thereupon prevailed on John's father to get them jobs with the Spreckels company. This time the Spreckels factory near Salinas had no positions open, but they were offered jobs in a branch factory at Manteca, a humid town at the head of the San Joaquin valley between Stockton and Modesto.

Steinbeck and Sheffield barely made it through mid-August, when they quit out of boredom and heat distemper. They drifted to San Francisco and quickly squandered their earnings looking for girls and frequenting Prohibition speakeasies. Since John was going to pass up the fall term at Stanford, Sheffield persuaded him to return with him to his home in Long Beach, where together they could spend the fall months writing and trying to get published commercially.

John agreed and moved south to the Sheffield house in September. He and Sheffield wrote furiously for a while, collaborating on shallow adventure stories and mailing them to pulp magazines in the hopes of making some quick money. They had no success, however, and were reduced to addressing Christmas Seal envelopes for spare change. By Christmas John was back in Salinas, where he importuned his parents to subsidize one final try at college.

He reregistered at Stanford for the January 1925 term, but this time he rented a tiny room in a shack off campus, in the backyard of a private home. The shack soon became a magnet to his aspiring-writer schoolmates, who would gather there in the evenings to quaff beer, exchange gossip and discuss their hopes. Steinbeck named it "The Den of Pegasus" — Pegasus being the mythological flying horse, which he took to symbolize his, and possibly the others', soaring ambitions. "If a horse can fly," Steinbeck said, "anything is possible."[9]

Steinbeck was still nominally in the prejournalism curriculum, but his passions remained with his literature courses. He also began to study, on his own, some of the contemporary young writers who had recently burst onto the American literary scene — writers like Ernest Hemingway, William Faulkner and F. Scott Fitzgerald — and established older authors such as Theodore Dreiser and Willa Cather. Of particular interest to him was the work of James Branch Cabell and Donn Byrne, and, whether consciously or unconsciously, he tried for a time to emulate them.

John encountered a further important influence during the spring term of 1925. This was in the form of Mrs. Elizabeth Smith. John had joined the university's English Club, an organization of bright and talented literature students who met weekly at the homes of various faculty members to offer their work for criticism and to discuss literature in general. Elizabeth Smith, an attractive outspoken divorcee in her early forties, was frequently host to the club's sessions in her home. At first Steinbeck stood in awe of her, as did others, for she was, in addition to being a charismatic teacher, an oft-published writer. Usually under the name of E. C. A. Smith, and sometimes under masculine pseudonyms, she had published stories in a number of national magazines, and one of her stories had been included with special praise in the annual called *Best Short Stories of 1921.*

Elizabeth Smith warmed to Steinbeck during the course of several English Club meetings. Amused by his combination of intellectual garrulousness and personal shyness, and by the writerly image he sought to strike with his eccentric clothing, she brought him into her circle of favorites. When she asked to look at one of his stories, the one he was proudest of, he gave her "A Lady in Infra-Red," sure that since Edith Mirrielees thought so much of it, she would too.

After reading it, Elizabeth Smith called Steinbeck to her home. Aware that she rarely wasted words and liked to be blunt in her criticisms, he appeared, fearing the worst. As it turned out, she was uncharacteristically mild in her criticisms of the manuscript and enthusiastic about its virtues. In her view, "A Lady in Infra-Red," in its bittersweet picture of a man's betrayal of his early dreams and the disillusion that descends on him because of his inability to accept the betrayal, was a theme worthy of a novel. Steinbeck had written the story partly as an attempt to justify and reinforce his belief in his own dreams for himself, and Elizabeth Smith easily detected the motivation. The theme was a noble one, she told Steinbeck, particularly so because it came from the pen of a young man who was stubbornly trying not to betray his own ideals. On one level, then, it was intensely autobiographical. Every budding author should make his first major work autobiographical, she told Steinbeck. The personal novel was useful because it enabled the young writer with little experience to write truthfully and with immediacy. It also afforded him a chance to polish his skills in characterization and action by forcing him to disguise himself in the writing. A superficially biographical novel in which the novice author blatantly appeared on every page was a bore, she exclaimed; the characters tended to be just as uncertain and colorless as the authors themselves. But the same kind of novel, with the author subtly submerged in the characters, could lead to exciting first-novel results. Elizabeth Smith added that if published as a short story, "A Lady in Infra-Red" would have little impact. But if expanded into a novel and published, it stood a good chance of receiving attention, with the concomitant benefit that Steinbeck would be viewed as a young author who was capable of dealing with important humanistic themes, instead of as just another writer telling stories to make a living. The primary virtue she saw in Steinbeck, she told him, was an impulse to create literature that meant something and stood for something, that prodded the reader into a recognition of human nature. However, she cautioned, she too would like to see Steinbeck abandon the excessively caustic narrative tone of most of his previous work, for it tended to confuse the reader. Why should the reader care for his characters if they suspected that he didn't?

Steinbeck was elated by Elizabeth Smith's reaction to "A Lady in Infra-Red." When he gave her a few more stories to read, she expanded on her favorable view of his talent, but again warned him about the bitterness in his voice. She urged him to "discard your acerb like a snake sheds it skin" and develop a gentler, more sympathetic style of humor vis-à-vis his characters. His satire came out as a sneer, she claimed, and until he wiped "the sneer off your face," his writing would never "amount to more than clever verbiage." He must not confuse literary toughness, a characteristic he professed to strive for, with literary bullying, the style to which he was presently in danger of becoming chained. Literary toughness was proper because it was part of the quest to create that which was true. The literary bully was satisfied merely with the counterfeit effect.

Elizabeth Smith became his mentor for the remainder of the spring term. Fired by her moral support and specific suggestions, he locked himself in the Den of Pegasus for two weeks at the beginning of May and immersed himself in the challenge of expanding "A Lady in Infra-Red" into a novel. Except for an overnight visit from the Redwood City secretary, whom he was still desultorily romancing, he saw no one other than Elizabeth Smith's seventeen-year-old daughter Polly, who delivered daily donations of food and coffee from the Smith home.

John blithely ignored whatever charms Polly might have possessed and slaved away at the task of transforming "A Lady in Infra-Red" into a novel. He had decided to expand the story by making it an allegorical saga of the entire life of its protagonist, Henry Morgan. Steinbeck's idea was to trace in fiction the story of the modest Welsh boy, Morgan, who left his home to seek an honest fortune in the West Indies, turned to privateering when he had no success, and was thereby forbidden from ever returning to the home in Wales for which he yearned.

Writing slowly in his minuscule script in a large book-keeper's ledger (a vehicle he would subsequently use in the composing of most of the first drafts of his books), Steinbeck became bogged down in the conflict between his natural inclination to write in a tone of caustic superiority and Elizabeth Smith's urgings that he empathize with his characters. Toward the end of May he had completed close to forty pages, but had become so self-critical that he was tearing up five or six pages for every one he completed. Nevertheless, he felt that he was on to something in the fragmented novel. Totally absorbed in it, he all but ignored his college classes. He prevailed upon Polly Smith to type the first forty pages, then showed them to her mother. She reacted positively and urged him further on.

At the same time, Steinbeck received another warning from the school. His neglect of his classwork had again placed him in academic jeopardy. At the end of May he made a half-hearted effort to set things right, but his preoccupation with his novel soon dissipated his resolve. Rather than face another round of scholastic embarrassment, when the term ended in June he announced that he intended to withdraw from Stanford for good. An astonished Elizabeth Smith tried to dissuade him, but he pointed to her favorable support of his writing efforts as his justification for leaving. He had wasted enough of his life, he said. He could never write a long, sustained novel while at the same time having to fulfill his academic responsibility. He was going to leave Stanford forever and embark on a full-time writing career. If he failed, then he would eventually find something else to do. But he could no longer wait to learn whether he was fated to fail or succeed.

All that was left for Steinbeck to do was to break the news to his parents. He returned to Salinas in mid-June with the idea of not telling them about his decision but of simply telling them that he would once again skip the fall term and work, as he had done the previous two years. Perhaps, he thought, by the end of the fall he would have completed the Morgan novel and had it accepted by a publisher. If so, he would be more easily able to persuade his parents of the wisdom his decision not to finish college. He quickly realized, however, that if he spent the next six months working again for the Spreckels company, he would have little time and energy to complete the novel. Therefore, he screwed up his courage and told his parents, on a take-it-or-leave-it basis, that he was out of Stanford permanently.

Not surprisingly, since they had prepared themselves for it after hearing reports from their daughter Mary, they took the news with gracious resignation. They saw no use in further beating the dead horse that was John's education. He was old enough to look after himself, and they decided that the better part of wisdom would be to provide him with their moral support in his desire to become a writer. If he indeed failed, he could always fall back on a career in the Spreckels organization. In an uncharacteristic expression of generosity, most likely influenced by his wife, John's father offered to subsidize him at a rate of twenty dollars a month so that he could finish his novel, which John estimated it would take him six months to do. The senior Steinbeck's condition was that if it failed to find a publisher, John would once again concede that he had no future as a writer and consent to rejoin the Spreckels company with a view to forging a career there.

Steinbeck wanted to explain to his father that the publication or nonpublication of one novel would not be a fair measure of his potential for success or failure as a writer. But John Ernst had the habit of thinking in absolutes, and Steinbeck was grateful enough for his subsidy offer to avoid arguing the question. Instead he accepted it, installed himself once again at the cottage in Pacific Grove, and set out to finish his fictionalized biography of Henry Morgan, which he had tentatively entitled

"The Pot of Gold." The title was an ironic reference to the booty of pirates such as Morgan and the proverbial illusory reward that waited at the far ends of rainbows.

By September, Steinbeck recognized that by his father's standards he would be a failed writer. He worked diligently through July and August on the manuscript but made little satisfactory headway. The character of Henry Morgan was ponderous and overlarded with Steinbeck's philosophical point-making. He knew its weaknesses, saw how they chained the action to a slow-motion pace, and recognized his tendency to go off on didactic tangents. But he couldn't help himself. After he finished nearly eighty pages he began to lose interest. He couldn't imagine any publisher's taking the work seriously. In a letter to his Stanford friend Carl Wilhelmson, himself still an aspiring writer, he expressed his mood: "At times I feel that I am playing around the edges of things, getting nowhere. An extreme and callow youth playing with philosophy. . . ."

Through September and October, Steinbeck took out his frustrations in letter writing, most of which was self-pitying. Although he still continued to practice the craft of writing in the increasing number of letters he wrote, most of his dispatches were tinged by an excess of self-centered melodrama. The year before, he had written to Wilhelmson: "It would be desirable to be flung, unfettered by consciousness, into the void, to sail unhindered through eternity. Please do not think that I am riding along on baseless words, covering threadbare thoughts with garrulous tapestries. . . ."[10] Nevertheless, this is what he was doing much of the time in his novel — covering threadbare thoughts with garrulous tapestries.

He was told as much by Edith Mirrielees in late October of 1925. Finally flinging down his pen in frustration, he closed up the Pacific Grove cottage and visited Palo Alto to show Elizabeth Smith what he had written. She received him coolly, miffed by his departure from Stanford against her wishes. She refused to read his manuscript and tell him where he had gone wrong. Hurt by her indifference, he took the manuscript to the stern Miss Mirrielees. After reading it, she advised Steinbeck to abandon it and return to Stanford. She still had no doubt of his literary potential, she said, but she did not think John would have the power to realize it until he spent several more years in study and practice.

But Steinbeck had made his decision: no more college. He went back to Salinas and told his parents that although he was unable to finish "The Pot of Gold," as he still called the abortive novel, he could not yet bring himself to admit that he had no future as a writer. Because he was compelled to break his agreement with his father, he said, it would be dishonorable of him to ask for any further financial help. Thenceforth he would undertake the struggle on his own. He had had a long-standing invitation from his sister Elizabeth to visit her and her new husband in New York, the literary capital of the country. Perhaps his writing prospects would improve if he exposed himself to the world of editors and publishers there. He would thus, he told his parents, make his way east. When his father asked sourly how he expected to finance his trip, John explained that a Stanford friend, whose father was in the shipping business, had arranged a berth for him on a Lucken-bach freighter leaving the port of Wilmington for New York, via the Panama Canal, a week hence. It was a "work-your-way" berth; that is, in exchange for a low fare he would have to do odd jobs on board, mostly of the housekeeping variety.

Despite their dismay, John's parents, to preclude him from pestering Elizabeth and her husband for money, pressed a hundred dollars on him to see him through until he could get a job in New York. Steinbeck then left for Wilmington, stopping on the way for a visit with the young man who had by then become his best friend, Duke Sheffield.

✻ ✻ ✻ ✻ ✻ ✻ ✻ CHAPTER ELEVEN

The ship, a rusting hulk called the Katrina, set sail from Wilmington in early November. When it reached Panama City a few days later, Steinbeck had a chance to go ashore. He had set "The Pot of Gold" in Panama and was pleased to see from the local sights that the story's scenes, created out of his imagination, were reasonably accurate. He received further confirmation when, a week later, the ship put in at Havana. His stay in Havana was not altogether a pleasant one, however. Whoring and drinking for several days with members of the ship's crew, he quickly exhausted his parents' hundred-dollar stake. In a newspaper article twenty-eight years later, he would describe arriving in New York with only three dollars left in his pockets. "I crept ashore — frightened and cold and with a touch of panic in my stomach."[11]

Steinbeck made his way to his sister's and brother-in-law's apartment in Brooklyn. Since it was too small to accommodate him, he borrowed thirty dollars and, with Elizabeth's help, located and rented a third-floor room in a walk-up tenement in

Brooklyn's Fort Greene Place. Then he wandered the borough's dismal, frigid streets in quest of work. After several days of fruitless search, homesick, frightened by New York's impersonal immensity and depressed by its harsh climate, he was ready to go back to California. He went to the Luckenbach offices and applied for a berth on a return ship. There was nothing leaving immediately, however, so he closeted himself in his room, penned a number of long, sour letters to Duke Sheffield and other friends in California, and wrote two short stories. He also looked up an acquaintance from his original Stanford class, Amasa Miller. Miller, nicknamed Ted, was in the process of starting a legal career in New York with one of the city's distinguished law firms. Straitlaced and impeccably dressed in the style of the important lawyer he hoped to become, Ted Miller took pity on the impoverished but doughty Steinbeck, whom he hadn't seen in several years. When John said that the reason he had come to New York was to pursue his writing vocation, Miller, who had a few remote contacts in the city's publishing industry, offered to try to use his influence to get John's work some attention. Steinbeck was grateful for Miller's concern and interest, and the two became more friendly.

Toward the end of December 1925, Steinbeck's brother-in-law arranged for John to get a job as a bricklayer's assistant on the construction of the new Madison Square Garden on Manhattan's Eighth Avenue. The job consisted of wheeling heavy barrows of cement up wooden ramps to the levels on which the bricklayers worked. It left Steinbeck so exhausted at the end of each day that by the time he made the long subway trek back to his room in Fort Greene, he was without any energy to write. He soon began to wonder despairingly if he was fated to spend his working life in the company of laborers and illiterates. Although the pay was enough to keep him well fed, all his money-earning ventures so far had been menial jobs in which only sure hands and a strong back were required.

A stroke of good luck soon changed his outlook. In February, soon before John's twenty-fourth birthday, his uncle Joseph Hamilton visited New York on a business trip from Chicago, where he owned a successful advertising agency. Son of John's maternal grandfather, the colorful Samuel Hamilton, Joe Hamilton knew little of John except for what he had learned in letters from Olive. He was aware of his sister's anxiety over her son's literary ambitions, but since he too had made a successful career out of writing, albeit advertising copywriting, he failed to share her worry. Instead, when he arrived in New York, he gathered John, Elizabeth and her husband around him and treated them to several nights of expense-account dining and entertainment, mostly theatergoing. He asked to read some of John's stories. Afterward, he advised him to give up his construction job and get work in a field where he would have a chance to practice writing — such as advertising. He offered him a job in his own agency, but Steinbeck had no interest in moving to Chicago. He then offered to use his connections to get him a writing position with a New York agency. John again declined. Advertising was not for him, he said; the only thing that interested him other than fiction was journalism.

Joe Hamilton was on a first-name basis with several important people in the vast Hearst newspaper empire. Within two days he arranged for John to be given a "cub" reporter's job with Hearst's New York flagship paper, the *American*. Steinbeck started out at a salary of twenty-five dollars a week as a general-assignment reporter working out of the newspaper's city desk. Daily he would show up for work and be dispatched to cover events of local interest. He often got lost trying to find his way about the city, and missed a number of stories. When he did fulfill an assignment, he tended to write his reports in a discursive essay style, embellishing them with occasional bursts of poetic imagery, and every piece he wrote had to be rewitten by a desk editor to fit the plain, urgent Hearst style. Steinbeck took to quarreling with the rewrite editors over their treatment of his reports, and after a few weeks he was transferred to the federal-court beat in downtown Manhattan.

When he went to work for the *American,* Steinbeck moved
out of his room in Brooklyn and rented another in a small hotel
off Manhattan's Gramercy Park. After he got his newspaper
job he began to see more of Ted Miller, who urged him to resume writing. Miller again promised John that with his contacts in New York's publishing world, he could at least get him
a fair hearing. So did another friend John made, Mahlon Blaine,
an artist-illustrator who knew a number of book and magazine
editors.

Steinbeck took their advice. During the next two weeks he
turned out three short stories based on his newspaper activities
and gave them to Blaine to pass on to his friends. Late in April,
while he was waiting for a reaction, he began to see regularly
a girl he had met a week earlier on one of his newspaper assignments.

Mary Ardeth was an aspiring actress who worked as a
showgirl at a nightclub in Greenwich Village. John had met her
on a night he had been sent to the club to report on the show.
He encountered her outside the club's entrance and, with uncharacteristic daring, complimented her on her looks. In the
conversation that followed he learned that she lived just around
the corner from him on Gramercy Park. He had just moved into
his new room and was unfamiliar with the area, so he asked her
for directions. Because it was a pleasant spring night, she offered
to walk him home. During the walk he found himself telling
her his life story, embroidering the facts with a generous amount
of fiction. She was intrigued to discover that he was from California, and wanted to know all about Hollywood. Having once
visited a movie studio in Los Angeles with Duke Sheffield, John
spoke of Hollywood with vivid authority and mock-weary condescension. Mary Ardeth seemed to hang on his every word.

John was astonished when she invited him up to her apartment. She made coffee and, as they sipped it, she told him about
her artistic ambitions. When she spoke, she looked at Steinbeck
with eyes that seemed to penetrate him. He felt both discomfort
and elation — discomfort because of his habitual shyness, ela-

tion because of the apparently sensual nature of her interest in him. Much to his further surprise, and due largely to Mary Ardeth's increasingly suggestive gaze, he ended up falling in love with her.

During the next week he lived in a dream world. Soon he was spending every night with Mary after picking her up at her club. He used his room only to work on his short stories in the evenings, after leaving the newspaper and before meeting her in the Village. Impelled by his euphoria, he began to ignore his newspaper work to spend more and more time on his own writing, hoping to sell some stories so that he could ask Mary to marry him. It did not take long before his superiors at the *American* took note of his frequent absences and listless attitude. By early May they threatened to fire him if he did not show an immediate improvement.

Steinbeck didn't care. Mahlon Blaine had sent his stories to Guy Holt, an editor at the Robert M. McBride book-publishing firm, and Holt had summoned him to the McBride offices. Holt liked the stories and told John that if he would do half a dozen more, he would be interested in publishing them as a book under the McBride imprint.

This was the first positive news of Steinbeck's embryonic career, and in premature self-congratulation he treated Mary Ardeth to an expensive dinner at the celebrated Luchow's restaurant. Mary thought John was too smart to be a journalist or a writer. She was beguiled by his intelligence and sharp wit. The writers and newspapermen she had come in contact with were poor, unreliable and usually rancorous men who lived lives of total self-absorption and bitter disappointment. When John had told her that his uncle had offered him a job in advertising in Chicago, and that he had turned it down to remain in New York, she had chastised him for being so foolish. Thus, she was unimpressed when John told her of Guy Holt's reaction to his stories. And when he followed this up by mentioning that once he had his first publication he would like them to get married, she again disappointed him by responding negatively.

He thought she loved him, he protested. She did, she said, but she had no intention of starting married life with someone whose ambitions did not include the achievement of financial security. If he were to give up his foolish writing ambition and accept the advertising job, she would look with more favor on his idea of marriage. He could still write his stories in his spare time.

Their dinner discussion led to a quarrel that lasted for a week. Steinbeck stopped going to the *American* altogether, feigning illness. He holed up in his room and furiously wrote three more short stories, as if by the very act of writing he could resist the temptation to comply with Mary's conditions and purge his disappointment in her. When the week was over, his longing for Mary overcame his anger. He went to her apartment one morning to engineer a reconciliation. When she failed to respond to his knocks, he searched out the building's superintendent. The superintendent handed him a note she had left for him. In it she said that their quarrel had made her realize that their relationship was impossible. She had returned to her home near Chicago for a while. When and if she came back to New York, she did not want to see him again. He did not meet her financial standards for a future husband, she wrote, and even if he chose to, it would only be because she had pressured him into giving up his real ambition. She could see now that John was stubbornly bent on being a writer. If they were married, she would never be comfortable knowing that she had caused him to relinquish his dream. And he would never forgive her. So, she concluded, "Goodbye, John, and good luck. I pray I shall see a book of yours in a bookstore before too long."

Steinbeck was shattered. For the next few days he wandered the city aimlessly, bemoaning the rotten turn of events and blaming his literary aspirations for the loss of his first love. He hardly took notice when he received word from the *American* that he had been dismissed. A few days later he wrote an impulsive letter to his uncle in Chicago saying that he had changed his mind and would like to go to work in his advertising agency. He also wrote to Mary, telling her of his decision and announcing that he would be arriving in Chicago as soon as he heard from his uncle.

Joe Hamilton responded first. In his letter inviting John to Chicago, he enclosed a check for his train fare. A day or so later, as Steinbeck was preparing to leave New York, the response from Mary Ardeth arrived. Her letter told him not to bother; upon returning home she had begun dating an old boyfriend, a young banker, and she had decided to become engaged to him.

Steinbeck had had a week to recover from his hurt over Mary's abrupt departure and to weigh more rationally his conflicting feelings. Thus his anguish over this final blow was probably tempered by his relief that her actions had settled the issue, for he promptly returned his uncle's check with a sheepish note of explanation and began writing again. By the beginning of June he had a manuscript of nine short stories, some new, some rewrites of stories he had written in California. Ready to take up Guy Holt on his proposal, he delivered the manuscript to the Robert M. McBride offices only to suffer the ultimate disappointment of his stay in New York. When he arrived at McBride, he was informed that Guy Holt had recently left to take an editorial job at the John Day Company, another book publisher. Having counted on Holt's commitments of six weeks before, he was startled. Another editor at McBride gave the manuscript a perfunctory reading. He informed Steinbeck that his stories were "not up to McBride's literary standards" and that, since Holt was no longer with the firm, it was under no obligation to honor his commitments.

Steinbeck checked this with Ted Miller and learned that it was true. After advising him to take all verbal commitments with a large dose of salt, even in so honorable-seeming a business as publishing, Miller suggested that his writer friend deliver the stories to Holt at John Day. Steinbeck did so, only to learn from Holt that the Day firm had no interest in publishing stories by an unknown writer. There was nothing Holt could do about it, he said. "Get some of the stories done by good magazines," he said. "Get yourself a name, and then we'll see."

Although seething with anger and disappointment, Steinbeck was polite to Holt. Perhaps in gratitude, the editor said that if John ever got around to writing a novel he would like to have a look at it. But he *was* writing a novel, Steinbeck said, thinking of the unfinished "Pot of Gold." He had been having trouble with it, he explained, among other reasons because it had too many influences in it from other writers whose work he had read and admired. Holt asked whose the influences were. Steinbeck mentioned James Branch Cabell and Donn Byrne, among others. Holt said that he knew Cabell and offered to introduce Steinbeck to him. John, feeling at the moment profoundly unworthy as a writer and overawed by the prospect of such an introduction, declined the offer. He used as an excuse his expectation that he would probably be disillusioned by Cabell. The amused Holt later mentioned this to Cabell, who promptly penned a note for Holt to give to Steinbeck:

> Dear Mr. Steinbeck: Sometimes I too wish I did not know the undersigned.
> [signed] James Branch Cabell[12]

Communications from notable writers notwithstanding, Steinbeck found himself no better off in his literary pursuits than he had been when he arrived in New York, except for the fact that he had accumulated a number of short stories. He halfheartedly applied for a few newspaper jobs but was turned down. By the end of June he was again practically penniless. With no further prospects in New York, and too proud to go back to his sister for more money, he returned to the Luckenbach steamship offices. This time there was a freighter due to leave shortly. Steinbeck made his farewells to Elizabeth and her husband, to Ted Miller and Mahlon Blaine, and headed by sea back to California.

When he arrived in mid-July, he had a brief reunion with his parents and then went to Palo Alto, where Duke Sheffield, having just married, had returned to Stanford to study for a master's degree. Steinbeck stayed with Sheffield and his wife for two weeks. He and Duke spent most of their time deep in talk about the ideas and notions they had developed in their many letters to each other while Steinbeck was in New York.

No longer, however, did John feel entirely comfortable with Sheffield. To him, Duke's wife Ruth was always a slightly hostile presence. Ruth, in fact, did not particularly care for John. She knew that he had tried to discourage Duke from marrying her, claiming in his letters that she would destroy his ambition with her yearnings for security and respectability. She then overheard John say that the fact that Duke had returned to Stanford to obtain a master's degree, so that he could teach, was a confirmation of his suspicions. Duke was sheepish about the matter in front of his friend, and that sheepishness caused Ruth to be defensive when John was around. Moreover, John had had the audacity to write her from New York an acerbic, almost vindictive, letter when he heard that she and Duke had gotten married. She had been offended and intimidated by his mock-humorous warnings about the exclusivity of Duke's and his relationship. She consequently distrusted him doubly, which made her husband that much more sheepish. The interaction between the three finally became so strained that at the end of two weeks Steinbeck packed his meager belongings and, when Duke and Ruth were out, left.

He made his way to Lake Tahoe to visit with another Stanford friend, Webster "Toby" Street. Toby was married and the father of a child but was still a student at Stanford. An aspiring playwright, he was spending the summer at his in-laws' resort lodge at Fallen Leaf Lake in the High Sierras near Lake

Tahoe, trying to finish a play he had started writing the year before when he and John had been members of Stanford's English Club.

Street was familiar with John's hopes for his novel about Morgan the pirate. Although his own play, which he called "The Green Lady," had been proving nettlesome, he promoted the virtues of the lodge as a place to write and got John a maintenance job for the remainder of the summer. Steinbeck was glad to have it, and when he wasn't working he and Toby spent many hours at night discussing their respective writing problems. As the end of summer approached, Toby decided to pass up the fall session at Stanford and remain at the lodge until cold weather set in. John, who was captivated by the rugged Sierra scenery, agreed to stay as well. Then, through Toby's mother-in-law, he heard that a winter caretaker's job was available at the nearby estate of a wealthy San Francisco widow. Resolving to spend the winter on his own in the high country so that he could make a final effort at "The Pot of Gold," he applied for the job and got it.

The estate was owned by Mrs. Alice Brigham, whose late husband had been a prominent San Francisco surgeon. When Steinbeck arrived for his interview he was awed by the beauty of the place, which was dominated by a large lodge-type mansion expensively furnished within. Behind it towered steep forests of giant pine leading up to the summit of Mt. Tallac, while ahead lay the vista of Fallen Leaf Lake framed against the wilderness of its opposite shore. Steinbeck was hired to begin work on October 15, and was shown a snug stone caretaker's cottage that would be his to live in.

After a trip to San Francisco with Toby Street, Steinbeck returned alone to Fallen Leaf Lake in October to settle in at the now-vacant estate. By the time the first snows came to the Sierras, he had the main house weatherproofed and had cut enough firewood for his own needs in the caretaker's cottage. By mid-November, except for a trek once or twice a week to the post office and store at the village of Camp Richardson, a mile and a half away, he was isolated by snow. He had little to do but contemplate the task for which he had sequestered himself there: the completion of his Morgan novel. To begin, he put aside everything he had written and started anew. But once again he became bogged down, distracted in part by the pristine beauty of the area, by his fears and insecurities, and by his loneliness. By early December he had set the novel aside once more and was spending most of his time toying with short stories and writing long letters to his friends in the outside world.

The long, harsh winter passed slowly. Steinbeck's only literary achievement was the publication, in March of 1927, of a short story he had first written at Stanford and then revised and sent off to a new magazine called the *Smoker's Companion*. Entitled "The Gifts of Iban," the story was another of his satirical efforts, a parable written from strong *Morte d'Arthur* influences but containing Steinbeck's developing thematic sense of innocence and hope transformed by events into disillusion and sorrow.

The locale of the story is a forested fantasy land peopled by animal-like characters — "web spinners," "dragonflies," "hummingbirds" and the like. The hero is Iban, a songster who lusts after the beautiful Cantha, plying her with gold and silver and promises of more delightful ethereal gifts. During the night they spend together, these gifts materialize. But when dawn comes they are discovered and are forced to wed to avoid disgrace. Despite their marriage, they are shunned by the populace of the forest, and this angers Cantha's mother. She cleverly poisons Cantha's mind against her husband and convinces her that Iban's ethereal gifts are worthless. At the end of the story, Cantha deserts Iban.

When Steinbeck first wrote it, the parable had a different thematic thrust: it was simply his wry vision of the eternal struggle between the sexes. When he rewrote it during his early weeks at Fallen Leaf Lake, however, he did so with Duke

Sheffield in mind. The revised story was meant to be a caution- ary tale for his friend on the threats that marriage poses to masculine dreams and ambitions. When he finished it he was afraid to send it to Sheffield. Instead, he mailed it to the *Smoker's Companion* with the request that if they printed it, they do so under a pseudonym. Thus it was that "The Gifts of Iban" was published under the name of John Stern.

Steinbeck received only a few dollars for the story and he was not inclined to boast about its publication. Nevertheless it was a milestone — his first piece of writing that earned money. What was more significant, however, was the fact that its theme foreshadowed the larger-scale but similar idea he had been try- ing to realize in his progression from the "Lady in Infra-Red" short story to the novel, "The Pot of Gold."

Although Steinbeck cogitated a great deal on "The Pot of Gold," he was unable to move himself to do any further work on it as winter melted into the spring of 1927. Instead, to salve his nagging conscience, he revived his long-dormant interest in marine life. His escape from the novel came as a result of a casual meeting in February, while he was at Camp Richardson fetching mail and food supplies, with a young man about his age named Lloyd Shebley. Shebley, who worked for the state's fish-and-game administration, had just arrived to open the nearby Tallac trout hatchery for the coming season.

Steinbeck and Shebley quickly became fast friends. A lover of nature and the outdoors, Shebley was a born conservationist and had a scientist's appreciation for the wonders of the cyclical patterns of fish and animal life. During March and April Stein- beck spent most of his spare time, of which he had a great deal, at the hatchery with Shebley learning about the breeding habits of fish and the migratory propensities of various wildlife. Most of May was taken up by the job of preparing the Brigham estate for the return of its owner, her daughter and family for the summer.

John remained at this job on the estate throughout the

summer and agreed to spend another winter there. Although he occasionally dipped into the manuscript pages of "The Pot of Gold," making a correction here, rewording a sentence there, he did little actual writing. Indeed, he had fallen into the mental habits of a nonwriter, finding much more pleasure in creating physical jobs for himself to do around the estate than in pursuing the one job he still professed he was born to do — write. He kept up this pattern into the fall of 1927 when, in answer to his plaints, a letter from Duke Sheffield arrived.

Most of Steinbeck's letters to his friends were about his difficulties with the Henry Morgan novel. To some it seemed that John had spent the entire year in the Sierras simply for the purpose of settling on a new title. Nevertheless, in discoursing on his literary problems, he had inadvertently managed to work some of them out. But he was beginning to bore some of his friends with his carefully elaborated excuses for not being able to carry out "The Pot of Gold." It took a letter from Duke Sheffield in September to jog Steinbeck out of his torpor. Seething with impatience, Sheffield excoriated him for his literary malingering and doubted his sincerity in wanting to be a writer. A "fish-or-cut-bait" attack loaded with cynicism and a touch of vindictiveness, it evidently struck to the bone. For suddenly Steinbeck reattacked his manuscript with a fury. Through the rest of the year and well into January of 1928 he wrote three to four thousand words a day, driven by a compulsion to finish the book and prove to Sheffield that he could carry off a complete novel — something that Sheffield had made a point of doubting in his letter.

By the end of January he was finished. Emotionally and physically depleted, he put the manuscript away without reading it and spent the next two weeks recovering his mental energy. Toward the end of February, when he felt he had acquired an objective distance from it, he retrieved the manuscript and read it. His disappointment in it was crushing. It "was no good," he wrote in a letter to Sheffield late in February. It had some "indubitably fine things" in it, he said, but taken as a whole it was, in his view, "utterly worthless." He lamented the fact that he had just turned twenty-six and had "done nothing to justify my years." He spoke of the cabin fever from which he was suffering and then returned to the subject of the novel. He described his self-delusion in believing that in Henry Morgan, his protagonist, he had been creating a heroic character only to find upon reading the manuscript that Morgan was nothing more than "a babbler of words and rather clumsy about it." He characterized the novel as "a monument to my own lack of ability." He was ready to discard it for good, but was not yet prepared to give up his writing dream. "I shall write good novels but hereafter I ride Pegasus with a saddle and martingale, for I am afraid Pegasus will rear and kick, and I am not the sure steady horseman I once was."

Much of Steinbeck's reaction clearly derived from his ingrained self-doubt, which was compounded by his isolation. For a first complete draft of a first novel, "The Pot of Gold" exuded a sense of thoughtful craft despite the banality of its story. Steinbeck's preoccupation with prose style shone foremost through its pages. His striving for keen observation was a bit muddied, but the cadences of his sentences and the occasional surprises contained in his images and word constructions gave the novel an authoritative authenticity.

There, in fact, was the nub of the matter. For a young man of doubtful self-confidence, Steinbeck wrote with compelling authority. It was as if the latter were in compensation for the former. Was his personal insecurity the inspiration of his forceful prose? What heights of authority would he be capable of if he could rid himself of his insecurity and lack of faith in himself? Or would the acquisition of genuine personal self-confidence somehow compromise his literary power?

These questions remained to be answered. Suffice it to say that, compelled to write out of an acute yearning for self-worth (not to mention self-aggrandizement), Steinbeck produced in his first full-length effort a flawed but forceful literary invention.

❄ ❄ ❄ ❄ ❄ ❄ ❄ CHAPTER TWELVE

Steinbeck's sense of failure was so great, however, that he felt he could no longer stay at the estate. The stark barrenness of the snow-laden Sierra surroundings mirrored his perception of his own lifeless talents. A furious early-March blizzard, which collapsed a portion of the roof of the estate's mansion, only sharpened his desire to leave. While repairing the damage, he received a note from Lloyd Shebley saying that Shebley would be returning at the end of the month, not to the Tallac hatchery but to a newer and larger one near Tahoe City, on the northwest shore of Lake Tahoe. Shebley mentioned that he would need a paid assistant for the summer to help him operate the facility and asked Steinbeck if he was interested in the job. John wrote back that he was. He notified Mrs. Brigham that he would be leaving the estate as soon as he got the winter's damages repaired.

Early in April, at the cost of forty dollars, John bought a thirteen-year-old car. He drove it to Tahoe City a week later to show it off to Shebley. Shebley told him that he had been okayed for the hatchery assistant's job, that it would begin the first week of June, and that he would be paid $115 a month for three months. On May 1, Steinbeck drove the 150 miles into San Francisco to report to Mrs. Brigham on the winter's damage to the estate and collect his final two months' pay. He quickly spent most of the money on a frenzy of girls and speakeasies, and then headed south for a visit with his parents in Salinas. On the way he stopped at Stanford for a reunion with Duke Sheffield. Sheffield's wife — the girl Steinbeck had locked horns with two years before — had recently died, and John arrived in a state of proper contrition for the manner in which he had treated her.

In the final month of his stay at Fallen Leaf Lake, Steinbeck, recovering from his frustration over "The Pot of Gold," had begun another novel. By the time of his departure, however, he had discarded it. Hence, all he had from his two years in the Sierras were his handwritten ledgers containing the first novel and some stories. Duke Sheffield asked to read the novel, so John reluctantly left the ledgers with him while he went on to Salinas. When he returned to Palo Alto on his way back to Lake Tahoe in late May, he found Sheffield to be at once quizzical and enthusiastic. He was quizzical because, after reading "The Pot of Gold," he couldn't understand the reason for Steinbeck's misery over it. Sheffield suggested a change here and there in the manuscript, but he thought that overall the book was excellent. "It's certainly not something I'd be ashamed of sending to publishers," he said with a touch of envy in his voice. Sheffield proceeded to elaborate on what he saw as the novel's virtues.

Although he trusted Sheffield's literary judgment, Steinbeck suspected that his friend did not properly understand the allegorical aspects of the novel and had praised it simply to encourage him. He thereupon showed it to his former teacher, Edith Mirrielees. Despite her approval, he was still unsure, so he sought out the one person whose opinion he was certain would be candid — Elizabeth Smith.

Steinbeck had written "A Lady in Infra-Red" as a satirical allegory about the compromises that modern civilization demands of men and their noble ambitions, and the disillusion such compromises provoke. It is quite likely that he had conceived of the idea for his story in these terms in order to portray the conflict he himself was going through, the conflict between his desire to be a writer and his need to please his parents by endeavoring to fulfill their expectations of him. Although he had been encouraged as a child to admire the nobility, the striving and the adventurous individuality of the great characters in literature — characters such as the knights of the Arthurian legends — he had at the same time been expected, even pressured, to live his own life in accordance with his parents' notions of security and respectability. This meant that he should seek to fit into his society with an acceptable career, that he become not an individual in pursuit of some great and noble achievement but an integrated unit satisfied to sacrifice his individuality to the social group of which he was a member.

From his early years, Steinbeck had struggled with this paradox. Inspired by his childhood reading, he had been instilled with a need to nurture and expand his individuality. Yet all around him he perceived that individuality was considered eccentric and undesirable. Coupled with this was his continuing perplexity over the question of the marked differences he saw in the behavior of humans in individual capacities and their behavior in groups. He had probed the question to some degree in college philosophy courses, but his perplexity had merely deepened. The only thing he could conclude was that the individual, permitted to express his individuality, was a more desirable form of humanity than the individual who was forced to suppress it for the sake of the group. Yet despite the fact that individuality was clearly the more desirable form of human existence — it was the only thing that gave man the opportunity to rise above the purely animal side of his nature — society demanded its suppression. There was something perverted in this fact of life, Steinbeck concluded.

The impulse to expose the perversion would become the engine of Steinbeck's forming literary vision. The literary method that he should pursue to carry out the exposure remained to be found. However, due to his early literary education, much of which revolved about allegorical and fabulist books, including the Bible, it was inevitable that he would eventually resort to the allegorical form to deliver his perceptions. And because his early writing endeavors tended to philosophical preachiness, it was doubly inevitable. As Edith Mirrielees had pointed out to him when he first started in her classes at Stanford, allegory, expertly carried out, was a very effective way to moralize without boring or offending the reader.

"A Lady in Infra-Red" had been Steinbeck's first real attempt at sustained allegory. In Morgan the pirate he had created a symbolic character pursuing a grail-like dream, only to have it shattered by the processes and pressures of the society he has become involved in, represented by the seductive woman in red of the title. Steinbeck was little aware of the stylistic niceties of allegory, however, and his execution of the short story was notable only for a heavy-handed satire that he mistook for pungent parable. The theme, nevertheless, was a mature one, which was what had prompted Elizabeth Smith to urge him to turn the story into a full-scale allegorical novel.

The final product of Steinbeck's three years of intermittent work on "The Pot of Gold" was a quasifictional biography of Henry Morgan from the time when, as a farm boy living in Wales, he yearns to go to sea to make his fortune. "To make his fortune" actually means, in Steinbeck's symbolic terms, to fulfill his individuality in adventure abroad rather than remain mired in the banal respectability of Welsh farm life. Young Morgan encounters a mysterious hermit with the Arthurian name of Merlin, who predicts that if the boy pursues his dream he will become a noble man. The boy thereupon ships out for the West Indies, but the ship's captain takes advantage of his innocence and sells him into indentured servitude. Four years later, no longer a naive youth but a shrewd young man, Morgan obtains his freedom and, with money stolen from his master, buys himself onto a privateering schooner and becomes its captain. Morgan roams the Caribbean in a series of successful raids for gold, diamonds and other booty and is soon a legend. His final triumph comes when he successfully raids the Spanish treasury in Panama City — the "pot of gold" of the novel's title. But along with his triumph comes an even more telling defeat. Living in Panama City is "La Santa Roja," the Red Saint (the lady in infra-red of the original short story). A legend in her own right, a woman of such exotic and seductive beauty that all men, but Morgan above all, dream of having her. After sacking Panama he takes her captive, only to find that the sweet and virginal beauty he had expected was instead "sharp, almost hawklike . . . the harsh, dangerous beauty of lightning. . . . [Morgan] was not prepared for this change of idea. He was staggered by such a revolt against his preconceptions."

Despite this initial disillusionment, Morgan demands that La Santa Roja give up her husband and sail away with him. She condescendingly rebuffs him by saying, "I have heard your words so often. . . . Is there some book with which aspiring lovers instruct themselves?" She says that his reputation for brazenness and daring had caused her to admire him, but that now, on meeting him face to face, "I find you to be a babbler, a speaker of sweet, considered words, and rather clumsy about it."[13]

Morgan, who has created an image of himself as invincible, who believes that he has fulfilled the hermit Merlin's prophecy of his human greatness, is stunned by La Santa Roja's contempt. Merlin had cautioned him that if he truly wanted greatness, he must always retain his child's outlook on the world. "You want the moon to drink from as a golden cup; and so it is very likely that you will become a great man," Merlin had said, "if only you remain a child. All the world's great have been little boys who wanted the moon. . . . But if one grows to a man's mind, that mind must see that it cannot have the moon and would not want it if it could. . . ." Merlin's image of the moon as a "golden cup" returns to haunt Morgan once he is rejected by La Santa Roja. The most prized booty of his raid on Panama City is a great gold cup. Morgan examines it reflectively and sees that it is engraved along its outer rim with the figures of "grotesque lambs," while inside, from the cup's bottom, the figure of "a naked girl lifted her arms in sensual ecstasy."

Steinbeck conceived of the gold cup as the symbolic grail of the novel and used it to bring the allegory to its climax. Borrowing William Blake's notion of the lamb as the universal symbol of childhood, Steinbeck deftly made his lambs grotesque in order to symbolize the distorted vision those who dream of greatness must possess. He placed the lambs on the outer edge of the cup to symbolize his belief that children concern themselves only with the externals of the world, while the naked woman within represented the adult vision of the real, carnal world beneath the golden surface of the childhood vision. In the naked woman, Steinbeck gave Morgan the option of choosing the sensual rewards of manhood as compensation for the shattering of his childlike self-image of greatness at the hands of La Santa Roja.

In the end, Morgan rejects the option. Instead, he tosses the golden cup onto a pile of diamonds, where it loses its childhood-manhood symbolism and becomes, simply, a token of wealth. Steinbeck has Morgan say that "Hereafter I shall be gallant for two reasons only — money and advancement." Seeing himself no longer as a hero, Morgan eventually cheats his fellow buccaneers out of their shares of the Panama City raid and retires with his riches to a life of bourgeois conformity and respectability.

Elizabeth Smith, who had been the one to suggest the symbol of the gold cup three years earlier, was impressed when she read the finished manuscript. She put aside her previous resentment of Steinbeck and praised his achievement in completing the book in what she praised as so artful a style. The novel's theme was well served by the symmetry of the allegory, and if the characters were a bit on the unrealistic side — well, that was all right, because "lost innocence" was the literary fashion of the day and John had captured it in a way that was far more interesting than the conventions of the "realists" who were writing to such popular acclaim. Her final contribution was to suggest that John change the title to "A Cup of Gold." He agreed, later dropping the "A."

With Elizabeth Smith's support of his new novel, Steinbeck left at the beginning of June for Lake Tahoe to take up his job as Lloyd Shebley's assistant at the fish hatchery. He was still vaguely unhappy with the book but was convinced that it was publishable. So on his way to Tahoe, he stopped in Sacramento and mailed the handwritten manuscript off to Ted Miller in New York. With it he sent a letter telling Miller that Edith Mirrielees had suggested the firm of Farrar and Rinehart as a possible publisher.

John started work at the Tahoe hatchery on June 4, 1928, moving with Lloyd Shebley into the adjacent fish-farmer's cottage. The hatchery was somewhat of a tourist attraction for the thousands of Californians who vacationed at Lake Tahoe. It was primarily a breeding plant for trout that were later stocked in the state's lakes and streams, and its massive fish-production capability, as well as its majestic stone-and-shingle architecture, was featured in the local tourist brochures. Steinbeck's duties consisted primarily of feeding the newly hatched trout and fingerlings and keeping the pens and outside areas clean. An ancillary task became the answering of tourists' questions, since Shebley was often away on fish-stocking expeditions. Because he knew little about the technical details of trout breeding, he often invented elaborate explanations to satisfy his questioners' curiosity. Much to his amazement, he one day received a notice of commendation from the state's superintendent of fish and wildlife. A tourist had evidently been impressed by John's courtesy and "knowledgeable" thoroughness in answering his questions, and had written a letter of appreciation to the super-intendent.

During Steinbeck's first two weeks at Tahoe he did no writing, having decided to await word from Ted Miller on the fate of "Cup of Gold." Instead, he devoted most of his spare evening time with Shebley to visiting Tahoe resort lodges in search of women. On these expeditions, usually in John's rattle-trap car, Shebley was the leader, since he had a bold libido and little hesitancy in expressing it. John, still reticent and unsure of his looks, although affecting a certain bravado, followed in Lloyd's wake. During the two winters at Fallen Leaf Lake, he had let his beard grow and had been pleased to note that it tended to soften the harsh planes of his face and reduce some-what the prominence of his nose. He had shaved it off the month before for his visit home, but now he began to grow a moustache in the hope that it would serve as a buffer between his nose and his coarse mouth. It must have helped, for like a pilot fish he was able to feed off Lloyd Shebley's "leavings" on more than one occasion during their nightly tourist-lodge forays.

Two weeks after sending the manuscript of "Cup of Gold" to Ted Miller in New York he was astonished to receive it back. With it came a letter from Miller informing Steinbeck that no publisher would even consider looking at a manuscript by an unknown author that wasn't cleanly typed. Miller urged him to get the job done as soon as possible, since he had primed several important book editors to read it in typescript.

With what were becoming his usual grumbling complaints about the difficulties of being a writer, Steinbeck set about the task. He foresook his nighttime ramblings with Shebley and, using the hatchery's typewriter, agonizingly two-fingered his way through thirty pages of reasonably clean typescript over the period of a week. After thirty pages, however, he could go no further; his fingers ached and his head swirled with frustration at the tediousness of the job.

It was Lloyd Shebley, having spent the previous few nights

womanizing on his own, who came to the rescue. He told John that he had met two girls — sisters — at a nearby lodge. Enamored of one of the sisters, he offered to get John a date with the other, who worked as a stenographer in an office in San Francisco. Surely, said Shebley, John could persuade the girl to type his manuscript, even if he had to pay her something out of his forty-dollar-a-week hatchery salary. Thus did Steinbeck meet the girl who was to become his first wife, as well as the expediter of his first novel.

The girl's name was Carol Henning. Twenty-two years old, she and her sister Idell were on vacation at Lake Tahoe. Shebley invited the two of them to the hatchery the next day. Steinbeck, expecting a plain, bespectacled, secretarial type, was surprised to find that the girl was, if not pretty, at least comely. Moreover, she was bright and agreeably aggressive — qualities he was unused to in the girls he had so far encountered.

Shebley took Idell Henning off to show her around the hatchery. Carol told John that Lloyd had mentioned that he was some day going to become a famous writer but needed typing help with a manuscript. Steinbeck confirmed at least the latter. Soon the two struck an agreement: she would spend the remaining days of her vacation typing "Cup of Gold" at a rate of five cents a page.

An accomplished typist, Carol Henning finished the job in short order, working in the hatchery's office. Occasionally she had to consult with John on an unclear spelling or a word made illegible by his tiny, cramped handwriting. At night she and John, along with Shebley and her sister, journeyed into Tahoe City to drink Prohibition gin and dance. On these occasions much of their talk revolved about Steinbeck's writing potential. He held forth on the grimness of his prospects and his determination in spite of it. Carol, basing her authority on her growing familiarity with "Cup of Gold," extolled his talent. She was clearly fascinated to be in the presence of a budding writer of John's obvious skill. He was fascinated by her increasingly en-

thusiastic devotion after each day's typing. By the time her
vacation was over and she had to return to San Francisco, they
were in love. Carol refused to accept payment for the typing
job.

Steinbeck sent the typescript of "Cup of Gold" back to
Ted Miller in New York in mid-July, keeping a carbon copy
for himself. At the end of August his job at the hatchery ex-
pired. Saying good-bye to Lloyd Shebley, he made his way back
to Salinas for a visit with his family and then spent some time
at the cottage in Pacific Grove, where he wrote a few stories
and mulled over another novel.

The novel he had in mind derived from "The Green
Lady," the play that Toby Street had had so much trouble writing. During the summer Steinbeck had visited Street at his in-
laws' resort at Fallen Leaf Lake and had made some suggestions
about how Toby might resolve his continuing problems with
the play, which Steinbeck liked. Street had lost all faith in his
writing ability, however, and was thinking of pursuing a career
as a lawyer. Nevertheless, because John liked the story and had
tried to help him out of the technical morass he had gotten himself into, Street "gave" Steinbeck outright use of it. Although it
didn't work as a play in Street's hands, perhaps it would work
as a novel in Steinbeck's.

John made little progress on the new novel while in
Pacific Grove during the early fall weeks of 1928. Toby Street
had written the play as a pseudo-Shakespearean fantasy. With
his allegorical juices still flowing, partly out of his certainty at
having failed in his allegorical efforts in "Cup of Gold," Steinbeck thought he could simply transform the fabulist substance
of Street's play into a symbolic narrative that would encompass
what continued to be his primary thematic concern: the individual loss of innocence and self-betrayal through social pressure. But after a couple of serious attempts to start writing "The
Green Lady" as a novel, he put it aside. The fragile fantasy
world created by Toby Street in his settings, characters and

dialogue adapted itself awkwardly to Steinbeck's more pedantic sensibilities.

Besides, his concentration was diverted by his increasing longing for Carol Henning. On the way to Salinas from Lake Tahoe in early September, he had stopped in San Francisco to see her. Their reunion after almost two months was an emotionally glorious and intense one. John's former college mate Carl Wilhelmson was living in a small flat in San Francisco, also trying to become a writer. Carol Henning shared an apartment nearby with her sister. Upon John's arrival Wilhelmson gave him the use of his apartment since he was leaving the city for a few days. John and Carol spent most of John's brief time in San Francisco in Wilhelmson's flat. Soon the two had vowed undying love for each other.

Carol immediately began to talk about marriage, which jarred Steinbeck only slightly out of his euphoria at having found so willing and adventurous a love mate. He resisted the idea with arguments about his lack of financial status and his determination to continue in such a state until he could succeed as a writer. She dismissed his misgivings by offering to continue working to support them. His stern Christian upbringing simply would not let him hear of such a thing. She pressed. He finally agreed to think about it during his visit to Salinas.

After seeing his family, he broke his promise to return to Carol in San Francisco and went instead to Pacific Grove to work on the conversion of "The Green Lady" into a novel. A letter to Carol explained his reasons, the primary one of which was his continuing reluctance to think about marriage when he was still without means or realistic prospects of making a living as a writer. He felt that to marry then would be to subject himself to all the external pressures of married life, including the need to make a living and support a family. He wanted her as his wife. But to marry her at that juncture would be a betrayal of his higher ambition, for he could not continue to write if he were forced to take on another form of work to fulfill the marital conventions. Nor could he permit her to support both of them, he explained, for his guilt over being a "parasite" would eat at his writing resolve. Self-betrayal, after all, had been the meaning of "Cup of Gold," which Carol had come to know so well. And the book he was preparing to write now would be an even better and more effective statement of that theme.

Steinbeck received no response from Carol during the three weeks he idled at "The Green Lady." Then, just after he put it aside and was indignantly contemplating a trip to San Francisco to learn why she hadn't written, a letter arrived. In it Carol said that although she had been hurt, she understood his reasoning and accepted the wisdom of it. She would not raise the question of marriage again, she promised, but she would like to continue seeing him. There was no reason they could not be married in spirit, if not in fact. That is, if he still felt about her as he had a few weeks earlier.

With that, Steinbeck returned to San Francisco and resumed the relationship. He moved in with Carl Wilhelmson and, after the initial bloom of his second reunion with Carol wore off, returned to the task of "The Green Lady." Wilhelmson was hard at work on his own second novel, and his writing discipline was a source of admiration and envy. For no other reason than that, Steinbeck forged ahead on his new novel with almost equal determination.

When he was not working at his writing ledger, John roamed the hilly streets and parks of the city with Carol. As the year came to an end, he began to run out of the scant money he had saved from his two years in the Sierras. He again worked in a department store during the Christmas season to keep himself going. A small cash Christmas gift from his parents got him into January of 1929. Then, as he started to look around for a permanent part-time job, he received an urgent letter from Ted Miller in New York. "Cup of Gold" had been accepted for publication.

❉ ❉ ❉ ❉ ❉ ❉ ❉ ❉ ❉ *Part Two*

❊ ❊ ❊ ❊ ❊ ❊ CHAPTER THIRTEEN

S teinbeck took the news with phlegmatic indifference, or
so it seemed to Carol Henning and Carl Wilhelmson. The only
thing that seemed to excite him about it was the irony of the fact
that the firm that had decided to publish his first novel was
McBride — the very same house that had given him so much
trouble with his short stories during his stay in New York two
years before. Carol was ecstatic. In her somewhat naive view,
the acceptance of "Cup of Gold" meant that John had attained
success as a writer. Consequently she began once again to drop
hints of marriage. Perhaps Steinbeck's lack of enthusiasm was
designed to discourage her. He finally had to explain to her
that the acceptance of one novel was neither a success in itself
nor a guarantee of success in the future.

With Miller's letter came a publishing contract from
McBride. As soon as Steinbeck signed and returned it, he would
receive a check for two hundred dollars, half of his advance
for the novel. The other two hundred would be paid upon publication, the date of which McBride estimated would be the

following August. There was a cautionary note in Miller's letter, however. He said that the McBride firm had been the eighth to see the manuscript. The previous seven, including Farrar and Rinehart, Scribner's, and Harper Brothers, had rejected it. McBride was in a struggle with insolvency, said Miller. John might be taking a risk by accepting their offer; he would probably get the initial two hundred dollars, but there was a question as to whether McBride would survive long enough to actually publish the book or pay him the balance due. On the other hand, it was unlikely that any other publisher would accept the manuscript should John decide not to go with the McBride offer. The prospect of soon receiving two hundred dollars overrode whatever qualms Steinbeck had due to Miller's warnings. He signed the contract and sent it back. A few weeks later he had the advance.

The money didn't last long, and by late spring Steinbeck was again looking for a job in San Francisco. He finally found one as a clerk in a department store. Afterward, he and Wilhelmson moved into another apartment. Once settled, he returned to the novelization of "The Green Lady."

He and Wilhelmson passed considerable time together discussing fiction techniques. Wilhelmson was far more academically inclined than his roommate and devoted much of his attention to studiously reading the novels and stories of the young writers who were gaining prominence in America at the time, particularly Faulkner and Hemingway. Steinbeck had little interest in modern fiction; his tastes still ran to the classics, and the closest he came to the modern period was his regular reading of the nineteenth-century American transcendental and pastoral writers such as Thoreau, Emerson and Whitman.

His interest in this literary-philosophical strain originated during his first winter at the Brigham estate at Fallen Leaf Lake, when Duke Sheffield sent him a copy of Thoreau's *Walden Pond*. Sheffield had suggested that Steinbeck read it in order to compare the spiritual values Thoreau had developed out of his self-enforced isolation to those Steinbeck had developed out of his own. In a series of letters to Sheffield, Steinbeck had expounded on his appreciation of Thoreau's ideas and equated them to his own. His most pressing philosophical problem during the previous years had been the paradox between the individual acting from his own uniquely human impulses and the individual acting from the more herdlike animal demands of the social group to which he belonged. Thoreau had championed the individual. This did not resolve the problem for Steinbeck, but it sharpened his perception of it. Thereafter he took to reading the essays of Emerson and his nineteenth-century contemporaries who, in their attempts to solve a similar problem, gave birth to the religio-philosophy of transcendentalism — an idealistic doctrine that defined man, the individual man, as the central element of the universe. The doctrine carried with it a paradox in its own right, however. For on the one hand it insisted that man, to properly fulfill his function, must remain intensely individualistic. On the other it demanded that the individual man be selflessly altruistic, providing succor, protection and resources to others — men, animals, things — as they provided these things to him. The paradox both confused Steinbeck and bewitched him. Resolving it had become his central intellectual preoccupation during his last year in the Sierras and the months he spent living in San Francisco. The preoccupation had infused the thematic content of "Cup of Gold" and continued to haunt him in his efforts to turn "The Green Lady" into a novel.

Carl Wilhelmson had little sympathy for Steinbeck's thematic concerns. He was, with respect to his own writing, more involved in the mechanics and techniques of fiction than in solving the philosophies behind it. His general thematic sensibility was pessimistic, in the fashion of the contemporary "Lost Generation" writers, whereas Steinbeck's was optimistic in the fashion of the nineteenth-century moral idealists. Wilhelmson thus favored a laconic prose style that operated at a distinct remove from his characters and endowed them with the quality of indiscrete laboratory specimens observed under an objective, ruthless magnifying glass. Steinbeck, on the other hand, was committed to a style that sought to enrich his characters with individuality and discreteness. He saw man's primary struggle as being one between his "individual" and "group" characters. Although man was doomed to sacrifice his individuality to the pressures of the group, the struggle itself — man's recognition of the dichotomy in himself and his self-conscious attempt to act on and resolve it — was a cause for optimism. Steinbeck, to describe him in the most general terms, was an idealist. Although his characters' moral and physical downfalls — in "Cup of Gold" and the in-progress "The Green Lady" — were inevitable, the allegories upon which their stories were supported supplied a redemptive quality. In their reflective musings on their fates, his characters at least came to the realization that their dismal destinies could have been different had they only been able to act out of different, more enlightened impulses. Wilhelmson's characters, on the contrary, were allowed to enjoy no such optimistic retrospective alternatives. Their fates were mechanistically predetermined, and as the readers of Wilhelmson watched his characters inexorably go down their respective drains, they were meant to acknowledge the singular nihilism of human life.

The discussions between Steinbeck and Wilhelmson often became intense arguments over the underlying philosophical purposes of fiction. Although both young writers were sardonic and ironical in their approaches, Steinbeck invested his irony in his themes while Wilhelmson stitched his into his prose. Wilhelmson was a determinist writer, which is to say that he only allowed his characters to reflect on the "what-is" aspects of their natural destinies. Steinbeck at this time was struggling to be a humanist writer; that is, he was compelled to dwell on the "what-ought-to-be" aspects of his characters' fates. This impulse had given "Cup of Gold" a preachy tone which, when he read the manuscript, Wilhelmson had criticized. As he looked over parts of the progressing novelization of "The Green Lady," he again detected a preachiness in the ironic effects Steinbeck was reaching for.

Steinbeck developed considerable respect for Wilhelmson during their apartment-sharing days of 1929, not the least of which derived from the fact that Wilhelmson was a more intrepid worker than himself. While John was only midway through the "Green Lady" adaptation, Wilhelmson was finishing his third novel and planning a fourth. He had already acquired a New York literary agency to represent him, had had his second novel accepted for publication, and seemed well on the way to a successful career. (Ironically enough, although Wilhelmson's early success meteorically outstripped Steinbeck's, he was destined to fade into obscurity as Steinbeck's star rose in the late 1930s.)

Wilhelmson's criticisms served inadvertently to reinforce Steinbeck's insecurities about himself as a writer, but they also reawakened in him an impulse to pursue a more naturalistic style of fiction — the type he had experimented with during his first writing sojourn at Pacific Grove. The reawakening was gradual, however. During the spring and summer of 1929, while working as a store clerk and at other temporary jobs, he continued to hammer away at the transformation of "The Green Lady" into fable form.

Carol Henning and Steinbeck were now practically living together, although they continued to maintain separate apartments. A headstrong and outgoing girl, Carol played counterpoint to John's introspective seriousness. She made friends easily and had a wide circle of acquaintances in San Francisco, many of whom mildly disapproved of her devotion to the outwardly surly Steinbeck. Her devotion was unshakable nevertheless, and when it became apparent that she was bent on deepening the relationship, most of her friends took pains to cultivate John. Some, though, took the cynical view that John's attraction to her was merely one of convenience; he kept her busy typing and retyping the manuscript of his new novel. They were sure that sooner or later Steinbeck would discard Carol as readily as he discarded dissatisfactory pages of manuscript.

Few understood the relationship, however. Although Steinbeck often made it appear that he was only suffering Carol's friends because of her, his devotion to Carol matched hers to him and his dependence was probably even greater. She was the first woman in his life to respond to him on what might be described as a spiritual basis. Sharp-minded, she judged him positively on his determination to be a writer and had come to share his ambition for himself. She was capable of cogent insights into his writing. Since most of her comments were favorable, they counterbalanced Carl Wilhelmson's more rigorous critical ones.

Carol was also vulnerable, however, and often became upset by Steinbeck's quicksilver changes of mood. He could be charming and likable one moment, hostile and impatient the next. Much of his mood changing had to do with his vacillating sense of himself as a writer, and was compounded by his uncertainty over the "form" he should finally pursue in his fiction. It also had to do with the fact that Carol and her friends were for the most part hardworking members of society, establishing careers in business and the like and bringing home weekly paychecks to attest to their pragmatic industriousness. At twenty-seven, he was beginning to wonder if he weren't letting life slip by him; in a few years, if he failed at writing, it would be too late to start another career. Carol continued to offer him financial support, but except for allowing her to buy them an occasional dinner, he Calvinistically refused.

Their relationship during the summer of 1929 fell into an alternating round of days of bitter argument about their future and hours of tender making up. Steinbeck's increasing dissatisfaction with himself, the cause of most of the spats, was not alleviated when, in August, *Cup of Gold* was published by McBride. He had arranged through Ted Miller for his New York friend, the artist Mahlon Blaine, to design the dust jacket.

Blaine's jacket was a disaster — a cheap portrayal of a swash-buckling pirate that gave the book the look of a boy's adventure story.

By way of further insult, the few reviews the book received generally dismissed it, and what little advertising McBride devoted to it plugged it solely as an adventure novel. Stuart Rose, the McBride editor who had originally accepted the novel, had left the firm prior to its publication. The editor who took over from Rose was indifferent to it. Steinbeck, having hoped to make some money from the book despite his own misgivings about its quality, was angry and disappointed. And when he heard from Ted Miller that certain bookstores in New York were stocking copies of the novel in their juvenile adventure sections, he knew all hopes of making any money were lost.

Carol shared none of John's bile. As far as she was concerned, he was a published author and, therefore, someone to be reckoned with. When twelve free copies of *Cup of Gold* arrived in San Francisco from New York, she got John to autograph ten of them and then proudly distributed them to her friends and family. The books were testaments to her faith in John, particularly with regard to her parents, who had taken a disapproving attitude toward her relationship with him. She saw the publication of *Cup of Gold* as a personal vindication. Steinbeck was embarrassed by it, even refusing to send copies to his own parents. Instead he refocused his energies on "The Green Lady," which he had decided to retitle after the ancient Vedic hymn "Who Is the God to Whom We Shall Offer Sacrifice?" Carl Wilhelmson criticized the length and awkwardness of the title, and it shortly became "To an Unknown God."

The book, though again a high-blown allegory dripping with symbolism, was Steinbeck's first "California" novel. It had started with Toby Street as a California piece. Steinbeck's disaffection with *Cup of Gold* had convinced him to follow the advice of Elizabeth Smith to forget foreign settings and write stories of California, which in her opinion was rich in material of triumph and tragedy. This was the principal reason he had been so willing to transform Street's play into a novel: it had a ready-made California setting that was considerably more finished and authoritative than anything he felt confident to invent.

He had long debates with Carl Wilhelmson over this. Wilhelmson was almost daily witness to Steinbeck's attempts to novelize "The Green Lady" and blamed his difficulties on the fact that John was locked into a theme and characters not of his own invention. In a way, the Morgan and Merlin characters of *Cup of Gold* were also borrowed rather than wholly invented figures. Wilhelmson maintained that so long as Steinbeck took the safe way of adapting existing stories and characters to fit his thematic ideas, he would never be taken seriously as a writer. He counseled John to abandon this method and start working solely out of his imagination. "Create a character," he said, "and then another. Put them up against each other on your first page. Then see where they take you. If they take you past ten pages, and they ring true, then you've got a story. Let the story shape what it is you want to say."

This was not revelatory advice, of course. Steinbeck had heard much of it from other quarters and had even discovered its virtues himself when he practiced his Monterey character sketches a few years earlier. But thus far he had been able to develop little confidence in his ability to match characters of his own invention to the import of what he thought he wanted to say by his fiction.

Wilhelmson's urgings did not go unheeded, however. Gradually through 1929, as Steinbeck struggled over transforming Toby Street's original play into a novel, the story and characters were themselves transformed. Steinbeck finally saw the light at about the time *Cup of Gold* was published. He briefly considered abandoning "The Green Lady" altogether, and indeed started a new novel based on characters of his own invention — a California novel.

The new work was really conceived not as a novel at all, but as a series of interrelated short stories. Steinbeck had told Duke Sheffield that the only real-life people he felt confident of basing fictional characters on were the colorful individuals he had known or observed when working at the various short-term jobs he had held — the Mexican laborers at the Spreckels plant and ranches, the hard-drinking roustabouts of the road-survey camps. The only trouble was that he didn't see how he could sustain these characters through the length of a novel. They were characters whose traits and eccentricities were more suitable to the short story. But Steinbeck had already written a number of short stories with little positive result, and he was convinced he had no future as a short-story writer.

This was an artistic dilemma that Sheffield helped him to resolve by reminding him of his interest in the Arthurian tales of Malory. Malory's *Morte d'Arthur* was in a sense a series of separate but interrelated short stories united by a common theme and recurring characters. It was Sheffield's idea that Steinbeck try something similar in a contemporary California vein: a novel about a segment of California life — the harsh, frontier aspects of it that Steinbeck was interested in — told in the form of interconnected short stories. Steinbeck liked the idea and gave it a good deal of thought, experimenting for several weeks with possible ways in which to realize it. In the meantime he reapproached "To an Unknown God."

By November there was little doubt in either John's or Carol's mind that they would wed. Carol wanted to marry immediately, but John was still reluctant to do so until he could get a better line on his future prospects. Although he had had a book published, it seemed to him that he was further away from success than ever. His view of success simply meant the ability to make a living as a writer, no more than a modest living.

Others were not so pessimistic. The publication of a first book was in their view a signal event in the life of a struggling writer and a favorable portent of things to come. Although John belittled *Cup of Gold* to his parents, they obtained copies and were enormously pleased both by the book itself and by the fact of its publication. Their attitudes toward John's pursuit of a writing career changed markedly as a result, particularly his father's.

In October, while awaiting his check from the McBride firm for the balance of his advance on *Cup of Gold*, Steinbeck extracted from his father a loan of one hundred dollars, to be paid back when the check arrived. (He didn't tell his father of Ted Miller's worry that McBride might not be able to make the balance of the advance.) The check did not come until December, but when it did, Steinbeck dutifully repaid his loan. So pleased were Olive and John Ernst with their son's integrity, and now so concerned that he have the time to produce his second book, that they offered again to "invest" in John's future. That is, John Ernst said that he would be willing to provide John with a regular subsidy of twenty-five dollars a month until such time as his son was able to earn a full-time living as a writer, provided that John agree to start paying the subsidy back once he achieved financial success.

Steinbeck accepted the proposal with alacrity, but also with some guilt. He was secretly sure his parents' sudden faith in his future was misplaced, since his struggles with "To an Unknown God," his putative second novel, gave him little hope of achieving the success they looked forward to. His guilt, however, propelled him into harder work. It was at this time that, out of a need to construct an alternative to the probable failure of "Unknown God," he began to write the Arthurian-type "short-story novel" that Duke Sheffield had suggested.

All he had at the beginning was a title, "Dissonant Symphony." The title had a twofold implication. One aspect represented John's intention to weave a group of disparate stories into a harmonic whole. The other was meant to symbolize the theme he intended to embrace — the struggle of man to retain his individuality while at the same time he sought to fit himself into the natural scheme of things.

In a state like California, the natural scheme of things was perpetually shaped by the vicissitudes of weather. Drought and moisture, which seemed to occur in harsh, unremitting cycles, dictated the fortunes of the average California rural and small-town dweller. They had been never-ending topics of conversation throughout Steinbeck's life in Salinas, since the economy of the town — indeed of his own family — depended so much on agricultural production. The farmers and ranchers who had settled the Salinas Valley had done so out of fiercely individualistic impulses. They soon learned, however, that their individuality was no match for the fickle and undependable California weather. To survive, they were forced to group together into cooperatives and associations, thus forfeiting their individualism. Those who refused to subscribe to the group movement invariably suffered personal and business failure. It was no small irony that once this happened, they proceeded to lose their individuality anyway, since they were thrust onto the public dole.

It was the conflict between the inherent individualism of the human soul and the group imperatives that rural California life dictated, that Steinbeck resolved to write about in "Dissonant Symphony." As it happened, he would soon complete the effort only to withdraw it from consideration for publication, claiming that he had failed to fulfill his intention. The effort itself, nevertheless, represented a singular turning point in his literary ambition. For by focusing his writing on the problems of contemporary rural California, he struck a chord in himself that sounded the discovery of his true function as a writer.

✤ ✤ ✤ ✤ ✤ ✤ CHAPTER FOURTEEN

Steinbeck's discovery did not come in the form of a sudden or miraculous revelation. He worked hard at "Dissonant Symphony" during the end of 1929 and the beginning of 1930. But he remained unsure of its worth as fictional subject matter — it represented a kind of naturalistic fiction he was unused to writing, after all — and continued to pursue his commitment to the more fanciful material of "To an Unknown God." It would take the continued encouragement of Duke Sheffield throughout 1930, and a fateful meeting with another man that same year, to convince John that the narrative material with which he was experimenting in "Dissonant Symphony" was his proper subject matter.

Steinbeck did nevertheless seem to go through a sudden jolt of maturity shortly after *Cup of Gold* was published. In a letter to A. Grove Day, another former Stanford student who was living in New Jersey and trying to establish himself as a writer, he described the experience as a "shedding of his poses" and attributed it to his two years of relative isolation in the Sierras. The letter, written in December of 1929, recounted his

Stanford days as a period in which he played a series of roles to create positive impressions of himself in his fellows' minds. During his extended stay in the mountains, he said, he had no one to impress. "Gradually all the poses slipped off and when I came out of the hills I didn't have any poses anymore."[14]

But it was not just the mountains that caused Steinbeck this intense period of reflection and maturity at the end of 1929. The fact that his parents were voluntarily willing to subsidize him, even though in a modest way, imposed on him an urgent sense of responsibility. His disappointment in *Cup of Gold* added an ingredient to the process. The reception it received hammered home the reality of his perception that a published book was neither a guarantee nor a harbinger of writing success. Indeed, he began to believe that the evident commercial failure of *Cup of Gold* would make publishers even more wary in their consideration of his next manuscript submission.

The most influential element of his rapidly changing outlook late in 1929, however, was Carol Henning. By December he had overcome his misgivings about complicating his life and had committed himself to marrying her within the next few months. She had convinced him that he would have nothing to be ashamed of if she contributed to their mutual financial support. Because of her typing work on *Cup of Gold* and on the successively tortured rewrites of "To an Unknown God," she felt that she had earned a proprietary interest in his career. Moreover, she not only was confident of his future as a writer, she also professed a deep love and need for him as a man.

As for Steinbeck, the overwhelming attention and tenderness he received from her, although it sometimes irritated him in its dependency, on the whole pleased him. After they were married for a time, however, this pattern in their relationship would change, causing each of them no end of unhappiness. But at the beginning of their life together, it was merely a minor flaw in an otherwise happy union of the kindred spirits of John Steinbeck and Carol Henning.

The marriage took place in Glendale, a San Fernando

Valley adjunct of Los Angeles, on January 14, 1930. They had left San Francisco a few weeks before to visit with Duke Sheffield and his second wife, Maryon, near Los Angeles's Occidental College, where Sheffield had obtained a teaching job after getting his master's degree from Stanford. Sheffield had urged Steinbeck to settle for a while near the Occidental campus. He was still trying to write, and the college had an active nucleus of several other aspiring novelists in its faculty. As a published novelist, he had suggested, John might be able to get a part-time teaching job at the college. The Los Angeles climate was good, and so was the company.

Sheffield and several other faculty members had embarked on an attempt to obtain a teaching position for John beginning with the opening of the new semester at Occidental in late January. John and Carol had remained with the Sheffields and, in anticipation of his getting the Occidental job, decided then and there to get married. Afterward they moved into a nearby run-down rental house in Eagle Rock, nestled in the hills separating Los Angeles from the eastern reaches of the San Fernando Valley. The teaching job never materialized, but the Steinbecks enjoyed their new surroundings so much that they determined to stay on. John still had his monthly twenty-five-dollar stipend from his father. Carol had become involved with some San Francisco friends in an attempt to successfully market a new Swiss product that could be used more neatly and conveniently than the traditional plaster of Paris in making sculpture molds and casts. The group was sure that the new substance would be immediately attractive to the movie industry and would one day even have mass-market appeal. If the venture were a success, Carol stood to make a considerable amount of money.

To celebrate their marriage, John and Carol purchased a puppy and moved into their first home. John had grown up with dogs and during his two-year stay at Fallen Leaf Lake had had the company of two Airedales belonging to the Brigham family. He held to the somewhat romantic outdoorsman's belief that no man is complete without a dog at his side. Since he had left home to go to Stanford in 1919, his travels had been too unpredictable to allow him to keep a dog of his own. But now that he was married and "settling down," it was time to bring a dog back into his orbit. The puppy was a Belgian shepherd and, like many of its breed, was sickly from the moment they brought it home.

In addition to tending the puppy, the Steinbecks devoted much of their time to refurbishing and decorating their house, for which they paid a rent of fifteen dollars a month. John did not let these diversions interfere with his revived literary determination, however. He diligently put about five hours a day into finishing the current version of "To an Unknown God," and then devoted an hour or two in the evenings to "Dissonant Symphony."

Neither, however, was working out to his satisfaction. Mostly because of his discussions during the previous months with Carl Wilhelmson, he had decided to change much of the original story on which "To an Unknown God" was based. It remained an allegory, but now had to do with a family of New England farmers who immigrated to California and encountered all sorts of difficulties, which produced both material tragedy and spiritual enlightenment. The fictional family was meant to be a composite of the separate forebears of Steinbeck's mother and father; he made them Irish, like the Hamiltons, but set their migratory trek from New England, like that of Johannes Adolph Steinbeck and his family.

Steinbeck's extensive revisions of the story crystallized in his mind the difficulties he was having with "Dissonant Symphony." The difficulties resided mainly in the fact that he was unable to work out a unifying leitmotiv for the separate characters he was writing about. He continued to like the idea of a novel told in the form of interlocking short stories, but found that the methods to which he had to resort in order to link his plots, characters and theme came across as forced and artificial. As well, they frequently sent the stories in directions he didn't want them to go.

In "To an Unknown God," he had settled largely on the Hamilton-family side of his ancestry from which to draw his character outlines, no doubt because the Hamilton family lore had been such a prominent part of his upbringing. His mother, aunts, and uncles had based much of their vivid family story-telling on the character and exploits of their father, the colorful and resourceful Samuel Hamilton, and John had grown up with a heightened consciousness of his maternal antecedents. His father, on the other hand, had always been Teutonically close-mouthed about his own family; he had been neither close to his parents and brothers nor given to graphic descriptions of his own upbringing. In musing about his paternal grandfather (such a lifeless, mysterious figure compared to his grandfather Hamilton) and concurrently about the seemingly insoluble problem he had created for himself in the format of "Dissonant Symphony," John suddenly stumbled upon a solution. The solution was his grandfather Johannes Adolph. Having heard but a few stories about him, he wondered what kind of man Johannes really was in comparison to grandfather Hamilton. Much of what he knew of Samuel Hamilton had come through the stories of his mother, Aunt Molly, Uncle Joe, and other relatives. Each had remembered him in his or her own way, and each story had added a new dimension to him. Steinbeck wondered whether, had his father's family been given to such story-telling, his grandfather Steinbeck would have assumed a similar vitality.

In constructing a number of invented stories about Johannes Adolph, told from what he imagined were the differ-ent points of view of his father and other members of Johannes's family, Steinbeck discovered the device by which he could realize his ambition in "Dissonant Symphony." He would create a character simply by having other people talk about him. The central character would never appear directly in the narrative but would exist only through the eyes of those who told of him. Each narrator's tale would be a separate story; the character about which each wrote would be the connecting link. This was not a new idea in fiction, but to Steinbeck it was a revelation. With this device, he could paint a richly colorful portrayal of life in California and the people who lived it. Moreover, the device would enable him to embrace a theme that reflected a philosophical position that, though not yet completely formed in his mind, was becoming increasingly important to him. This was that there were no immutable truths in the lives of people; the "truth" of an individual was only what others saw of him, and such truths were always elusive and often contradictory.

The philosophy was somewhat tied into his thoughts about himself after his two years at Fallen Leaf Lake. He had claimed that prior to his isolated stay there he had lived his life in accordance with what he believed others expected him to be. His lonely sojourn in the Sierras had caused him to shed his various personas and simply be himself. Or so he thought. Had he really managed such an accomplishment? Was it possible to exist without poses struck for the benefit of others? He had claimed that it was. But having made a number of friends in San Francisco and having gotten married, he was no longer sure. He would use "Dissonant Symphony" to explore the question further.

In the meantime, in April of 1930, Steinbeck finished what he thought was the final version of "To an Unknown God" and mailed the manuscript, cleanly typed by Carol, to Ted Miller in New York. The McBride firm had a contractual option on it, which meant a first-refusal right. John undoubtedly expected them to exercise the option, for he cautioned Miller in his accompanying letter to make sure that McBride printed an acknowledgment to Toby Street in the book when it was published. He looked forward to another cash advance to buttress his and Carol's meager finances; the marketing of the new Swiss molding device had not worked out, and Carol had been forced to lean on her parents in San Jose for money.

Late in May, word came from Miller that McBride had rejected the novel. The Steinbecks' puppy had just died, and the bad news sharply compounded John's grief. Although he was not totally happy with "To an Unknown God," he was convinced that it was a great improvement over *Cup of Gold* and could not understand why a publisher who had been willing to invest in an inferior novel should be unwilling to take on a superior one. He rationalized his disappointment by convincing himself that McBride, on the basis of its mishandling of *Cup of Gold*, was an inferior publisher and didn't, after all, deserve to publish his second novel. He urged Miller to send it to other publishers and vowed not to give up his hopes for the book. What he didn't know was that the principal reason for McBride's rejection lay in the fact that the Depression, in full swing in New York, had sharply reduced the firm's already slender capital resources. Other publishers were suffering similar problems. It was the worst possible time for a barely-known writer to get published — especially one dealing in obtuse allegories. The nation, and its publishers, wanted not the sermons of muddled philosophers but the escapist adventures of sales-proven writers.

"To an Unknown God" was rejected by a number of other houses during the summer of 1930, including such eminent ones as Harper Brothers and Farrar and Rinehart. Steinbeck, bolstered by the ministrations of Carol, Duke Sheffield and, from a distance, Carl Wilhelmson, refused to give in to his despair. He finished "Dissonant Symphony," compressing what was to have been a long work of interlocking short stories into a hundred pages and changing the central character from one based on his Steinbeck grandfather to one who more closely resembled John Ernst, his father.

He had told John Ernst of his idea regarding his grandfather when he had first started to toy with the notion of using Johannes Adolph as his model for "Dissonant Symphony." Steinbeck's father had been intrigued by John's intention. He had misunderstood it, however, thinking that John was setting out to write a fictionalized but pleasant family history. When John gave him the finished manuscript to read, the elder Steinbeck was astonished to discover that his son had written a darkly psychological and depressing study of mental aberration. It was not the book he had expected. Deeply dismayed, he implored John to destroy it and turn his attention to more commercial things.

Steinbeck was not that pleased with it himself, for in his view he had failed to fully realize his short-story-as-novel conception. But with "To an Unknown God" making no progress in New York, he decided to put his family novel out for publishing consideration. Feeling guilty about Ted Miller's diligent but unrewarded efforts to place what he called the "God novel" with a publisher, and not wanting to burden Miller with yet another manuscript, he sent it directly off to a *Scribner's Magazine* contest in New York. At that time, as the publisher of Hemingway, Fitzgerald and Thomas Wolfe, Charles Scribner's Sons seemed the most daring and ambitious of firms. Steinbeck vowed to his father that if they rejected "Dissonant Symphony," he would destroy it and try something else in a similar form.

In mid-July John and Carol received notice from their landlord that they would have to vacate the house they had so arduously restored. The landlord, admiring their handiwork, had decided to give the house to his soon-to-be-married daughter as a wedding present. John and Carol briefly looked for another place but were discouraged by the rents. Since they had no further financial prospects in Los Angeles, and since it was apparent that John would be earning no more money from his writing in the immediate future, they decided to move back to Pacific Grove where they could live rent-free in the Steinbeck family cottage. The impetus to do so was heightened when Steinbeck's father used his political influence as county treasurer to get Carol a job as a secretary with the Monterey Chamber of Commerce.

They made the move in late August. Once settled in at the little house on Eleventh Street, Carol took up her job at the chamber of commerce and John began a new novel. He worked on it into the fall. But peppered by continuing rejections from New York of "To an Unknown God" and hearing nothing from Scribner's about "Dissonant Symphony," he tore up the new work in disgust after completing forty pages.

During this time, he and Carol spent an evening at a party in nearby Carmel, which had developed into a fashionable artists' and writers' colony. Their host was an old acquaintance, John Calvin, who had achieved some success as a writer of adventure books, mostly for teenage boys. Several other commercially successful writers were at the party, and John found their cavalier attitude toward their work contemptible. They made it clear to him that they cared little about literary excellence and wrote solely to make money. His bile became so acute that it provoked in him an expression of anti-Semitic feeling that belied his insistence later in life that he had held no racial or other such prejudices as a young man. Describing the party a week later in a letter to Carl Wilhelmson, he wrote, "These writers . . . are the Jews of literature. They seem to wring the English language, to squeeze pennies out of it. . . . A conversation with them sounds like an afternoon spent with a pawnbroker."[15]

Despite his feelings, the experience of partying with a group of literarily crass but financially successful authors must have awakened in him an urge to emulate them. Or perhaps he was fired by a desire to hammer home his contempt by showing them that he could write the sort of commercial trash to which they devoted their careers; they had, after all, claimed that writing commercial literature was not so easy as it appeared. Whatever the case, Steinbeck immediately set out to write what he thought would be a "commercial" piece, a short mystery novel. Working furiously, he completed the two-hundred-odd-page manuscript in nine days and immediately sent Carol's typescript to Ted Miller. In his letter to Miller he apologized for the work, which he had titled "Murder at Full Moon," and said that he had only written it so that he could get some money to repay a debt that was making him miserable. He realized that he was temporarily sacrificing his artistic integrity for the sake of personal integrity (his need to make good his debt) and cautioned Miller to "remember that when this manuscript makes you sick. And remember that it makes me a great deal sicker than it does you." He insisted that if the story found a publisher it be printed under a nom de plume.

Steinbeck's continuing poverty was beginning to weigh heavily on him. Carol's secretarial salary, added to the monthly twenty-five dollars they received from his father, was enough to get them modestly by, but he was beginning to feel increasing guilt over his inability to do the providing. Although she valiantly tried to disguise it, the pressure had begun to drain Carol's vitality as well.

She was offered an opportunity in November to go into partnership with a woman friend in a small advertising agency in Monterey. Starting a business in the Depression seemed a foolhardy thing to do, and she would also have to give up her chamber-of-commerce job. Yet Monterey was in a period of commercial growth. The United States Army operated expanding facilities in and around the town, giving the area a certain amount of immunity from the effects of the Depression. The main industry, fishing and canning, continued to thrive — the cheap tin of sardines had become a staple of many a Depression-era dinner table. What's more, plans were being made to dredge the harbor, build a breakwater and turn Monterey into a deep-water port.

Although she disliked secretarial work and was eager to go into the advertising venture, Carol was forced to hesitate, uncertain of the wisdom of giving up her chamber-of-commerce salary for the immediate absence of income the new business would impose. Steinbeck, in the expectation that "Murder at Full Moon" would have a quick and lucrative sale, urged her to take on the new venture. Finally, obtaining a small stake from her father with which to go into partnership and establish an office, she did.

The debt to which Steinbeck alluded in his letter to Ted Miller apologizing for "Murder at Full Moon" was a dental bill. During his years at Stanford, followed by his trip to New York and his two-year stay in the Sierras, John had subsisted on a regimen of cheap foods laden with sugar. While in Eagle Rock after his marriage to Carol, his teeth, suffering the decaying effects of his diet, began to bother him. By the time they had moved back to Pacific Grove his mouth was aflame with periodontal disease. A series of visits to a Monterey dentist had alleviated the immediate problems, but it was clear that Steinbeck was going to require a considerable amount of further remedial treatment to save his teeth. Unable to pay the bill for the initial emergency patching up he had needed during the fall of 1930, he was unable to return to the dentist for the more extensive treatment he should have had. He finally had to borrow money from Carol's father to pay his bill so that he could get further treatment. It was to repay him — a matter of personal honor and integrity — that he gave as his reason for writing "Murder at Full Moon."

John's dental crisis, a source of physical agony and further financial anxiety, was not without its benefits, however. For it was while visiting his dentist one day in the fall of 1930 that he met the man who would, by the force of his singular intellect and insight, synthesize and transform Steinbeck's confused artistic aspirations.

❀ ❀ ❀ ❀ ❀ ❀ ❀ CHAPTER FIFTEEN

The man was Edward F. Ricketts, a slender, bearded young scientist from Chicago who operated a marine laboratory and biological-supply firm out of a ramshackle former warehouse on Monterey's waterfront.

By all accounts, Ed Ricketts was a most unusual man. Although formally educated at the University of Chicago in the science of invertebratology, his expansive mind ranged over a vast spectrum of human interests. He ran his lab and specimen-supply business in a casual, almost haphazard way and enjoyed most his expeditions along the California coast and up the state's rivers to collect the specimens that he would later supply to high school biology labs and medical research facilities. He also conducted experiments on fish and other marine and animal life in his own lab, and then wrote highly original papers on the evolutionary process for scientific journals.

But his scientific vocation was only one small facet of his personality. An extremely articulate, almost glib man who both wrote and spoke on almost any topic imaginable with the authority and originality of superior intelligence, he was also a hard drinker, a womanizer and an adventurous, sharp-eyed cynic with a trenchant wit. All of these traits instantly attracted Steinbeck to him in a combination of wonder and envy. Ricketts found in Steinbeck something of a kindred spirit — a man of intelligence and curiosity who was basically shy like himself; a loner, seeking the independent life, who masked his shyness with an outspoken if sometimes naive intellectualism. Moreover, Steinbeck had retained an interest in marine biology; that he knew something about the subject further enhanced his acceptability in Ricketts's eyes.

By January of 1931 the two had become fast friends. It was not quite a friendship of equals, however. As spring arrived it became clear that, by dint of his superior intellectual brilliance and originality, if not deeper sensitivity, Ricketts was slightly more the leader and teacher, Steinbeck the follower and student. Much of this stemmed from the fact that Ricketts had to make no effort at incisive reflection and analysis, whereas Steinbeck did. Where Steinbeck was deliberate in his thoughts and ideas, often plodding after them into blind alleys, Ricketts's mind operated with balletic ease, grace and precision. Where Steinbeck was assailed by doubts even about the utility of his own large philosophical notions, Ricketts expressed no hesitancy about his. Steinbeck's thought processes tended to turn a single concrete idea into a morass of confused, unresolvable possibilities. Ricketts's on the other hand could mercurially reduce countless disparate ideas to a single cogent, concrete and unified vision.

Despite his intimidating intelligence and the slight disparity in the intellectual balance of their relationship, Ricketts was never anything less than a sympathetic companion to John as their friendship ripened during the spring. Steinbeck almost daily visited Pacific Biological Laboratories to watch Ricketts at work and sometimes assist him. Ricketts, already a well-known character along the Monterey waterfront, which was known as

Cannery Row, would bring John into its dockside saloons for long beer-drinking and discussion sessions. Steinbeck marveled at the ease with which Ricketts could shift from discussing his theories about life to bantering with a group of cannery workers or a prostitute from one of the several brothels near the waterfront. He was equally at home with the rough-hewn as he was with the refined of Monterey.

Steinbeck had previously observed the denizens of Cannery Row from a distance, but now, through Ricketts, he had a chance to experience their life at first hand. The life on the Row often led the two friends into debates about one of John's favorite but unresolved subjects: the dichotomy between the animal and intellectual tendencies in man. Most of Cannery Row was inhabited by people whose existence was almost exclusively animal in nature. Food, drink, shelter, sex and the often self-destructive striving for status were their sole concerns. To Steinbeck, this was confirmation of his belief that such people made poor models for literature. Ricketts saw them in a different light. He expounded the view that the impoverished, semiliterate characters who peopled Cannery Row were ideal models for the kind of philosophical fiction Steinbeck wanted to write. Nothing was more poignant than the hopeless conflict between poor people's efforts to drag themselves out of their impoverished, unremittingly oppressed state, and the impossibility of their succeeding because of the very state in which their minds were imprisoned. Their aspirations grew out of their human mental processes; their inevitable failures stemmed from their animalistic reflexes. Write a book about these people, urged Ricketts, and show every reader how thin the line is between his own animal and human nature.

It was this sort of realistic philosophizing that Ricketts was given to, and it impressed Steinbeck. Between them, the two developed an intellectual give and take, with Ricketts almost always the succinct summarizer of the ideas that flowed between them. Much of their talk was about Steinbeck's literary direc-

tion — or at that time the lack of it, since after the evident
failure of "To an Unknown God" and "Dissonant Symphony"
he was in a quandary about what to do next. During the spring
he gave carbon copies of both manuscripts to Ricketts to read.

Ricketts acknowledged his new friend's literary striving
but told him that he thought, on the basis of the manuscripts,
that it was diffuse and uncertain. The same was true, he said, of
the published *Cup of Gold.* Steinbeck was obviously trying in
these works to avoid coming to emotional grips with his mentally
conceived thematic principles and goals. "The good writer," he
said, surprising John with his pithiness, "must tell lies to show
the truth. But he must lie only to his reader, not to himself."

According to Ricketts, Steinbeck had been lying to himself
by his obsession with allegory and symbolism. His allegories in
Cup of Gold and "To an Unknown God" were clearly more
concerned with thematic form than with substance. What was
the point of using characters as symbols when much more was
to be learned from them, and experienced through them, as
realistic people. Allegory was a form of preaching, and the only
people who preached were those who were unsure of their beliefs. That was what was good about science. Scientists cannot
preach their truths; they must let the evidence they compile,
based on their experiences and observations, and untainted by
human manipulation, speak for them. Darwin had spoken of
evolution not because it was some pet philosophical theory, but
because his studies convinced him that its truth was inescapable.

A good writer must tell lies, Ricketts concluded, but only
to gain his reader's attention. Once he had his attention, he
must then put together the evidence — through the untainted
thoughts and actions of his characters — that will lead the reader
to accept the inescapable truths of the human condition, and
thus the truth about himself. The good writer must be "a scientist of the imagination."

Of the three novels and several short stories Steinbeck had
given him to read, Ricketts had liked "Dissonant Symphony"

most, not for what it was, but for what it could be. He agreed with the experiment in form — the novel comprising interconnected short stories — but thought that Steinbeck's execution of it was shallow and halfhearted, and tendentiously sermonistic in the bargain. Again, he said, John's preachiness — drawing conclusions for the reader — was symptomatic of a failure to believe in his material.

By probing, criticizing and discoursing with Steinbeck in this manner, and by exposing him to the scientific regimen of his marine laboratory, Ricketts managed over a period of time to reshape many of John's deepest literary ideas and writing proclivities. Since he was indeed unsure of his art, Steinbeck found in Ricketts's visceral certainty and authority an anchor on which to secure himself. What made Ricketts's insights different from those of such friends as Duke Sheffield and Carl Wilhelmson, aside from the fact that they came from a much more brilliant and incisive man, was the fact that he had no literary ambitions for himself. He was a superb writer of biological monographs but was no more capable of writing fiction than John was of inventing a laboratory process. It was partly because his critical perceptions were unpolluted by dreams of personal literary glory that Steinbeck so readily absorbed them. But it was more so because the force of Ricketts's authority, coupled with his own floundering anxiety about his writing, left him no choice.

One day in the spring of 1931, John, Carol and Ricketts were returning in Ricketts's car from a visit to Salinas. Steinbeck had invited the biologist to meet his parents and had shown him around Salinas, claiming that one day he would write a huge novel about the people of the town and valley in which he had grown up. On the way back to Monterey, John took them on a short detour to see the ranch of his late aunt, Molly Martin. The ranch was located in a picturesque valley known as Corral de Tierra, which was nestled in the rocky hills between Salinas and Monterey. John recounted to Carol and Ricketts some of the local lore of the isolated valley, which he had learned as a boy during his visits to his aunt. The most vivid of his tales was one that had to do with a family that had moved into the valley in the 1870s and had seen everything they did turn into disaster. They built a beautiful barn only to have it burn down; they purchased a herd of cows only to have them ravaged by disease. Many other residents of the valley believed them to be cursed. When they were finally forced by circumstances to abandon their ranch and leave the valley, many local residents were convinced that they had left their curse behind. After they were gone, the valley continued to suffer disasters.

A few days later Steinbeck was at Ricketts's laboratory helping him to label and pack frogs for shipment to several school labs. Ricketts mentioned that he had been thinking of John's curse tale and wondered aloud if it wouldn't make good material for a short story or novel. His initial idea was for John to use it as a fictional framework to debunk the dependence of most people on religious and mythological belief — another topic they had discussed at length. A pet theory of Ricketts's was that one of man's greatest deficiencies as a species was his inability to adapt to his changing environment. In that sense animals, lacking the intellect to subscribe to beliefs, were superior to man. They evolved and adapted in accordance with the demands placed on them by their environments. Man, on the other hand, although blessed with an intellect, was also cursed by it because it resisted adaptation and change. This was nowhere more evident than in his religious beliefs, went Ricketts's theory: most men still lived in the Dark Ages, clinging to beliefs and doctrines that were ancient even then.

Ricketts's suggestion was casual, but as he expanded on it the idea lodged firmly in John's mind. Further discussion, which included talk about his desire to write another California novel, his unsuccessful short-story-as-novel experiment in "Dissonant Symphony," and his hope of one day writing a "big" novel about Salinas, refined the idea. Ricketts suggested that John abandon "Dissonant Symphony" but reemploy its form to write a book about a "cursed" valley and the people in it. The idea began to germinate.

Steinbeck had suffered a number of further rejections on the three manuscripts still circulating among New York publishers. "To an Unknown God" had practically run out of publishers. "Murder at Full Moon" was by then even being rejected for serialization by the cheap pulp magazines. "Dissonant Symphony" had been returned by Scribner's with a brief note saying that it was unacceptable. Ted Miller was able to hold out no further hopes.

A visit from Carl Wilhelmson, although he was still full of encouragement and constructive criticism, did little to buoy Steinbeck's spirits. Wilhelmson had already had two novels published, his third had been accepted, and he had acquired a distinguished literary agency in New York to represent him and negotiate his publishing contracts. As often happens in the darkest hours of one's life, however, Wilhelmson's visit planted a seed that would in time help hoist John out of his despair. He had recently received a letter from Ted Miller in which the New York lawyer suggested that John's manuscripts might fare better in the hands of a full-time literary agent than in his; besides, said Miller, his legal career and personal problems were consuming so much of his time that he was no longer able to devote much attention to marketing John's works.

The letter at first depressed Steinbeck. What reputable literary agent would want to deal with manuscripts that had already been so roundly rejected by the publishing community? He mentioned his problem to Carl Wilhelmson. Wilhelmson immediately recommended that John tell Miller to deliver his manuscripts to the literary agency of McIntosh and Otis. Mavis McIntosh, one of the partners in the small but active firm, was Wilhelmson's personal agent, and he promised to write to her immediately, recommending John.

In his reply to Ted Miller, Steinbeck asked him to deliver the manuscripts of "To an Unknown God" and "Murder at

Full Moon" to McIntosh and Otis. A week later, at the beginning of May, John received a letter from Mavis McIntosh. In
it she agreed to take him on but dismissed "To an Unknown
God" as disjointed, confusing and inconsistently paced. Seeing
commercial possibilities in "Murder at Full Moon," she urged
Steinbeck to send her more stories of that type. She added that
from her limited reading of his "serious" work, she thought he
might do well as a portrayer of certain contemporary aspects of
American life, particularly in California. He wrote well when
he directly described characters and places, she said; it was only
when he sought to hammer home points with quasipoetic effects
and philosophical musings that he lost her interest.

Steinbeck was at once disturbed and heartened by the
letter. He was not yet willing to give up on "the God novel" and
he wondered about her literary qualifications in view of the fact
that she thought the murder tale had merit. But her remarks
about his promise as a portrayer of "aspects of California life"
accorded with his thoughts about the "curse" novel Ed Ricketts
had been encouraging him to write. Moreover, despite its critical stance, the overall tone of Mavis McIntosh's letter was
sympathetic and optimistic, which nourished his failing spirit.
Only a few weeks before he had told Ted Miller, "Perhaps I
have been kidding myself all these years, myself and other people. . . . [Perhaps] I have nothing to say and no art in saying
it. It is two years since I have received the slightest encouragement. . . ."[16]

By August, whatever optimism Mavis McIntosh and her
partner Elizabeth Otis had provided John by their letters in
praise of his work had vanished. McIntosh was trying to find a
publisher for "To an Unknown God" and the murder novel,
while Elizabeth Otis had entered the picture as the agent for
his short stories. Steinbeck, at her request, had sent her a sheaf
of stories. Although by then he had conditioned himself to expect the worst from any manuscript submission he made, the
agency's encouragement had given him hope that something

positive would soon happen. His disappointment was acute, then, when the stories were returned to him — pleasantly assessed by Elizabeth Otis, but unsold. Shortly thereafter he heard from Mavis McIntosh that she had had no success in trying to place "To an Unknown God." Drawing from the comments she had received from the editors to whom she had submitted it, she sharpened her own criticism of it. Yet, she said, if John would rewrite in it a fashion that would give it more unity and cohesion, she was sure she could find a publisher for it.

The prospect of rewriting a novel that he had spent two years struggling over at first repelled Steinbeck. For the most part he could agree with McIntosh's critical remarks. But although he assured her that he would be willing to redo it, he had little sense of how or where to begin. Instead, he had Ted Miller deliver the manuscript of "Dissonant Symphony" to her. He wrote and explained that he was currently working on a novel in the style of "Dissonant Symphony"; he did not expect her to try to market the "Symphony" manuscript but wanted her to see the form so that she would know what to expect when he sent her "The Pastures of Heaven." This was the ironic title he had decided to give his book about the cursed valley known as Corral de Tierra.

McIntosh's reaction to "Dissonant Symphony" is unknown, but when she received the manuscript of "The Pastures of Heaven" she was unimpressed. Steinbeck had slaved through the fall at the new work with a determination and discipline that reflected the imperative he felt to produce a book that would carry his career forward rather than backward, as the contemplated rewrite of "To an Unknown God" would have done. Mavis McIntosh thought "Pastures" had little chance, but halfheartedly promised to circulate it to publishers. Steinbeck, further disheartened by her pessimism, finally began to think seriously about rewriting "the God novel." If McIntosh's estimates of "Pastures" was correct, it would mean another year of groaning impoverishment for Carol and himself.

Carol's advertising venture had failed. Out of work, she had spent several weeks cooped up with her husband. The climate in the cottage grew rapidly tense. Carol increasingly sought to pry emotional support from John to compensate for her failure to make a go of the advertising agency. He, investing all his emotions and energies in his feverish attempt to finish "Pastures of Heaven," was unable to respond. They frequently argued, their spats turning into battles in which both took positions that grew irrevocably fixed and became the bastions of a creeping alienation. Another problem was money. John was remorseful over his inability to provide, and began to blame her for enticing him into the trap of marriage. As 1932 dawned, both were sure that the future held nothing but further misery and defeat.

❊ ❊ ❊ ❊ ❊ ❊ ❊ CHAPTER SIXTEEN

The year indeed began with dismal prospects. The publishing firm of William Morrow rejected "The Pastures of Heaven" in January, and Steinbeck, aside from wrestling with his marital difficulties, was glumly facing up to the rewriting of "To an Unknown God." In a note to Ted Miller, he said, "I'm pretty damn sick of my consistent failure. Everyone says nice things and no one buys my books."

But then came some unexpected good news. In February, on his thirtieth birthday, John received a wire from Elizabeth Otis announcing that the agency had sold "The Pastures of Heaven." The publisher was to be Jonathan Cape and Harrison Smith, the American subsidiary of the prestigious British firm Jonathan Cape, Ltd. The Cape and Smith editor who had accepted the manuscript was Robert Ballou, a former literary editor of the *Chicago Daily News*. To Steinbeck's astonishment, Ballou was so enthusiastic about "Pastures" that he offered contracts on John's next two novels as well, sight unseen. The advance money would not be much, but Steinbeck would at least, and at last, have a small measure of security. The development also meant that "To an Unknown God" would finally have a publisher. Steinbeck had already started his rewrite when he learned of the Cape and Smith offer, and now he bent to the task with optimism. Deliberation and thoughtfulness replaced the urgency and confusion with which he had begun the rewrite a few weeks before.

The reworking of "To an Unknown God" had crystallized out of a number of conversations Steinbeck had had about the troublesome novel with Ed Ricketts after he had sent the "Pastures" typescript to McIntosh and Otis and received their gloomy assessment of its marketability. In tracing the fortunes of the migratory New England family on its arrival in California in his first version of the novel, Steinbeck had imposed all sorts of religiously oriented psychic artifices on the story to carry forward his theme of human self-delusion. It was precisely these deus-ex-machina factors that had provoked the unanimous criticisms of the novel as disjointed and artificial, including Ricketts's.

Ricketts's view of life was exclusively Darwinistic, animalistic, naturalistic. Psychic disorder and its consequences came not from a conflict between man and his "Maker" but from the struggle between man and his natural surroundings. Outlining his complex ideas with ease and simplicity, Ricketts had gradually convinced Steinbeck that a portrait of the Wayne family (the protagonists of "To an Unknown God") doing battle with the elements, rather than with religious myths, would give the novel a reality and immediacy that it sorely lacked. California had just been released from the throes of a severe ten-year drought, and there was documentable evidence to prove that this natural phenomenon had unleased countless psychological and behavioral aberrations in the state's population. Once the drought had broken, people returned to normal. Ricketts suggested that John rework the story of the Waynes to show their awakening to the powers of nature and their consequent discarding of puritanical New England religious beliefs.

Steinbeck was not ready to altogether abandon his much more fanciful goals in the novel, but he responded positively to Ricketts's idea of using the drought as a central element in the story. He was still intent on executing the allegorical aspects of the book. But he thought he could incorporate Ricketts's notions (which were gradually, but not yet completely, becoming his notions) to give the story the desired coherence and reader interest. It was in this spirit, then, that he pressed forward with the rewriting of "To an Unknown God" during the spring of 1932.

Matters with respect to "The Pastures of Heaven" were destined not to proceed as smoothly as he had anticipated in February, however. When Cape and Smith made its offer, the firm was fighting a quiet battle against Depression bankruptcy. The contracts for "Pastures" and the two subsequent books were not forwarded to Steinbeck for several months, when the firm was reorganized under the name of Jonathan Cape and Robert Ballou, Inc. Even after signing the contracts, Steinbeck still received no money, for Ballou quickly became involved in a company dispute and left the firm for another — Brewer, Warren and Putnam. Fortunately for Steinbeck, Ballou was able to persuade his new employers to assume the three-book contract. But by September of 1932, when he signed new contracts with Brewer, Warren and Putnam, John still had not received any money and was forced to borrow one hundred dollars, using the contracts as collateral. Carol had been given a job by Ed Ricketts as an assistant in his laboratory, but her fifty-dollars-per-month salary eased their financial stress only barely. And John was still accumulating dental bills.

Steinbeck worked assiduously through the summer and fall of 1932 on "To an Unknown God." With Carol working once again, and with the contractual expectation of a modest amount of money, the tension in their marriage eased somewhat. Lasting emotional damage had been done, nevertheless, and their relationship gradually became infused with an air of distrust. Their respective moods were sharpened by the death of their second dog, an Airedale terrier they had acquired to replace their Belgian shepherd. Steinbeck was particularly fond of the dog, which he called "Tillie," and in his mind had invested it with almost human qualities. In his frustration over the delayed payments on his book contract and his anguish regarding the re-writing of "the God novel," he blamed Carol's indifference for the death of the dog.

Robert Ballou had originally projected the printing of "The Pastures of Heaven" for the summer of 1932, but the con-tract delays in New York caused the book's appearance to be postponed until late fall. Upon its publication John and Carol traveled back to Los Angeles, where they remained into early 1933 while John finished the rewrite of his long-suffering "God novel." He sent it off to Ballou in February under the slightly transposed title of "To a God Unknown." The transposi-tion had been suggested by Ricketts, who felt that the previous title, "To an Unknown God," gave the novel a misleading re-ligious character. In the meantime, a few reviews of *The Pas-tures of Heaven* had appeared. Most were unfavorable, accusing Steinbeck of obsessively dealing with mentally defective char-acters.

By February it had become clear that "Pastures" was going to earn Steinbeck no further money than the small advance he'd received for it from Brewer, Warren and Putnam. Then came word from Ballou that because of the national economic situa-tion, the firm might not be able to fulfill its contractual obliga-tion to publish "To a God Unknown" and a subsequent novel. Following that, Olive Steinbeck was stricken with a serious ill-ness. John and Carol had been preparing for a trip to Mexico. Instead, they were forced to return to Salinas to help look after John's mother; at the age of seventy, John's father, his own health deteriorating, was incapable of caring for his wife.

Olive had long suffered from high blood pressure. Her problem was now complicated by a hardening of the arteries, which left her in a state of rapidly advancing senility. In May, she was attacked by a stroke that permanently paralyzed the left side of her body, left her incoherent, and demanded that she have full-time care. John's sister Mary had married several years before and was living in Los Angeles with her husband and two young children. She was unable to spend long periods of time in Salinas. Beth and Esther were also otherwise occupied with their lives away from Salinas. Since John had no reason not to, and because he now felt a powerful sense of loyalty and duty to his mother and father, he and Carol moved back into the house in Salinas and began a deathwatch over Olive that lasted through the steaming summer and into the fall.

Olive Steinbeck was placed in the Salinas Valley Hospital at the time of her stroke, and to keep expenses down Carol helped to nurse her while John looked after his increasingly feeble and distraught father at home. During the summer he wrote little but spent long hours reflecting upon his past ideas, particularly those that had been shaped or refined by his discussions with Ed Ricketts, and upon his future. Robert Ballou had finally confirmed the bad news that Brewer, Warren and Putnam would not be able to publish "To a God Unknown." He had said, however, that he was going to strike out on his own and hoped that Steinbeck would let him publish that novel under his new imprint. Steinbeck was dubious, but he had little other choice. He was sure that "To a God Unknown" was as cursed as the valley about which he had written in *The Pastures of Heaven,* and he saw scarce likelihood of its ever being published. While in Salinas, he worked on a few short stories, but was too distracted by his mother's hospitalization and his father's growing anxiety about her to embark on another novel. Besides, cast about as he did, he could think of nothing to write about.

As the summer progressed, however, and he reflected with more intensity on his purpose and ambition as a writer, as well as on his mother's certain impending death, a number of philosophical notions that had long nagged at him began to jell in his mind. He and Ed Ricketts had several prolonged discussions about the nature and mechanics of death during John and Carol's occasional brief visits to Pacific Grove during the summer. Largely as a result of Ricketts's insights into the whole process of life and death, John began to form a more concrete idea of what it was he wanted to say in his writing.

The idea was based on the individual-group and man-animal dichotomies that Steinbeck had been worrying over for a number of years. The accumulation of explanations that Ed Ricketts had offered during the previous eighteen months gradually synthesized in John's mind until he perceived a coherent whole. At its heart was the observed phenomenon that when acting as a group, men do not exercise their own ordinary natures but behave on the basis of the group nature, a separate and distinct mechanism. Borrowing Ed Ricketts's interpretation of things, he saw groups as being "as separate and distinct from the individual men that compose them as individual men are separate and distinct from the bodily cells of which they are constituted." The group is at once dependent on and independent of its individuals, just as the individual is at once dependent on and independent of his cells. The independence of the group evinces itself in its collective nature — that is, the nature of the group is distinct and separate from the nature of any of its members. "Just as a bar of iron has none of the properties of the . . . atoms which make it up," Steinbeck wrote at the time, "so these huge creatures, the groups, do not resemble the human atoms which compose them."

Steinbeck described his discovery as having "splashed" on him like a revelation of monumental dimensions. Although philosophers since ancient Greek times had made similar discoveries, it was obvious that for Steinbeck it was a novel and, because of his belief in its eye-opening truth, exciting perception. His excitement remained for many months unbounded, and it acted as an antidote to his depression over his mother and his stalled career. In fact he later attributed the timing of his insights to his mother's illness. It was pondering the death of the cells in his mother's semiparalyzed body that had gotten him to thinking, with Ed Ricketts's help, about the differences between a person's cells and the whole person. From there it was a logical jump to the resolution of the problem of the difference between the individual and the group, of why the two entities acted in separate manners.

The group has its own memory, its own emotions, its own active and reactive impulses, Steinbeck concluded, all of which are unique to it and separate from those of any and all its members. It was this separate nature that gave the group — or "the phalanx" as he came to call it — its transcendent power and momentum in human affairs. Steinbeck decided that his new theory, and the exposition of it, would be the thematic stuff from which he would thenceforth make his fiction. All he had to do now was to find an appropriate subject and a method with which to express it.

During the initial stages of his mother's illness and hospitalization, Steinbeck's father led him through a number of nostalgic reminiscences about their earlier days. Among them was the story of John's boyhood acquisition of his chestnut pony. Elizabeth Otis had been hounding Steinbeck for some more short stories. He had written a few after sending "To a God Unknown" to New York in February. Now, when not working out his "phalanx" theory, he passed the time in Salinas writing a few more. Responding to Otis's criticisms about the unnecessary satirical archness of his previous stories, he was consciously trying to change his style to the ironic naturalism popularized by such writers as Hemingway and Fitzgerald. His father's recollections prompted him to write a story in this new style about a boy in Salinas and his pony. John had been thinking more and more about trying to write a kind of epic novel about Salinas and its valley. But his recent philosophical synthesizing had temporarily overpowered his novelistic impulses. During the summer, therefore, he worked on his stories, including the one about the boy and his pony — the theme of which dealt with the boy's passage from innocence to manhood — with the idea of forming them into another short-story-as-novel project like *The Pastures of Heaven.*

He worked intermittently at "The Red Pony," as he called it, and several other stories about the valley — most inspired by his father's increasingly senile reminiscences — throughout June and July. But it was his mental convolutions over the phalanx theory that occupied most of his thoughts. He wrote long cryptic essays to himself about it, as well as dozens of extended letters to friends such as Duke Sheffield, Carl Wilhelmson and George Albee, an aspiring writer a few years younger than Steinbeck whom John had befriended during his and Carol's first stay in Los Angeles and from whom he had borrowed the hundred dollars against his three-book contract. As he said in a letter to Albee that summer, "I have my new theme out of all this [phalanx theorizing]. I am scared to death. . . . In fact it has covered my horizon completely enough so there doesn't seem to be anything else to think about. . . ."

But he was indeed thinking about other things. His mother continued to weigh heavily on his mind. So too did his rapidly declining father, to whom John was finally able to direct some overt affection. Carol also became an increasing source of concern. Her daily attendance at his mother's side was a selfless demonstration of loyalty to him. But while it muted their hostility and drew them closer in certain aspects, it also acted as a drain on Carol's energy and enthusiasm for life. She gradually assumed a dispirited air; whereas she had always been attentive to John's ideas, she now found his heavy philosophizing tiresome, as though he was drifting further and further away from the simple ambition of storytelling on which he had rationalized their poverty.

The one positive aspect of the summer was the news that Robert Ballou had finally gotten enough money together to start his own modest publishing venture and had begun production on "To a God Unknown," with plans to publish it in the fall.

During John's residence in Pacific Grove the year before, he had met a young Monterey high school teacher named Susan Gregory. Sue Gregory was partly of Mexican descent and had cultivated a folkloric interest in Monterey's poor Mexican *paisano* population, most of whom lived in a community of shanties on a flat in the hills above the town. Because of its ex-clusively Mexican character, the community was called locally, and somewhat derisively, Tortilla Flat. Sue Gregory, an aspiring poet as well as a teacher, had managed to find in the poverty and illiteracy of the inhabitants of Tortilla Flat a dignity and humor that inspired her to write poems about them. Ricketts, in his continuing urgings to John that he give up his metaphysical fic-tion and concentrate on writing about the colorful characters of Monterey, had referred him to her. Ricketts had proposed that John study the *paisanos* in much the same way that he studied his marine specimens and then try to write something that would illuminate the balance between the human and animal nature in man — a metaphysical theme, to be sure, but framed in the simplest, most naturalistic way. Sue Gregory was to be his introduction to the people of Tortilla Flat, just as Ricketts had been his introduction to those of Cannery Row. Sue Gregory had taken John on several occasions into the flat and regaled him with stories about its inhabitants that underlined both their native dignity and their survival and humor in the face of adversity. John agreed that they would make interesting short-story subjects.

A year later, as he whiled away the summer in the sad Salinas house jotting down book ideas and struggling through an occasional short story, his mind returned to the *paisanos* of Tortilla Flat. He dashed off a couple of brief stories and found that the writing experience brought him back to the simple fun-damentals of storytelling with which he had experimented years before. Not only that, but the experience of writing humorous sketches about characters real to his senses but foreign to his sensibilities managed to at least momentarily block out his ever-darkening concern over his mother and father, and to serve as a further counterpoint to his intensive, tortuous philosophizing. He tried a few more stories and discovered that, while writing simply and straightforwardly, he could still work his new thematic ideas into them.

Gradually a plan emerged in his mind. During the summer he had picked up his childhood copy of *Morte d'Arthur*. Browsing through it, he reflected on his vague ambition to someday "translate" the old language of the Arthurian legends into modern colloquial English. He also reflected on the influence the Malory book had had on his own work so far. He realized that he had not yet utilized the form as he had hoped to. Although *Cup of Gold* had borrowed from it in characterization and symbolism, and "To a God Unknown" in its allegorical-quest qualities had remotely derived from *Morte d'Arthur,* only *The Pastures of Heaven* had been a conscious attempt to draw from its form. But "Pastures" had gone off on other tangents so that the form had lost its intended Arthurian identification. Now, as he thought of his *paisano* stories, he wondered if he couldn't give a book about Tortilla Flat an authentic Arthurian ring. Without some cohesive formal thread, a series of stories about the *paisanos,* no matter how poignant and amusing, would probably fall on deaf editorial ears, as had so many of his previous short-story efforts. But if he could successfully draw them together into a novel format, much as he had done with the stories in *The Pastures of Heaven* but with more clarity and simplicity, he might have the makings of a powerful book. And Robert Ballou was still obliged to publish the next book-length work he submitted.

As summer turned to fall, Steinbeck finished "The Red Pony" and sent its ten-thousand-word typescript to McIntosh and Otis, along with several other short stories. Then he turned his fragmented writing attention to developing his book of *paisano* tales, which he would eventually call "Tortilla Flat."

John's father's health worsened during the fall as his anxiety over his crippled, dying wife intensified. In October John and Carol moved back to Pacific Grove, taking John Ernst with them. A new puppy was added to the spartan household, this one an Irish terrier that Steinbeck named Jodie. *To a God Unknown* was published by Ballou in November, but its appearance produced no joy. As far as John could see, his previous books not only had not sold but had acquired for him nothing in the way of an audience or a following. *To a God Unknown* had once been his most precious and pampered literary possession, but he cared little for it now. His new ideas, still being synthesized out of Ed Ricketts's quicksilver mind, had turned him in a new direction. And they had provoked a new artistic struggle — this between allegory and naturalism as a writing method. Besides, as he often said, once he had finished a book, "I have little interest in it. By the time one comes out I am usually tied up in another."

Although he clung for a while to the hope that *To a God Unknown* would earn him some money, if not repute, he was quickly disabused of it. The few reviews the book received lacked enthusiasm. Thus far he had earned about $870 for his seven years of steady writing — an average of $125 a year. He glumly faced the fact that *To a God Unknown* would not appreciably add to his average. Indeed, if he did not succeed in producing something more commercially lucrative in the year to come, the average would plummet.

Most writers of Steinbeck's period, like those of every period, took a special pride in their published books. Initially a writer's struggle is to get published, and many would-be writers never achieve even this. Those who do, be it with one or several books, tend to view their books as symbols of singular self-significance and accomplishment. One or more published books tend to have a mystical quality in the minds of authors. Whether the books are profitable or not is usually a consideration of secondary importance. The books themselves — the fact that they have been published — are reward enough. The mystique of being a writer has been fulfilled. Only veteran authors, those who have published a number of books, tend to outgrow this mystique and remain unimpressed by the fact that they have been, once again, published.

Steinbeck, whether instinctively or not, had assumed the attitude of the veteran from the start. With three books to his credit, he remained unimpressed by his achievement when most other writers would have gloated with satisfaction. His indifference was due in part to the fact that his books were commercial and critical failures, but it was also a function of his generally dour nature. He had developed a contempt for writers who displayed their books as though they were priceless symbols of their own uniqueness and importance. To be sure, he desired an audience for his writing and remained convinced that he had compelling things to communicate. But he geninely viewed writing as work and was able to take his satisfaction from the act of working. To be paid handsomely for it would be a splendid thing, but that was not his main concern. That is why, in the face of his continuing financial adversity and his disappointment over the financial prospects of *To a God Unknown,* he was able to think of nothing but pressing on. He remained stubbornly certain, despite Carol's increasingly petulant misgivings, that he would one day make a mark sufficient to support them. Hence no matter how much spiritual discomfort he felt over his failure thus far, he gave no serious thought to giving up fulltime writing. Robert Ballou and Mavis McIntosh were both predicting that the road to financial success was just a short distance away. Steinbeck, although he was grateful for their encouragement, distrusted it as mere supportive flattery. In his realistic view, affected as it now was by his sense of the complexity of his new thematic vision, it would take at least another five years of writing before he gained a measure of success.

What he needed still was a method. He was confident of the phalanx ideas that had come together in his mind with such suddenness over the summer, but he still needed to work out a new method of writing that would serve as their vehicle. He had previously resisted his friends' entreaties that he pursue other styles than the ones he had written in. And even though he had eagerly soaked up Ed Ricketts's philosophical ideas, he had been slow to respond to Ricketts's criticisms of the obtuseness of his literary execution. But now John was convinced that because the truth of his new thematic theory was so complex, he would have to express it in the simplest of terms — terms of characters and stories — to convey it properly. He had long heard comments that the characters he had been inventing in his books and stories were too abstract and philosophically conceived to be "felt" by the reader. Unable to "feel" a character, no matter how fully the character was realized philosophically, the reader would not identify with him. The reader would be unable to directly experience or vicariously live through the character — the secret of all good fiction, according to several people with whom Steinbeck shared his concerns.

Although John's intellect retained a strong residual belief in the effectiveness of abstract allegorical writing, his instincts began to swing toward the idea of the naturalism that his friends were promoting. For a while he had trouble dealing with the differences between naturalism and realism in fiction. He had developed a mighty distaste for formal literary realism — the simple, faithful recording of the mundane events in the life of a character. He insisted that such writing was capable of no enlightenment except of the sociological sort, and art was not sociology. "The festered characters of Faulkner are of no interest to me," he wrote, "unless their festers are heroic." On another occasion, he said, "The detailed accounts of the lives of clerks don't interest me much, unless, of course, the clerk breaks into heroism."

There it was, the crux of Steinbeck's artistic problem. He had always been compelled to write "heroic" literature. But he had confused heroism, and heroic characters, with grandiosity. His confusion was understandable, since he had been raised on the heroic proportions of the Bible, *Morte d'Arthur*, Shakespeare and the eighteenth-century English fabulists. For a long time he had believed that the only literature worth writing seriously was the blatantly heroic, overlaid with message and sermonistic suggestion. He had not yet completely caught up to his time — a time in which character examination was literarily de rigueur, a time shaped by the precepts of psychoanalysis and sociology. Few American readers, having been exposed to the fascinating but seemingly ordinary characters of Hemingway, Fitzgerald, Faulkner, Sinclair Lewis, Theodore Dreiser, and the like, were interested in fictional symbology and allegory. They wanted to see ordinary people like themselves transformed into extraordinary people through the twists of circumstance and event.

During the summer and fall of 1933, as he sought his new method by working on the group of straightforward character studies that included "The Red Pony," a few *paisano* stories, and several others, Steinbeck discovered that the style was comfortable if not inspiring. He was not yet ready to trust it completely, but it did awaken in him an appreciation for the difference between naturalism and realism. He found that he could conceive "ordinary" characters and transform them into extraordinary — in their own ways, "heroic" — ones. It was not his hated realism. Yet it was far different in style from his ingrained fabulism. For the lack of a better word, it was naturalism. And although he was uncertain of its value, he would soon become convinced of it.

❅ ❅ ❅ ❅ ❅ CHAPTER SEVENTEEN

Steinbeck had no way of knowing that things would soon begin to break favorably for him, financially as well as critically. Thus he was not concerned only about artistic problems as he and Carol settled back with his father at the cottage in Pacific Grove in the fall of 1933. Money, or the lack of it, became foremost in his mind.

Olive Steinbeck's hospitalization had begun to drain her and her husband's savings, and John felt badly about continuing to accept his monthly subsidy. He felt even more troubled by the likelihood that his mother, although terminally ill and help-less, would linger on for an extended period of time. What small inheritance he expected from her — enough to tide him over for another year or so — would be dissipated by the expenses of her prolonged medical care. He was worried about his father on the same account. John Ernst had slipped into a geriatric melan-choly which, coupled with his intensifying medical problems, would soon require large outlays of money from his savings. If he ended up in the same state of prolonged illness as his wife, the resulting expenses would completely wipe out that which John was hoping to be able to split with his sisters by way of inheritance. Not only that, but the Salinas house and the cottage in Pacific Grove, which to John and Carol had become home, would have to be sold.

John found it difficult to write as he worried over these matters and at the same time tried to fight off the interminable distractions of his parents' respective problems and Carol's growing irksomeness. Steinbeck had given up fighting with her; instead he had taken to reacting to her attention-getting ploys with long, sullen silences interspersed by brief, raging outcries that sent her into lengthy sulks of her own. In more rational moments, however, they were able to analyze their differences and temporarily patch them up. Their life together became an almost ritualistic interweaving of tenderness and bitterness. They both recognized that they had set themselves on a road that could very likely end in marital disaster, and they resolved over and over again to get off it. But their growing ambivalence toward each other — particularly John's toward Carol because of her inability to lessen her emotional dependence and demands — deprived their resolutions of staying power.

Carol found a new job in Monterey with California's Emergency Relief Administration. Further dispirited by the Depression-besieged people she was required to deal with, she began to spend her spare time writing poetry. (Some who knew John and Carol at the time say that her poetry writing was an effort to involve herself in John's vocation and thus express her independence and win back his affection.)

John in the meantime had his first piece of good news from New York in a long time. Elizabeth Otis had managed to sell his long short story, "The Red Pony," to *North American Review* for a nominal sum. The question of money was of no import. *North American Review* was one of the country's better literary showcases, and thousands more people would read "The Red Pony" than together had read his first three novels. Although

Steinbeck was fond of the two-part story, he had not attached a great deal of significance to it when he'd sent it to Elizabeth Otis. It was markedly different in its ironic simplicity and tender honesty than anything he had written in the past, true. But it was not representative of the style and method Steinbeck had been hoping to find for his future work at the time that he wrote it. In a way, it was simply a private memorial to his father and himself; at least it had started out that way. That it was much more — that it had a nobility and universal quality that would appeal to readers — he had hoped but not expected. The editors of *North American Review* had raved about it, though, and when Elizabeth Otis conveyed their enthusiastic comments, John began to suspect that he might have hit on something effective in the story's resonant style. What made the experience even more satisfying was that the editors wanted Steinbeck to write more stories for the magazine in the same plain but evocative style. As Duke Sheffield was later to say, in the boy Jody, his father, and the other figures in "The Red Pony," John had finally created poignant characters the reader was able to "feel," and feel closely. Steinbeck had done it almost inadvertently. Yet the fact that he had done it did not escape him. Once the story was bought for publication, he began to seriously consider its style as the one he had been so purposively seeking.

Despite being the author of three published novels, Steinbeck was unknown nationally. Whatever fame he enjoyed was local. That is, Monterey and Salinas knew of him as a writer. In many quarters, however, it was a negative fame, since not a few members of the local populace took delight in deriding his evident lack of success in the face of his bold and ambitious pronouncements about himself. With the publication of "The Red Pony" in two consecutive monthly issues of *North American Review* at the end of 1933, however, "John Steinbeck" was a name that became lodged in the minds of a nation of readers. He suddenly had a following that eagerly awaited his next piece of fiction.

The next was to be "The Murder" (not to be confused with the unsold potboiler "Murder at Full Moon"), a story about a young California man of Anglo-Saxon stock who marries a girl of semiliterate Slavic background. The rather prim husband is introduced to a code of values strikingly different from those he was brought up to adhere to. When he discovers his wife one night in bed with her male cousin, he is so shocked that he murders the cousin and beats his wife into insensibility. His tragedy is that he cannot accept such an alien pattern of conduct. Steinbeck's point in the story, borrowed from Ed Ricketts, was that people whose ethnic traditions and mores are different from those of the average American should be treated in the light of those differences, even if they are so alien as to be incomprehensible.

Steinbeck wrote the story during the fall of 1933, shortly after "The Red Pony" had been accepted and while he was still putting together the stories of "Tortilla Flat." His preoccupation with the Tortilla Flat tales had awakened in him an ideological humanistic concern for the problem of ethnic differences in human relations, particularly in the rapidly expanding populace of California, as had Carol's work with the Emergency Relief Administration. Carol had been shocked at the patronizing and often insulting treatment given to Monterey County's foreign population — the main victims of Depression unemployment — at the hands of E.R.A. administrators. She saw a clear ethnic and racial prejudice at work, and frequently brought her complaints home to John about it. He had seen much the same thing in his visits with Sue Gregory to Tortilla Flat, and the combination of impressions, filtered through Ed Ricketts, inspired the idea of writing a story that would encompass a humanistic theme.

In style, the story was by turns ironic and compassionate, without crass satire or sermonizing. For the second time in a row John had managed to write "feelable" characters, and his underlying idealistic social message was well received. "The

Murder" was published in the April 1934 issue of *North American Review* and would subsequently win the O. Henry Award as the best short story of the year. More significantly, it marked the beginning of Steinbeck's career as a writer of "social protest." Although there was little in the way of social protest in "The Murder," there was a palpable social consciousness that presaged his most significant and successful works.

In retrospect, one is compelled to recall the words of Steinbeck's high school English teacher, Ora Cupp, who questioned the sincerity of his later devotion to social idealism in his work. "These people were good copy," she said. "Let the reader cry over them. . . . I'm willing to wager there were times when . . . he stood off and grinned at his own indignation." One is also compelled to recall Steinbeck's own words, written late in his life in *Travels With Charley*, about the absence of any racial or ethnic prejudice in his life.

Why? Because despite its literary virtues, "The Murder" is suffused with an underlying feeling of ethnic superiority. Steinbeck had grown up in an Anglo-Saxon Protestant household and in an ethnically and racially divided town in which the Anglo-Saxons were the elite. Although humanists to a degree, the Steinbecks were not without a sense of their own intellectual and behavioral superiority. Their middle-class respectability had repelled John as a young man, but more lately, with his parents on the verge of death, he had rallied to their side with a belated sense of love and duty and probably guilt. As they approached death, he gained an appreciation of the stability and integrity of their lives. Because both Olive and John Ernst had, in 1933, reverted to the childlike or animal states that senility and paralysis produce, he was better able to view their former states of vitality with gratitude.

We have already noted that Steinbeck was the repository of a reflexive anti-Semitism as a young adult. Because anti-Semitism was powerfully endemic in Christian, Anglo-Saxon America, this was not surprising. But it gave lie to his later claims that he was without racial and ethnic prejudice. In its curious way, so too did "The Murder" and other works he was later to write. Despite their throbbing social consciousness and idealism, they were often to be infused by a narrative attitude that subtly looked down on or patronized their subjects. His aim was compassion, but it was always to be mixed with a certain condescension — as it was in his cautionary tale about the Slavs in "The Murder."

It is not unreasonable to assume, then, that the critical success of "The Murder" provided the pragmatic Steinbeck with a powerful impetus for the direction and tone of his future writing. This is not to say that his motives in turning to social protest were as cynical as Ora Cupp suggested. It is merely to say that after many years of indeterminate toil, Steinbeck had finally found a general subject matter that hinted of success. He was still searching for the proper milieu, and had happened on a significant discovery — social dysfunction.

Most pioneering scientists have stumbled accidentally on their great discoveries. Pasteur did not set out to discover sterilization; Fleming did not have penicillin in mind as the purpose of his laboratory experiments. But once they happened on their discoveries, they pursued them with avid belief in their worth. So too did Steinbeck with respect to social protest (although it was not called that in the 1930s). He had always had an idle fascination with the ethnically different and had even entertained an intellectual sympathy for the poor and oppressed of his society. With the success of "The Murder," his previously vague and abstract notions about social dynamics were transformed into more defined and urgent ideas vis-à-vis the conceptual horizons of his writing. The more he thought about social dysfunction as a subject, the more convinced he became that he could effectively exploit it. And the more he used that subject, the more he would come to believe in its ideological worth. What's more, it provided the opportunity to incorporate in his writing his need to illustrate character heroism. And it fit well into his theories about the group soul versus the individual soul.

John had just finished the manuscript of "Tortilla Flat" and sent it to McIntosh and Otis for forwarding to Robert Ballou when his mother died on February 19, 1934. More relieved than saddened, he spent little time in mourning. Instead he plunged into the writing of a number of further stories for *North American Review.* "Tortilla Flat," written in the form of the Arthurian tales but about a group of "real" characters, marked the final transition from Steinbeck's early work to the kind of fiction he was about to embark on. Into it he worked some of his ideas of heroism and group character while still giving it an overlay of allegory and satire. Its characters were naturalistic, but its theme smacked of Steinbeck's lingering impulse to symbolism. The numerous short stories he wrote after it was finished, however, reflected his drift further away from symbolic fiction and his deepening engagement in naturalistic writing.

One of the stories he produced in the spring of 1934 was "The Raid," a narrative about an aging American Communist labor organizer and a young worker he takes under his wing to train. Labor unrest was rampant in California at the time, particularly on the large produce farms of the Salinas Valley. Trade-union leaders, many of them militant Communists, were seeking to organize the workers and provoke strikes. The big landowners countered by hiring armed goons to discourage the dissidents. Steinbeck sympathized with the poorly paid farm-workers, but his sympathy was tempered by Ed Ricketts's frequent perorations against the Communist organizers who, he claimed, were only interested in manipulating and exploiting the masses for their own political aggrandizement. They cared little about the plight of the workers, Ricketts insisted, and were bent merely on imposing another form of oppression on them — the dull and joyless oppression of proletarianism.

Much of the philosophy in "The Raid" came out of Steinbeck's discussions with Ricketts, but John was able to use his writing skill to underline the theme with trenchant action and characterization. The story also planted in him an idea whereby, through a more ambitious work, he could fully test his phalanx theory. Consequently, once he finished the story, he began to make notes for a novel about Communist aspirations, individual political fanaticism, and group or mob psychology. In "The Raid," the Communist organizer and his protégé were oblivious to the personal desires of the workers and sought only to convert them into a unified, manipulatable mob. In the novel that he contemplated, Steinbeck wanted to expand on this theme, to study in full scale the manner in which the behavior of a group differed from that of its members acting and thinking on their own.

"The Raid" was sold to *North American Review* in the summer of 1934, bringing John a few more dollars. In the meantime, he was experiencing resistance to the "Tortilla Flat" manuscript. Robert Ballou had shied away from it, claiming that his small company's financial troubles (to which the unsuccessful publication of *The Pastures of Heaven* had clearly contributed) made it impossible for him to publish it. Besides, he didn't much like the manuscript. Nor did several other publishers to whom Mavis McIntosh submitted it. Nor did Miss McIntosh, who thought it trivial and without clarity of meaning. Steinbeck made some minor adjustments to the manuscript to clarify the meaning, and then turned his energies to his new novel, which he would eventually call, after a line in Milton's *Paradise Lost,* "In Dubious Battle."

Steinbeck's emendations to "Tortilla Flat" did nothing to attract the interest of the additional publishers to whom Mavis McIntosh sent the manuscript during the fall of 1934. Unbeknown to John, however, while he was toiling at a first draft of the novel that would become *In Dubious Battle,* his fate was taking a happy turn.

A bookseller in Chicago by the name of Ben Abramson had

read the two installments of "The Red Pony" in *North American Review* the winter before and had been impressed. He ordered copies of *To a God Unknown* and *The Pastures of Heaven* (*Cup of Gold* was by then out of print), read them, and began to promote them to his customers as the work of a writer who would one day be important. He particularly liked *The Pastures of Heaven,* and when "The Murder" appeared in the April 1934 issue of *North American Review* his enthusiasm for Steinbeck's potential solidified. One day Abramson was visited in his bookstore by Pascal Covici, a man who headed a small, financially troubled, but first-class publishing house in New York called Covici, Friede. Abramson sang Steinbeck's praises to Covici and pressed a copy of *The Pastures of Heaven* on him, urging him to read it during his train journey back to New York.

Covici did so and was as impressed as Abramson. On his arrival in New York he contacted McIntosh and Otis and inquired about Steinbeck's contractual obligations on his future works. Mavis McIntosh said that John had none, Robert Ballou having turned down the manuscript of "Tortilla Flat." Covici asked if it were still available, and when McIntosh said it was he asked to see it. In January of 1935 Covici made a publishing offer on it to McIntosh. In the bargain he wrote to John and said that he would like to become his permanent publisher. Not only would he publish "Tortilla Flat" and future works, he would also reissue John's previous novels.

Steinbeck had heard similar enthusiastic commitments before and was duly unimpressed, particularly since he had learned from Mavis McIntosh that Covici, Friede was in a shaky financial state. Besides, he was now deep in "In Dubious Battle," his most ambitious sustained writing effort so far, and he had begun to view "Tortilla Flat" as a trifle, more on the order of the numerous short stories he had written the year before than a serious novel. Nevertheless, he was grateful for a publication contract at last, particularly in view of Mavis McIntosh's doubts about "Tortilla Flat," and for the money it promised. He signed the contract in February and agreed to submit "In Dubious Battle," when it was finished. Later that month he sent the typescript of "In Dubious Battle" to McIntosh and Otis.

In one sense the novel had gone badly. By the time he was well into it, Steinbeck had discovered that his characters would not behave according to his thematic plan. His phalanx theory remained intact, but it seemed not to work as an envelope for his story of migratory apple harvesters and Communist efforts to organize them. When he tried to impose upon the characters behavior and motivation that accorded with his theory, the action became leaden. Finally he abandoned his larger thematic purpose and concentrated on letting the characters follow their own inclinations. As a result, he produced a different book than he had set out to. His theory needed more refinement.

Not that "In Dubious Battle" was any the less for its changed focus. Upon abandoning his original thematic vision, Steinbeck concentrated on perfecting the style he had discovered in writing "The Red Pony" and several of his subsequent short stories. So objective did his narrative viewpoint become that his depiction of the novel's protagonist, Jim Nolan — the young, radical protégé of the veteran Communist agitator, Mac — almost slid beyond naturalism into the mannered realism Steinbeck professed to despise. Yet it was precisely the realistic aspects of the book that, when it was published a year later, would thrust Steinbeck into the mainstream of America's popular literary world.

After sending the manuscript to New York, Steinbeck renewed his quest to find a way to write what he now perceived as his "big novel" — a book that would embody the mighty phalanxial world view he had continued to develop and refine in his mind. Most of his letters at this time were devoted to expostulating his theory to his friends. In a note to Wilbur Needham, a book critic for the *Los Angeles Times*, he wrote: "I should like to discuss with you a plan of work so difficult that it will take several years to do and so uncharted that I will have to remake the novel as it is now understood to make it a vehicle."[17]

Steinbeck was kindly disposed to Needham and even more so to Joseph Jackson, book critic for the San Francisco Chronicle, because they had given The Pastures of Heaven and To a God Unknown favorable reviews — no doubt in part because of the two books' California settings. But his opinion of reviewers in general had become one of almost automatic contempt. Aside from the fact that most of the reviews of his novel had been slighting and superficial, Steinbeck could not understand the whole review process. He felt that the only people remotely qualified to review or criticize books were those who wrote books, not journalists and essayists. But those who wrote books were at the same time unqualified, he fervently believed. His conviction was based on the axiom that those who live in glass houses should not throw stones. A novelist had no business critically reviewing another novelist's work, for to do so presumed a perfection and omnipotence as a novelist on the reviewer's part that simply did not exist. As for journalists and essayists, as far as Steinbeck was concerned they were literary mercenaries and worse, "typewriting whores" who sold their meager services for a by-line and lived like parasites off the sweat and anguish of the real writers they presumed to criticize.

Steinbeck grew increasingly voluble about his contempt for book critics and criticism. He understood of course why the process existed and could appreciate how it could contribute to the success of a book. He simply could not comprehend why it existed in the way that it did. There had to be another, better, fairer method of judging books. He swore that he would never accept a commission from any publication to review another writer's work. He would keep that vow throughout his life. But he would never let up on his unpaid reviews of the work of reviewers.

In March 1935 another of Steinbeck's short stories, "The

White Quail," appeared in *North American Review*. About a marriage destroyed by the wife's growing obsession with her security and protection from the vicissitudes of an uncertain world, the tale was the first to come directly out of Steinbeck's immediate personal experience. Although he was not particularly fond of children,[18] Steinbeck had for some time wanted to have a child, primarily in the expectation that a child would enrich Carol's life and free him of her emotional dependence on him.

In "The White Quail," the wife walls herself off from her husband in an obsessive attempt to rigidly organize her life so that there will be no pain or fear. The symbol of her obsession is a neat garden she creates and tends. She insists that it remain unchanged, and when a white quail settles in it she sees the fowl as an extension of herself. But then a cat appears and stalks the quail. The wife demands that her husband shoot the cat to remove the threat to the tidily ordered and static world she has constructed. Instead, he accidentally slays the beautiful quail, an act that symbolizes his real desire to destroy the wife who has isolated herself from him.

The theme of the story repeated a point that Steinbeck had made in a more diffuse way in the "Dubious Battle" novel. In portraying both the Communist fanatics and the capitalistic landowners who lock horns over the uneducated labor force in the novel, he depicted them each as being obsessively wedded to a status quo. The capitalists fight the Communists in order to keep things the way they had always been. The Communists fight the capitalists to destroy the old order but to establish a new and rigidly unchanging one. The itinerant apple pickers, caught in the middle, are the victims of these superficially contrary but essentially identical status-quo obsessions.

Steinbeck, although he took care to avoid any overt sermonizing in the novel, incorporated his views on this paradox in the character of Dr. Burton, a physician who treats the wounds of the embattled laborers and their leaders. (Steinbeck drew the sympathetic character of Doc Burton from the real-life model of his friend Ed Ricketts, whose nickname was Doc, and in so doing acknowledged that powerful impact of Ricketts's mind on his own.) Doc Burton repeatedly warns the Communist zealots of "In Dubious Battle" that nothing in life can be maintained without change, that change is inevitable. By this device Steinbeck not only ridiculed Communist aspirations as being as empty as those of the enemy, he also framed his own philosophical perception that what was wrong with the world was that so many people irrationally feared and resisted the inevitability of change.

This theme, drawn directly from Ricketts, had become an overriding concern of Steinbeck's during this period. But Ricketts had merely crystallized what Steinbeck had observed as such a fear in himself. He had suffered a sharp alteration in his relationship with Carol. He had experienced a profound sense of change in his life during the fatal illness of his mother and the wasting away of his father. His relationship with his sister Mary had changed; she was no longer the adoring sibling but a busy housewife and mother who had little patience with her brother's literary and sociological theorizing. Everything around him had been changing, mostly in an unhappy way, but he seemed to remain mired in his own personal situation. Ricketts had defined his problem for him, however, mostly in terms of biological and other scientific precepts applied to human life and ideas. And once John had comprehended and integrated Ricketts's views on change into his own thoughts, they became a clearly perceived and powerful element in his artistic raison d'être. He had written about the relationship between change and shattered illusions in *Cup of Gold, The Pastures of Heaven* and *To a God Unknown*. But he had been able to conceive his notions in such indeterminate and unsure terms that he had been forced to take refuge in these books in stylistic artifice and quasipoetic effect. If he had failed to formulate an effective fictional framework for his ideas about group action in "In Dubious Battle," he had at least narrowed down the human conflict between change and stasis. One of his intentions in the novel was to show that people who attempt to overcome the ceaselessly changing order of nature, by pursuing ideologies that seek to prohibit such change, only succeed in creating disharmony and tragedy for themselves. The dubious battle of his title was precisely this. "The White Quail," which he wrote during the period he was working on the novel, was born of his desire to focus more closely on this theme. The novel had other points to make, and his notion about the natural inevitability of change and the human compulsion to resist it might have gone unnoticed. "The White Quail" enabled him to deliver the point undiluted.

At about the time "The White Quail" was published, Steinbeck learned that "The Red Pony" had been selected as one of the best short stories of the year before. His satisfaction with this news was shattered, however, when he learned that Pascal Covici was reluctant to publish "In Dubious Battle." Covici claimed that much of the Communist-party ideology as represented by Steinbeck in the book was incorrect, and he feared that the novel would be dismissed as naive and false. Short of that, he was afraid that it would be attacked by both radical and conservative elements in America as grossly misrepresentative. When he urged Steinbeck to rewrite it, John angrily refused. By then, several other publishers had seen advance copies of *Tortilla Flat* and one, Macmillan, had already expressed an interest in signing up his next book. Steinbeck was ready to take "In Dubious Battle" away from Covici, Friede and send it to Macmillan. Only the intervention of Elizabeth Otis resolved the argument between Steinbeck and Covici.

Up until then, Mavis McIntosh had continued to handle John's long fiction while Elizabeth Otis marketed his short stories. John had yet to meet either personally, having conducted all his business with them through the mails and by wire. Through their correspondence, however, he had formed a more favorable opinion of Elizabeth Otis than he had of Mavis McIntosh. Otis, aside from being more morally supportive of his fiction ambitions, was less stiff and formal in her letters than McIntosh.

Elizabeth Otis, aware of the dispute over "In Dubious Battle," read the manuscript and found Covici's fears unwarranted. If he were really afraid that the book would suffer widespread political attack, she agreed with Steinbeck that such an attack might create the kind of national controversy that would enhance the sales of the book and establish John as a "name" writer. She took her views to Covici and persuaded him that no matter what he thought of the politics of "In Dubious Battle," he had a very commercial book on his hands. Covici finally agreed to publish it as it was and Steinbeck's ruffled feathers were smoothed. Thereafter, Elizabeth Otis became the principal agent for all his work. She and Steinbeck would eventually become devoted friends as well.

The high tension over the manuscript of "In Dubious Battle" and Elizabeth Otis's talk of its potential for controversy convinced John that it might well make a splash, that it might be the book that would finally give him his long-due step up on the ladder of writing success. He was wrong, however. For *Tortilla Flat,* the book he had dismissed as insignificant, was about to make its formal appearance.

❋ ❋ ❋ ❋ ❋ ❋ CHAPTER EIGHTEEN

The only unhappy aspect of the publication of Tortilla *Flat* in May 1935 was that it came just a few days after the death of Steinbeck's father.

Following Olive Steinbeck's death the year before, John Ernst had gone steadily further downhill. He had left John and Carol in Pacific Grove to return to the house in Salinas, where he was cared for by a married couple who moved into the house with him. His arteriosclerotic enfeeblement grew progressively worse during the year, and at the beginning of 1935 his eldest daughter Esther took him to Watsonville to live with her. He died there on May 23. *Tortilla Flat* was officially published May 28.

The concurrence of events was particularly sad for John. A few months before, in a moment of lucidity, the senior Steinbeck had confessed to his son that he had never in his life achieved any of the things he had dreamed of achieving. This, he said, was the reason he had been so tolerant of John's ambition, and in his last years so supportive; he did not want his son to suffer the bitter regret that he had.

The confession haunted John during the last months of his father's life. Never close to John Ernst, often secretly contemptuous of his middle-class values, he was now stricken with a guilt-laced combination of love and pity for him. "If only we could have seen each other differently years back," he lamented to Esther. He recognized that much of what he was was due to his father. Indeed, as he had grown older, he had perceived more and more of his father in himself. That which was good — integrity, simplicity of taste, straightforwardness — came from his father. As well as that which was not so good — shyness, intolerance, remoteness, vindictiveness. As with his mother, the death of Steinbeck's father was more a relief than a shock. "I feel very badly," he said when he learned of it. "Not about his death, but about his life."

John Ernst's death, nevertheless, came at what for John was a favorable time. The senior Steinbeck's estate remained large enough to provide John, once it was divided among him and his sisters, with modest financial relief. He anticipated that by carefully managing the proceeds due him, he and Carol could live in a worry-free state for the next few years. As it happened, however, they did not have to rely on his father's financial legacy. The publication of *Tortilla Flat* took care of that.

The quasifictional book about Monterey's *paisanos* was published with an unusual amount of care by Pascal Covici. He commissioned Ruth Gannett, an accomplished artist and the wife of the respected critic Lewis Gannett, to illustrate the book with droll line drawings. He also primed the interest of the book-review fraternity with prepublication publicity. When the book was released it was, as a result, reviewed widely. And many critics, including Gannett himself, enthusiastically recommended it for its trenchant Depression-age humor and pathos.

During the summer the book reached the national bestseller list, and Steinbeck found himself a literary celebrity. The sudden recognition both startled and enlightened him. Having all along viewed *Tortilla Flat* as a lighthearted diversion from his much more weighty writing endeavors, he was astonished that the critics took it so seriously. Yet as is often the case, on discovering that he had written a book that in its comical and satirical aspects was indeed a serious piece of literature, Steinbeck learned something about what it was in his literary sensibility that pleased critics and readers. Despite the bawdy humor of its low-life characters, the critics treated *Tortilla Flat* as incisive social commentary. In writing about the social underdogs of Monterey in the way that he had, Steinbeck had accidentally created a channel of identification in the mass readership of America. The critics saw it as a tale that depicted the nobility of the human spirit in the face of hopeless adversity. General readers appreciated it because it showed how people who suffered more deprivation than themselves managed to sustain their spirits and survive.

By July the book was well known throughout the country. Steinbeck's first royalty check was delivered to him personally by Pascal Covici during a trip he took to San Francisco a few months later. It was the first face-to-face meeting between the two. Not much older than Steinbeck, Covici was much like his new author, shy and deliberate, but a man of strong opinions and an editor whose reputation for quality publishing was rapidly on the rise in New York. Known by the nickname "Pat," he was as impressed by Steinbeck as the writer was by him. The two worked out Covici's misgivings about "In Dubious Battle" during the following days and their relationship began to take on the dimensions of the lifelong friendship it would become.

Not all the critics liked *Tortilla Flat*, of course. A number denigrated the book as a callous glorification of idleness and illiteracy, while others viewed it as merely a failed attempt at bittersweet humor. But the momentum of public acceptance spiraled, and by September Steinbeck began to grow weary of the publicity and controversy that attended it. The book was nominated for the California Commonwealth Club's gold medal for the year's best book about California. But not everyone in the state was pleased with it. The Monterey Chamber of Commerce, once Carol Steinbeck's employer, was particularly exercised by what it took to be Steinbeck's ridiculing of the town and its respectable citizenry. As Steinbeck later recalled, the chamber of commerce issued a press release denying that such a place as Tortilla Flat or its *paisano* inhabitants existed. It would change its tune eventually. *Tortilla Flat* had put Monterey on the map. A new wave of tourism would begin, sightseers drawn to the town to ogle the "nonexistent" *paisanos* dwelling in the shantytown on the hill. And to catch a glimpse of the author.

Before the publication of *Tortilla Flat*, Steinbeck had at once enjoyed and suffered anonymity in the tiny house in Pacific Grove. In his desire for recognition, he had endured his anonymity as a symbol of the public's unjustified rejection of his work. By September his notoriety made him wish for a return of his former obscurity. Tourists, literary pilgrims, newspaper interviewers and a varied assortment of cranks and beggars made their way to the cottage in droves.

John and Carol finally escaped the din by taking the trip to Mexico they had been unable to make when his mother was first stricken. This time, using some of the money from his father's inheritance, they were able to travel in a more comfortable style than they would have earlier. The trip was not just to get away from the fuss over *Tortilla Flat*, however. John had promised Carol the trip once his father had died and the inheritance money was in hand. Its primary purpose was to give the two a chance to rehabilitate their marriage.

In this respect their automobile journey through Mexico was salutary. The effect was enhanced when, upon their arrival in late October in Mexico City, where they planned a two-month stay, John received a wire from Elizabeth Otis informing him that she had sold the movie rights in *Tortilla Flat* for four thousand dollars. The money, added to his inheritance, represented the final installment in Steinbeck's struggle to achieve his freedom from financial need. There would be additional significant sums once the major book-sales royalties from *Tortilla Flat* became payable, and for the first time in his adult life Steinbeck was able to relax about money. He and Carol could live comfortably for several years on what *Tortilla Flat* promised to earn, and John could write with considerably more reflection and deliberation than he had been able to up to then.

Because of this, he seriously considered taking the time to do a major rewrite of "In Dubious Battle," not to change it so much as to tighten and strengthen it. He had remained stubbornly impervious to the continuing criticisms of the manuscript by two of the subeditors at Covici, Friede once he obtained Pat Covici's commitment to publish it as is. But with the success of *Tortilla Flat,* he began to have second thoughts. He knew that it would be examined upon its publication with a hypercritical eye by the book-review establishment. And he sensed that because it would be so different in tone and treatment from *Tortilla Flat,* it would automatically provoke sharp resistance, its literary merits to the contrary notwithstanding.

When he cabled Covici from Mexico City about his idea, he found that he was too late. The book was already well into production and Covici, Friede planned to publish it in January, only a few months hence. Pat Covici sought to mollify Steinbeck by telling him that his sudden concern for the novel was the standard reaction of every writer who had his first success. Once a book is a success, said Covici, everything that follows is seen by its author in a different light. Writing is no longer an effort to achieve a reputation, it is a striving to protect and expand it.

Steinbeck accepted Covici's reasons for not reworking "In Dubious Battle" readily enough, but he did not cease to worry about the impact the book would make. Everyone connected with it agreed that, in the light of *Tortilla Flat,* it would generate considerable controversy. Steinbeck consequently began to feel the stirrings of a new kind of pressure. "In Dubious Battle" was only the second of the five novels he had completed with which he was reasonably pleased. He felt that he had achieved a large measure of his intention even though he had not been able to infuse it with the larger thematic dimensions he had originally visualized for it. The first novel that had given him a degree of pride had been *To a God Unknown*, and it had failed dismally.[19] Would "In Dubious Battle" suffer a similar fate? Steinbeck, despite the controversy he anticipated, was sure it would. This drove him to an equal worry over what he would write next. He was now strongly committed to work of a contemporary social-pathos character, but not in the humorous terms of *Tortilla Flat*. An innately angry man himself, he wanted to arouse anger in his readers, not humor. And yet, with his only successful book one whose acclaim derived from its humorous overlay, he was profoundly unsure of his ability to do so. So, as he and Carol tarried south of the border into January of 1936 and waited for *In Dubious Battle* to make its appearance in the United States, John's new anxieties mounted.

The predicted controversy over *In Dubious Battle* materialized shortly after the book was released that month. The United States was living through a period of intense social and political upheaval as it emerged from the Depression under the administration of Franklin D. Roosevelt. Communist political and economic theory, tested in the crucible of the Russian Revolution twenty years earlier, had been woven into the fabric of New Deal democracy by ivory-tower intellectuals and tough trade unionists alike, and was in the process of being adopted and glorified by a large portion of the emerging generation of postcollegiate idealists. The sudden rise of Nazism in Germany in the early thirties had sharpened sympathy for Communist ideology in this country, as of course did the Depression, the causes of which many traced to the undemocratic disparity between America's small ownership class and its much larger working class. Numerous books — fiction and nonfiction — had been published that embraced socialist and outright Communist ideals, as had books which disputed them. The country's consciousness, especially in intellectual circles, had been sharply raised on the issue of Communist ideology. The nation was filled with savants who claimed to be the "true" interpreters of socialist theory as refined by Lenin and the Soviets from the writings of Karl Marx, and as represented by the American Communist Party.

In Dubious Battle, an engaging but bleak and pessimistic book, merely added to the din. As expected, it was attacked by both left and right. Its literary and humanistic merits went largely ignored. What struck home was its ruthlessly contemptuous dismissal of dogmatic ideology in any form. Communists and capitalists alike felt betrayed by Steinbeck's harsh depiction of the manner in which the common man is exploited by political ideologues of all stripes. Many unsophisticated reviewers and readers nevertheless interpreted it as a pro-Communist book and viciously attacked Steinbeck as a traitor to America's democratic ideals. Those who saw it as a distorted portrayal of the Communist cause dismissed it as libelously naive and stupid.

Having returned from Mexico to Pacific Grove with Carol, Steinbeck received the reviews with mounting ire. Although pleased that *In Dubious Battle* was having a good sale, he often claimed to prefer that it sell badly but be interpreted correctly, than sell well and be misinterpreted. His animus toward reviewers and critics rose to steeper and sometimes irrational heights. Typical was his reaction to a review in *The Nation* by Mary McCarthy, a graduate of Vassar and an aspiring novelist, who was earning a reputation as a brilliant, acerbic left-wing writer. McCarthy's review of *In Dubious Battle* was sharply critical, describing the book in such terms as "wooden," "pompous" and "childish," and averring that its author had little aptitude for philosophy, social problems or labor strategy. Some months before, *The Nation* had published a mildly unfavorable review of *Tortilla Flat.* It was *The Nation's* practice to place its reviewers' by-lines at the end of their reviews. The writer of the *Tortilla Flat* review had been a woman named Helen Neville. Immediately preceding her review had been a review by Mary McCarthy of another book. Since McCarthy's name appeared just above the Neville review of *Tortilla Flat*, Steinbeck had identified her with the unfavorable comments about the *paisano* novel. His friend Joseph Jackson, book editor of the *San Francisco Chronicle*, had taken Helen Neville to task in print for her review of *Tortilla Flat*. Steinbeck had thought he was chastizing Mary McCarthy. Thus, when McCarthy's review of *In Dubious Battle* appeared in *The Nation*, he testily rationalized its patronizing tone by claiming that McCarthy had been waiting to "ambush" his next book so that she could get even for Jackson's criticism of "her" review of *Tortilla Flat*.[20]

Shortly after *In Dubious Battle* was published, Broadway theatrical producer Herman Shumlin secured the dramatic rights and announced his intention of turning it into a play. Although the play would never come off, the preparations made for it had a significant influence on Steinbeck's future course as a writer, which he continued to worry over.

For one thing, Shumlin hired John O'Hara, an established and celebrated writer of realistic fiction, to convert the novel into a play. O'Hara soon showed up in Pacific Grove to confer with Steinbeck on the adaptation. It was John's first personal exposure to a writer of O'Hara's reputation, although it could fairly be said that Steinbeck was by then of even greater stature than O'Hara, who was known mainly as a short-story writer. The two men were very much alike in literary style and personality (each suffered acute doubts about the worth of his talents, each was in similar ways shy but intellectually combative, and each had experienced widespread critical dismissal as writers while enjoying a large measure of popular acceptance), and immediately liked one another. They began a friendship that was to continue for the rest of their lives.

O'Hara was an easterner, however, a sharp-witted lover of New York artifice and Ivy League values, whereas Steinbeck oozed with the kind of West Coast sincerity that easterners took

pleasure in sneering at. Not that O'Hara lorded his sophistication over John. But Steinbeck was considerably more impressed
by O'Hara's hard-edged manner and spiffy clothes than O'Hara
was by Steinbeck's earnestness and his plain, tattered surroundings. Moreover, O'Hara, who was three years younger than
Steinbeck, had stopped in Pacific Grove on his way to San Francisco from Hollywood, where he had been paid outrageous sums
to write screenplays. He regaled John and Carol with artfully
told "inside" tales of the movie industry. Steinbeck had already
had one or two feelers from Hollywood to write scripts, but had
turned them down on the ground that he had no aptitude for
such work. O'Hara, whose principal acclaim had been based on
his gift for realistic dialogue in his stories and novels, chided
Steinbeck. Anyone who could tell a story like John, he said,
could write filmscripts in his sleep.

During their discussions about the adaptation of *In Dubious Battle,* Steinbeck confessed to O'Hara his anxiety about
what he would write next. He outlined his phalanx theory and
bewailed his inability to find a novelistic form in which to embody it. O'Hara suggested a play. Steinbeck demurred, again
citing his lack of feel for rigid dramatic structure. Present for
some of their talks were Toby Street, himself a failed playwright, and Ed Ricketts, whose incisive brilliance impressed
O'Hara as much as it had others. The talk, much of it philosophical and scientific, kept coming back to Steinbeck's problem
of finding a form with which to frame his epic theme of the
inherent conflict between group man and individual man. Out
of it came the suggestion from O'Hara that John experiment
with the idea of writing a novel in the form of a play, just as he
had earlier written *The Pastures of Heaven* as a novel in the
form of short stories.

The notion stuck in Steinbeck's mind and began to gather
force, more from his interest in finding a vehicle for his phalanx
theory than from a desire to try his hand at playwriting. Toby
Street, by then working in Monterey as a lawyer, was particularly

supportive of the idea, and Ed Ricketts provided further thematic grist. Soon the idea of the experiment itself became more compelling than the philosophical notions it was supposed to serve.

On his return from Mexico in January, Steinbeck had resumed writing short stories while waiting for inspiration to strike in regard to a new novel. In anticipation of O'Hara's visit, he had read some of the younger man's stories in back issues of *The New Yorker* and was impressed by the dramatic immediacy imparted by their simple, seemingly pedestrian style. He had tried his hand at the method in a couple of brief stories of his own, but was disappointed; the style did not seem to work for him. Another story he had been working on, in his own style, at the time of O'Hara's arrival was a tale of life among the hired hands of a remote Salinas Valley ranch. The story, which he had tentatively called "Something That Happened," was, in its in-progress state, a continuation and refinement of a number of his previous works' themes — the loneliness of the individual, the cruel, oppressive ironies of nature, the defeat of personal ambition, the shattering of illusions — all contained in another envelope of hopeless Arthurian striving among hapless, tragicomic characters. The story had a spare, haunting quality. But the characters were uneducated laborers who spoke in the idiom of the back country, and one of the main characters was a moron. Steinbeck suspected that the story failed because he had been unable to keep his own voice and viewpoint out of its telling. He had been unable to stop himself from imposing interior feelings and thoughts on people who, even if they experienced them, could not analyze or verbalize them.

After O'Hara's visit, however, he began to view the story differently. As the idea of a playlike novel took shape in his mind, he saw that he might elucidate the feelings and thoughts essential to the story's themes through O'Hara-type dialogue. He started to rewrite and soon realized that he'd found his new novel.

As Steinbeck reworked and expanded the story of George and Lenny, the itinerant ranch hand and his mentally defective sidekick of "Something That Happened," the tale took on a more cohesive narrative and thematic flow. He wrote the dialogue first — long uninterrupted stretches of talk between the two men who find themselves in a predicament. As in a play, he introduced additional characters — each with his own story — to move the action along. Soon he had another Round Table, except that instead of medieval knights it was composed of modern-day equivalents — a bunkhouse full of ranch hands each pursuing his own individual grail, be it women, whiskey, solitude or, as in the case of the two central characters, a financial stake to buy their own small spread.

Once he had the outline of the novel in dialogue, he proceeded to fill in the description. He wrote episodically, again as in a play, carefully shifting from one scene to the next. He employed all the devices of the dramatist, foreshadowing later climactic events so that the reader knew early on that something terrible was to happen, and building a lean strain of tension and suspense. Since the dream of George and Lenny to acquire their own patch of land was destined to be shattered by the tragic events of which they themselves were to be the unwitting architects, Steinbeck settled on the title "Of Mice and Men." It came from Robert Burns's famous phrase, "The best laid schemes o' mice an' men gang aft a-gley." The phrase was from a Burns poem that lamented man's enslavement to forces of nature that he cannot control and that relentlessly but indifferently destroy his ambitions and illusions. The title was suggested by Ed Ricketts, who had led Steinbeck to the Burns poem as an illustration of the scientist's naturalistic and biological determinism. The poem was the quintessence of Ricketts's philosophy and it served to reorganize and integrate in Steinbeck's mind a number of previously imprecise naturalistic perceptions.

Steinbeck worked with expanding enthusiasm on "Of Mice and Men" through the remainder of the spring of 1936. As he proceeded, he felt a singular power grow from the narrative objectivity he was able to achieve. He soon became convinced that it would work both as a novel and, with much of the description transformed into stage direction, as a play. The characters were forming fully and interestingly out of the realistic dialogue; the plain realism of the talk was heightened by the characters' inadvertent revelations to one another, as well as by the mood and atmosphere set by Steinbeck's highly concise and artfully intense descriptive passages. Evocative but economical writing, such as this from the beginning of "Of Mice and Men," Steinbeck had rarely achieved before in any sustained way:

A few miles south of Soledad, the Salinas River drops in close to the hillside bank and runs deep and green. The water is warm too, for it has slipped twinkling over the yellow sands in the sunlight before reaching the narrow pool. . . . On the valley side the water is lined with trees — willows fresh and green with every spring, carrying in their lower leaf junctures the debris of the winter's flooding; and sycamores with mottled, white, recumbent limbs and branches that arch over the pool. On the sandy bank under the trees the leaves lie deep and so crisp that a lizard makes a great skittering if he runs among them. Rabbits come out of the brush to sit on the sand in the evening, and the damp flats are covered with the night tracks of 'coons, and with the spread pads of dogs from the ranches, and with the split-wedge tracks of deer that come to drink in the dark.

Evening of a hot day started a little wind to moving among the leaves. The shade climbed up the hills toward the top. On the sand banks the rabbits sat as quietly as little gray sculptured stones. And then from the direction of the state highway came the sound of footsteps on crisp sycamore leaves. The rabbits hurried noiselessly for cover. A stilted heron labored up into the air and pounded down river. For a moment the place was lifeless, and then two men emerged from the path and came into the opening by the green pool.[21]

This opening passage is effective for two reasons. One is that Steinbeck instantly establishes the substance of his major theme: by having two humans suddenly intrude on the natural calm and order of the remote Salinas River glade, he presages the conflict between man and nature that he will later develop in a more elaborate manner. The second has to do with style. With its rhythms, selectivity of detail and sense of specific place, Steinbeck sets a narrative tone that he sustains almost flawlessly throughout the book. The vision reproduced in the opening sentences has a sharp ring of authenticity and authority, and the contrast between the picturesque peace of the river glade and the intrusion on it of the two men, causing the rabbits and the heron to flee, creates an instant tension. The reader is compelled to proceed, and as he does so he will be drawn immediately into the magnetic web of description and dialogue that follows.

It was the most accomplished beginning of any of Steinbeck's novels. That, and his success in spinning out of it a fascinatingly naturalistic story, suggested that he was finally approaching the realization of his powers as a writer.

✼ ✼ ✼ ✼ ✼ ✼ CHAPTER NINETEEN

"Of Mice and Men" came to little more than thirty
thousand words — an extended short story. Steinbeck wrote
it in just over two months, having had to rewrite a long section
of the manuscript that his dog had chewed up. He sent Carol's
typescript to Covici with a detailed explanation of his purpose
in writing it. If it was too short to be published as a novel, he
said, it could be easily converted into a playscript.

During the spring, John and Carol had decided to leave
Pacific Grove because of the constantly increasing infringe-
ments on their privacy. They also felt that a change of scene
from the busy seaside to a quieter inland site would be helpful
to their relationship. Carol enjoyed gardening, and John required quiet as well as seclusion. Consequently they purchased
a lot with a splendid view in the hills west of the town of Los
Gatos, midway between Monterey and San Francisco. Through
Carol's father, they arranged to have a small house built on
the two-acre property. Carol spent much of the spring and
early summer at the site, supervising the construction and

landscaping. John, in the meantime, having accepted a commission from the *San Francisco News* to write a series of articles exposing the woeful conditions under which California's migrant farm-labor forces lived and worked, set out to do firsthand research.

His first stop was the Gridley Migrant Camp above Sacramento. Agricultural-labor turmoil was now rampant in California. The scene Steinbeck had forecast in *In Dubious Battle* had become a reality, only more bloodily so, with statewide strikes and armed rebellions crippling harvests and threatening the stability of the traditional agricultural industry. Many farmers' associations even blamed Steinbeck for the situation, claiming that his novel of the year before had fueled the strife.

Although John resented much of the mindless publicity he had received during the previous year, he reveled in this exposure. It gave him an opportunity to answer his critics by assigning the blame where it really lay, in the feudal-lord attitudes of the farmers and landowners, and of the state government that had for so long enabled them to exploit and oppress the labor force with impunity. Nevertheless he developed a concern for his safety. Farmers' associations had spawned vigilante groups and strikebreakers to protect their lands from the left-wing organizers who were roaming the state inciting work strikes. While at Gridley, Steinbeck was told by a camp administrator that if he traveled south on the summer harvest circuit with a group of migrants, as he had planned to do, he would likely run into trouble since photos of him had been circulated among vigilante groups.

Although worried, he ignored the warning and decided to use the vigilante problem as the subject of one of his series's pieces. He traveled south through the San Joaquin valley, detouring to Salinas to observe the strife that had invaded his home town. He ended up near Bakersfield, the valley's southern terminus. There he met a man named Thomas Collins, a government employee trained in psychology who managed a model government labor camp that operated under the auspices of the Federal Farm Security Administration. The camp, informally known as Weedpatch, was a welcome relief from the squalid camps operated by the private-enterprise farmers' organizations. Populated mostly by refugees from the Dust Bowl areas of Oklahoma, Texas and Arkansas, the camp offered modest but neat living quarters and other amenities to those who were able to qualify for it.

Collins and Steinbeck, each working in his own way for a common cause, quickly became friends. Collins gave John a recently published book on the psychology of vigilantism and mob behavior that provided him with new insights into his philosophical notions of group man and a hook upon which to hang his projected article on the vigilante groups of the valley.

Steinbeck finished his newspaper series in August, condensing it at the same time into an article for *The Nation*. The points he made were basically factual repetitions of his themes in *In Dubious Battle*. He disparaged equally the farmers' organizations, the state and the labor unions, and focused most of his sympathetic attention on the plight of the impoverished, abused workers. He wrote in a crisp, objective style which, although detached, created the angry effects he sought.

Steinbeck was enough of an empiricist to know that change and reform did not occur overnight. Although his fascination with California's downtrodden may originally have been inspired more by a pragmatic need to find a locus from which to write than by a genuine reformer's compassion for the oppressed, his firsthand experience of the conditions at Gridley and throughout the valley left him seething with genuine outrage. He worried, however, about falling into the trap that so many reform-minded people had. The trap was demagoguery and simple-minded evangelism — the very impulses he had attacked in *In Dubious Battle*. So he withheld any overt expression of his anger in his articles and instead shaped his almost laconic eyewitness accounts in such a way that they would overpower the reader solely by objective description.

Much of the literary discretion he practiced derived from the influence of Thomas Collins. Collins, though not as natively brilliant as Ed Ricketts, was much like him in the clinical detachment he brought to his work and to his view of life. He burned with a passion for social reform and a will for bringing it about. But he, like Ricketts, distrusted sudden or violent change on the ground that it was contrary to the natural process and destroyed more than it benefited. He likened change to the putting together of a picture puzzle, with each step in the process dependent on the previous step and productive of the next.

One of Collins's hopes was to publish a book consisting solely of the official weekly reports he sent from the camp to Washington. He believed that such a documentary format, filled with dry statistical data about disease, death, criminal activity and the like, would have a much more shocking effect on the nation than books in which facts and impressions were manipulated by their authors to create specific reactions. This was the scientist in Collins — a plain, unadorned exposition of the facts would have more impact than dozens of literary perorations. Steinbeck, whose own clinical sense was becoming well developed through his association with Ricketts, agreed to edit such a book and otherwise have his name associated with it.

The two went to work, but the project was short-lived. Steinbeck was told by Covici in New York that such a book would have no commercial potential. He argued with that, but in the end decided to abandon the work. The *San Francisco News*, after receiving his articles, delayed publishing the series for fear that its decidedly anticorporate bias would erode its advertising revenues. Steinbeck was so angered that he resolved to start at once a novel about the migrant laborers — a book that would be a sequel to *In Dubious Battle* but that, instead of concentrating on the politics of the labor conflict, would focus on the lives of the exploited workers themselves.

On his return from Bakersfield in August, John moved with Carol into their barely completed house off Greenwood Lane near Los Gatos. While Carol put the finishing touches on the house and property, John began his new novel. He planned to base it on a vigilante incident and place it in and about Salinas. Recalling his edifying discussions with Tom Collins on mob psychology, he hoped that in the vigilante concept he had finally found a useful vehicle for the exposition of his urgent phalanx theme — the natural conflict between group man and individual, or lonely, man. To Steinbeck, the idea had become more and more certain as the true explanation of man's compulsive self-destructiveness. If he could only integrate and harmonize his literary method with his philosophic vision, he was sure that he would produce a work that might revolutionize man's ideas about himself.

When asked by his old roommate George Mors, still living in Los Gatos, why he simply didn't write a straight book of philosophy in which he could lay out his theory in detail and precision, Steinbeck claimed that books of philosophy invariably fall on deaf ears. "You cannot tell people how they should feel, act and think," he said, "unless you can enforce what you tell them." That was the trouble with philosophy and religion, and why criminal and civil law were needed in society. People only learn about themselves by experiencing themselves. The only effective revelation was self-revelation. Great fiction provided people with the opportunity to experience themselves through their identification with characters and events. He did not want to tell people what they should be. He wanted only to enlighten them about what they are. Through such self-discovery, they would then have the chance of becoming what they ought to be. If nothing else, this was the superiority of fiction over philosophy and religion and the social sciences, he said to Mors.

John worked hard through the fall on his new project.

But because he was attempting to meld two contrary visions — one philosophical, the other literary — he found the going tough. He gave his incipient novel the unlikely title of "L'Affaire Lettuceburg." It derived partly from his intention to satirize the pretensions of Salinas's chamber-of-commerce mentality, but was in larger measure simply a slang appellation that stemmed from some long-lost joke of Steinbeck's youth, probably related to the fact that the town derived much of its income from growing lettuce, as well as to the townsfolk's pre-occupation with making money (another kind of "lettuce").

The pain of his struggle over the vigilante novel was assuaged to a considerable degree by opinions from Covici and others at his firm that the "Of Mice and Men" manuscript was not only suitable for publication as a novel, but was John's best work so far. Shortly thereafter, the *San Francisco News* published his articles on the migrant workers under the title "The Harvest Gypsies." The series drew further ire from some local circles, but also brought a spate of requests for him to lecture and write more on the subject. Steinbeck rejected all the requests, continued to labor on the vigilante book, and spent much of his spare time writing letters to friends in which he endeavored to refine his phalanx philosophy. Almost every weekend he and Carol drove to Pacific Grove, where John chewed over his troubles on the vigilante novel with Ed Ricketts.

Of Mice and Men was an immediate best-seller. Published in early February of 1937, its sales approached one hundred thousand copies by the end of the month. Moreover it was chosen by the Book-of-the-Month Club. Steinbeck was suddenly looking at the prospect of earning more money in the coming few months than he had over his entire lifetime.

He decided to use some of the money to take Carol on an extended trip, first to New York, then to Europe. He was particularly interested in going to Russia. He had "struck a bad snag" in "L'Affaire Lettuceburg," he said to Elizabeth

Otis at the beginning of 1937. He didn't know how long the book would take to write. "The subject is so huge that it scares me to death." With the vigilante novel growing ever more problematic, he was considering putting it aside and writing a book about Soviet Communism as a way of further refining his phalanx theory. To do so, he would have to see Russia at first hand. Before they left, John learned that George S. Kaufman wanted to direct *Of Mice and Men* as a play in the fall. Kaufman, famed as a director of insouciant Broadway comedies, wrote to Steinbeck with a list of suggestions about how to convert the novel into a stage script. On March 23, John and Carol sailed from San Francisco on a passenger freighter for New York via the Panama Canal. For Steinbeck it was a sentimental journey. During it, he worked on converting *Of Mice and Men* into a play.

Upon their arrival in New York two weeks later, Steinbeck found that Elizabeth Otis had sold the film rights in *Tortilla Flat* for a hefty sum. He also discovered that he was a bigger celebrity than he'd imagined. He was quickly introduced to New York's literary smart set by John O'Hara and George Kaufman and was immediately lionized by the newspapers. He hated the experience, feeling uncomfortable in the midst of so much glib brainpower and preferring quiet, private sightseeing tours with Carol. Soon his shy and dour manner caused invitations to literary and show-business soirees to cease. His earnestness and seriousness were a bore to most of the local literary lights.

John worked for a while with Kaufman on the playscript — the contracts had been signed and a production date was set — and then gratefully sailed on the next leg of his and Carol's journey. They arrived in Sweden in May.

Steinbeck was not unknown in Europe. *Tortilla Flat* and *In Dubious Battle* had already been published in several languages. Steinbeck was pleasantly surprised to learn that European critics, particularly in England and Scandinavia, had approached the books with an intentness that he felt was lacking in America. In the United States the concern had, he felt, been too much with him. There was little he wanted to add about his work, yet commentators and interviewers had hounded him for elaborations and personal information. In Europe they more or less left him alone but discussed his books in pleasingly intelligent detail. It was the difference, he thought, between a society obsessed with celebrity and one interested only in ideas. "That is why Europe has endured so long," he remarked to Carol.

Their visit to Russia was both edifying and disappointing. Whatever possible intellectual attractions the theory of Communism might have had for Steinbeck were quickly dispelled by the regimentation and limitations on individual freedom and thought that he witnessed in the Soviet Union. Life was as drab and hopeless for the great mass of Russian people as it was for the impoverished migrants of California. The Russians tried to celebrate Steinbeck as the champion of the American proletariat, but he would have none of it. On the voyage from Sweden back to New York later in the summer, he decided to abandon the idea of writing a book about Russia. There was, after all, no individualism in the country against which to set the group behavior notions that were at the core of his thinking.

His visit nevertheless sparked the idea of returning to and revising the basic material of his uncompleted vigilante novel. In writing about the migrants in a more focused way than he had been able to do in In Dubious Battle, he would show America that its treatment of its stoop-labor minority was as evil as the Soviet Union's treatment of almost its entire population. By showing America that it was no different from Russia in its indifference to human striving and dignity, he might provoke some sort of accelerated reform.

Steinbeck compiled a large sheaf of notes about his revised book idea on the voyage back to New York. But by the time of his arrival in early August he was ready to discard them. He still could not match his philosophical imperatives to the demands of storytelling, and he doubted that another try at the vigilante book would work.

During John and Carol's European trip, Pascal Covici published a special edition of Steinbeck's short story "The Red Pony" in an effort to capitalize on his author's rising popularity and generate another movie sale. Steinbeck had at first been reluctant to permit it, but Covici convinced him that since *Of Mice and Men,* a slender book, had sold so well, "The Red Pony" would make an attractive book venture as well, particularly if John stretched it out by adding a third section to the two that had been published in *North American Review.* Since the original two parts were really separate but interrelated stories about the life of a boy on a California ranch, an additional story centering on the boy would not only be natural, given Steinbeck's interest in the short-story-as-novel form, but would flesh the work out sufficiently to forestall criticism that Steinbeck and Covici, Friede were trying to bilk the public by printing as a book something that had already appeared as a story.

It was this that Steinbeck had been wary of. But he capitulated on the condition that he be given time to add two more sections to "The Gift" and "The Great Mountains," the original two parts of "The Red Pony." He had written the first during the time he had "struck a bad snag" on the vigilante novel at the end of the previous year. Called "The Promise," this first of Steinbeck's additions continued Jody's adventures after the pony that had been given to him in the original story died, and traced further Jody's transition from the innocence of boyhood to the hard realities and disillusion of manhood.

Steinbeck had brought the story to New York with him in March on his way to Russia. Covici was so enthralled with it that he wanted to proceed instantly with the publication of it and the two original stories as a book. John continued to argue against it, insisting that a fourth story was still needed. He didn't know when he would have the time to write a fourth story, however, what with the urgent work he still had to do on the dramatization of *Of Mice and Men* during the trip abroad. Covici held out for immediate publication, wanting to strike while the iron was hot. Aside from the prospect of the fall production of the play, John had no work in progress, and Covici, Friede would therefore have nothing of his to publish during the coming year. It was important, Covici argued, to keep him before the book-buying public, and a creative publisher's job was to do just that — even when the writer had nothing new in the way of a book to be published.

Steinbeck finally gave in. On his return from Europe he found that Covici had put out *The Red Pony* in a special, luxuriously bound limited "gift" edition at a price of ten dollars. John was angry at Covici. Surely now the public and the critics would consider not the book itself but its price. Even the fattest of novels sold at that time for only four dollars. He would be lambasted for lending himself to such a commercial sham. His anger died, however, when the feared denunciations failed to materialize and the book quickly sold out. As Covici pointed out, the sale reflected the fact that John was a "star." His celebrity was no transient thing. On the contrary, the reading public viewed him as a writer of unique importance and had bought out *The Red Pony* as a testament to its faith in the longevity of his reputation. All he had to do was keep turning out novels and stories in his style, and the public would keep buying them.

Covici's words frightened Steinbeck nevertheless. For he was in the process of concluding that his "style" had failed to properly serve his philosophical ambitions and was mulling over the prospect of developing a new style, something that would take him beyond his California material. Would the public accept such a change?

It would remain to be seen. For now, his literary concerns were still rooted in California. He had more work to do on the *Of Mice and Men* play adaptation. And he was still trying to find a path to a novel on the migrant harvesters.

It was Steinbeck's first visit to New York in summertime, and the summer of 1937 was more than ordinarily hot and humid. He was accustomed to heat, but to the dry, baking heat of Salinas, not the moist steam-bath climate of New York. After a few days he found it impossible to accomplish any fruitful work in his and Carol's hotel quarters. The two were thereupon invited by George Kaufman to stay at his summer house in fashionable Bucks County, Pennsylvania, so that John could put the final touches on the dramatization.

The play version of *Of Mice and Men* was scheduled to open at New York's Music Box Theatre on November 23. John and Carol returned to the city from Kaufman's farm in mid-September. Both itched to get home, but Kaufman wanted Steinbeck to remain for the casting auditions, the October rehearsals and the out-of-town tryouts, so that he would be available for script revisions. Steinbeck remained for the casting,[22] but because, as he said, "I had this new book on my soul," he refused to linger in New York any longer. Instead he and Carol bought a new car and made a leisurely drive back across the country to Los Gatos. He was not a theater man, he later claimed, and once the production got underway he would feel like excess baggage. He left it to Annie Laurie Williams, a member of the McIntosh and Otis agency who specialized in theatrical properties, to look after the play's interests.

The Steinbecks arrived home in mid-October after stopping in Chicago to visit with the family of John's uncle, Joe Hamilton, and spending some time touring the Dust Bowl area of Oklahoma. While in Chicago they fell in love with a bloodhound puppy from a litter being raised by a neighbor of the Hamiltons. They bought it for shipment to them in California once it was old enough to travel.

The Broadway premiere of *Of Mice and Men* the following month was a stunning critical and popular success. It promised a long run and a substantial increase in the already considerable income Steinbeck was earning from his work. Nevertheless, his refusal to stay in New York through the play's rehearsals and his unwillingness to appear at the opening deeply offended George Kaufman and several others who had worked on the production. Kaufman, already puzzled by John's personal remoteness and lack of amiability during their pre-production working sessions, credited Steinbeck's attitude to the fact that he, Kaufman, was a Jew. Kaufman had heard gossip, months before when he was trying to acquire the stage rights to *Of Mice and Men,* that Steinbeck had expressed misgivings about Kaufman's involvement in the play. "What would a wiseacre New York Jew know about people like George and Lenny?" Steinbeck was purported to have said to someone that no one else seemed willing to identify to Kaufman. Steinbeck's alternating unease and diffidence evidently confirmed Kaufman's suspicions that Steinbeck disliked Jews. And although John wrote him a warm letter of appreciation after the opening of the play, Kaufman would refuse to talk to him for years.

The book Steinbeck "had on my soul," which, according to him, was the reason he had so abruptly returned to California, was, as it would turn out, *The Grapes of Wrath.* Out of the mélange of literary and philosophical musings and false starts on the vigilante book during the previous year, a single powerful idea had begun to germinate in his mind during the play preparations. It took more definite shape as he and Carol wended their way back to California by way of the Dust Bowl states. It would be, as he said once he started writing it, his climactic novel. Once finished with it, he would have to go on to some other form of writing.

❊ ❊ ❊ ❊ ❊ ❊ CHAPTER TWENTY

Steinbeck's fame, cemented by the hit production of Of *Mice and Men,* brought him considerably more personal bother than pleasure. Since he had become identified in the public mind as a spokesman for the poor, he became the recipient of an endless stream of letters from supplicants throughout the country who sought to persuade him to share his riches. The flow of curious visitors to Greenwood Lane hoping to catch a glimpse of him or, even better, get his autograph or sympathetic ear, sharply increased. There then came what was almost inevitable to any man of sudden celebrity: he learned that he was being sued by a woman, whom he had once known only slightly, as the father of her illegitimate child.[23]

What bothered him most, however, was the fact that many of his old writing friends – fellows like Duke Sheffield, George Albee and Carl Wilhelmson – had begun to react to him in a completely different manner than that of former days. The camaraderie and candidness of his relations with these men seemed to have slipped away like blood from a wound.

They were the wounded, and their wounds now festered with envy and resentment. Of them all during their twenties, John had seemed the least likely to succeed as a writer despite the stubbornness of his ambition. His success now caused them to reexamine their own ambitions, and they did not like what they discovered.

The first with whom John fell out was George Albee, from whom he had borrowed (and repaid) the emergency hundred-dollar loan a few years before. Albee, like the others, believed that success had caused Steinbeck to become excessively self-absorbed, self-centered and self-important. Superficially he was right, in essence wrong. John had always been self-absorbed and had never, in his literary discussions with his various friends, given their work or ideas a fraction of the attention he gave his own, whereas they had been much more generous in their sympathies. John was now being quoted nationally about his work. He was saying nothing different than he had said in his private discussions with his friends, and with no less self-importance. The fact that his pronouncements were now being broadcast as though they were the latest wisdom, however, grated Albee. Undoubtedly out of professional jealousy he took an "I-knew-Steinbeck-when" attitude and even claimed credit for being the inspiration for many of John's ideas.

As for Sheffield and Wilhelmson, they too found it hard to be pleased by their friend's success. Although they did not snipe at John the way Albee did, they found him much more difficult to perceive as the literary and social comrade of a few years before — particularly after he put everyone on notice that there would be no more casual drop-in visits to the Los Gatos house and that advance phone calls were required. Later in life Steinbeck claimed that he did this because his publicity had destroyed his privacy and his ability to work for long, uninterrupted periods. The claim was understandable, of course, except to old friends who, vaguely resentful of his success in comparison to their own lack of it, were ready to put the worst possible interpretation on John's actions.

At thirty-five, Steinbeck seemed to many in the literary trade an unlikely repository of the narrative skills and thematic insights that had shone through his most recent work. Numerous critics distrusted his talents, and he was not altogether wrong in suspecting that they were waiting for him to fail. It was with trepidation, then, that he began work on "Grapes of Wrath," the novel that would become his magnum opus.

In November, Steinbeck had only the vaguest notion of the shape his new novel would take. By rewriting, he was still trying to form it out of the material of the vigilante story. As such, it continued to be troublesome. All he knew for certain was that it would center on the migrant farmworkers and that, now, he would endeavor to use the mass migration that had brought them to California from the Midwest as the vehicle for his subtextual study of group forces and dynamics. He also knew from his trip through Oklahoma that he would have to do more firsthand research on the migrants and that the book would be a long time in the writing. Before he plunged in, therefore, he took pains to see that his income continued to flow.

The successful publication of *The Red Pony* had finally convinced him that there was merit in Pat Covici's desire to exploit his past writings to their fullest possible extent, particularly with regard to the lucrative movie industry. Steinbeck reminded his agents that although he had no interest in writing for Hollywood himself, several of his previous books were suitable for sale to the movies. *Tortilla Flat* had already been sold, of course, and several studios were vying for *Of Mice and Men* as a result of its success on Broadway. Steinbeck was sure that *Cup of Gold,* with its high-seas-adventure background, would make a popular movie. He forbade them to try to sell *In Dubious Battle,* but urged them to peddle separately several of the stories in *The Pastures of Heaven.*

Covici, in the meantime, wanted to follow *The Red Pony* with a collection of Steinbeck's short stories. *Esquire* magazine had recently purchased several of Steinbeck's unpublished stories, and Covici felt that a book of stories, conventionally priced and featuring the three parts of the *The Red Pony*, would be profitable. Steinbeck didn't know it, but Covici, Friede was experiencing financial difficulties, largely due to Pat Covici's extravagant spending policies. The success of Steinbeck's last three books had rescued the firm from an earlier disaster, but the profits generated by John's works had been squandered by Covici's unsuccessful efforts to expand the quantity and quality of the firm's list. He needed another Steinbeck best-seller fast. He could not wait for John's next novel, so he pressed him for the short-story collection. John agreed — other well-known writers had recently published successful volumes of short stories — but he wanted time to revise some of the stories that would go into the book and to write the fourth segment of *The Red Pony*.

Another project that occupied Steinbeck during the fall was a play version of *Tortilla Flat*. The success of *Of Mice and Men* on Broadway had inspired a number of producers to study other Steinbeck works for their stage possibilities. John Kirkland, noted for having turned Erskine Caldwell's best-selling book *Tobacco Road* into a popular play, had taken an option on *Tortilla Flat* and sent a draft playscript to Steinbeck for his comments. John was disturbed by much of Kirkland's treatment, feeling that the New York writer had excessively distorted the humor of his *paisano* characters in order to pander to New York audiences. He predicted that the play would be a failure, and when it opened on January 12, 1938, he was proved right. The play was vilified by the critics and closed after four performances. The *New York Herald Tribune*'s review was so damning that it provoked Kirkland to track down its author, Richard Watts, and physically assault him in public. The resultant publicity over this incident overshadowed the failure of the play. Carol, who had gone to New York to represent John on opening night (his concession to Elizabeth Otis's plea that he not repeat the mistake he had made by failing to attend the premiere of *Of Mice and Men*), reported back that the Kirkland production was a disaster in every respect.

The critics, dismissing the play as a cheap exploitation of a good novel, held Steinbeck blameless. Hollywood producers stepped up their efforts to persuade him to write movie scripts. Steinbeck continued to reject their offers with singular determination. With the exception of In Dubious Battle, which he valued too highly, he still had no objection to Hollywood's turning his stories into films. But he was convinced that a screenwriter's credit diminished a serious novelist's credibility. Such literary luminaries as Faulkner, Fitzgerald, Hemingway and John O'Hara had succumbed to the financial lure of Hollywood. Steinbeck believed that film writing had nothing to do with literature. Even if it did, he had learned from O'Hara and Kaufman that Hollywood writers had no autonomy over what they wrote, and what they wrote was almost always written to order.

It was a badge of pride to him that he had never written to order, nor yielded the autonomy of what he had written to his publishers or anyone else. Adaptation of his work by others was not the same thing, he rationalized. He had permitted John Kirkland to impose his own craft on the play version of Tortilla Flat. Now a road company of Of Mice and Men was being organized to perform the play across the country. Because some of the language of the New York production was considered a bit ahead of its time in its graphicness, and because the sexuality of some of its scenes was a bit too visually implied, John was asked by Kaufman for permission to make changes in the original script so that the play could be performed without controversy in the provinces. Steinbeck agreed without hesitation.

The year 1938 began in central California with a deluge of rain that broke the state's long drought cycle. As was usually the case after a drought, the rain came in excess, turning the farmlands of the San Joaquin Valley into an ocean of mud and ruined crops. It brought financial disaster not only to the farmers but to the vast army of itinerant pickers about whom Steinbeck had written with such controlled anger in "The

Harvest Gypsies." *Life* magazine contacted Steinbeck and asked him to accompany one of its photographers through the labor camps and write the text for a photographic essay on the plight of the migrants. Steinbeck agreed, and when he toured the camps late in February he was more astounded than ever by the privation and suffering endured by the migrants, and by the continuing indifference of the local governments that supported the farmers' organizations. Particularly hard hit were the farmworkers who had migrated to California from the Dust Bowl regions. Because the state and county governments refused to recognize them as legitimate residents of the state, they were not entitled to what little relief was provided to workers who could prove that they were natives of California.

During the spring, Steinbeck alternated the reworking of the vigilante novel with visits to various labor camps in the San Joaquin Valley. The rewriting continued to go badly, principally because he was still trying to superimpose his phalanx theories on a narrative that simply would not accept them. Finally, in May, after having gotten halfway through a new draft, he decided to abandon the vigilante idea altogether and start over again. In the meantime, he gave permission to a private California foundation, The Simon J. Lubin Society, to reprint "The Harvest Gypsies" as a booklet. The booklet appeared under the title *Their Blood Is Strong*, and Steinbeck insisted that all proceeds from its sale go toward migrant-worker relief. Also during the spring, Steinbeck learned that *Of Mice and Men* had won the New York Drama Critics Circle Award as the best play of 1937.

During the previous year the land adjoining his Greenwood Lane property had been sold to a developer. The winter of early 1938 had brought construction crews into the neighborhood to build a nest of houses nearby. John and Carol, deciding to look for another place to live, found a fifty-acre farm-ranch for sale deeper in the hills west of Los Gatos, three miles away. Although John loved the outdoors, he was reluctant to become involved with a farm because of the maintenance demands and other distractions. Carol's passion for gardening and cultivating overpowered his reluctance, however, and they purchased the place during the summer of 1938. In the fall they moved into the existing ramshackle farmhouse while Carol supervised the building of a new home nearby. They planned to move into the new house when it was finished and then refurbish the original residence as a guesthouse. As far as Carol was concerned, the ranch would be their home for a long time to come, perhaps forever. She planned to rent a small apartment in San Francisco so that they would have a place to stay whenever they wanted a taste of city life. But the ranch, to be gradually restored to its original pretty and productive state, would be their permanent lair.

John was not so sure. He acceded to Carol's desire for the ranch mainly to avert the growth of further tension between them. Their trip to Mexico after his father's death had restored the health of their marriage for a time, but John's sudden success of the following year had gradually renewed the strain. Carol had greeted her unexpected financial prosperity with a burst of domesticity that had at first amused and then perplexed John. Where before she had been content to live under the plainest of conditions and in the simplest of surroundings, now she seemed to aspire more and more to all those middle-class values that he had long despised. In his eyes she was seeking to isolate herself, and him, from the outside world. He was pleased at the prospect of being insulated from the irksome effects of his notoriety, but Carol's impulses went beyond that. Upon settling in at the remote ranch, it was as if she had attained the pinnacle of her life's ambition. She was content to live the secure, quiet existence afforded by the ranch and to gather about her all the things that would provide them with comfortable self-sufficiency. In transforming herself in this way, she subtly demanded the same form of contentment and satisfaction from John. He, however, could feel little in the way of contentment. He would return from his visits to the labor camps with grim tales of their squalid conditions. His anger and guilt were an intrusion on Carol's increasingly cocoonlike organization of their life in the pastoral surroundings of the ranch. She grew less and less interested in his concerns and soon even began to resent them as a form of disorder in the otherwise idyllic world she was trying to create. John's frustrating struggle to find à suitable mode for the book he was trying to write added to the tension, for he had little time or inclination to discuss the problems of curtain color and wallpaper pattern that preoccupied Carol as their new house moved toward completion. Moreover, he had begun once again to wish for a child, citing their prosperity as a reason why they could now safely have one. Carol apparently continued to reject the idea.

Their habitual spats increased in frequency and began to take on a spiteful ugliness that theretofore had been absent. John had started writing his totally new version of the aborted "L'Affaire Lettuceburg" late in May. By July he had finished forty thousand words. Although he had only made a dent in his story (he was sure now that the book would be the longest of his career), he was confortable with it and felt certain that he had finally come to grips with the form he had been agonizing over. Much of the anger that would emanate from the book, once it was published as *The Grapes of Wrath*, came genuinely from John's outrage at the farmworkers' situation. Some of it nevertheless derived from the gradual souring of his relationship with Carol. Many of the days and even weeks he spent on the writing of it during the fall of 1938 were periods when he and Carol were barely able to be civil to one another. Ironically, the more furious he felt toward Carol, the better he felt about what he was writing.

Covici, Friede's publication in book form of fifteen of Steinbeck's short stories had come at the beginning of the summer. The volume, called *The Long Valley*, included the three stories of *The Red Pony* plus a fourth, entitled "The Leader of the People," which John had written the winter before. Also included were "The White Quail" and "The Murder," which had been published earlier in *North American Review*. Another story, "The Snake," had appeared in the *Monterey Beacon*, a tiny avant-garde magazine, in June 1935. The rest of the stories, some of them quite good and most dealing with themes that Steinbeck had pursued in his novels, were fresh to John's audience. A number of the previously unpublished pieces came from the long period of short-story writing he had engaged in during the time of his mother's illness in the summer and fall of 1933, when he was working out his phalanx theories under the tutelage of Ed Ricketts.

As Pat Covici had anticipated, *The Long Valley* received wide review attention. The critical consensus was generally lukewarm on the new stories, however, and the book did not enjoy an immediate large sale. Even if it had, it would have been too late to help Covici, Friede out of its financial difficulty. The firm declared bankruptcy in the summer of 1938. Steinbeck had settled on "The Grapes of Wrath" (from "The Battle Hymn of the Republic") as the title for his new migrant-worker novel, and as he toiled on it through the weeks after the Covici, Friede failure, he naively wondered whether any other publisher would be interested in it. His worries were calmed by Elizabeth Otis, who informed him that publishers were standing in line for the chance to take him on. As it happened, on the strength of his association with John's previous books, Pat Covici was offered a job as senior editor at Viking Press, provided that he brought all of Steinbeck's past and future works with him. Viking had become one of the country's most successful "literary" publishers under its founder and chief executive, Harold Guinzburg, and its principal editor, Marshall Best. Despite their occasional differences, Steinbeck and Covici were by now good friends and John was more than happy to remain with Covici. He therefore approved of the arrangement. His books would soon become among the most valuable assets of Viking Press, which would be his publisher for the rest of his life and Pat Covici's employer for the balance of his.

Once Steinbeck got steady control of "The Grapes of Wrath" during the summer, he worked with tireless determination to finish it. Throughout the writing process he grew increasingly confident of his purpose and method. Yet as was typical of him by now, he grew increasingly afraid as well that the book would be a critical and commercial failure. The reviews of *The Long Valley* had indicated that the critical community was growing tired of the California focus of his work and of his apparent preoccupation with the vagrant and illiterate elements of the state's population. Because many of the stories in *The Long Valley* bore more than passing resemblances in theme and characterization to his novels, some critics wondered whether Steinbeck wasn't locked into a pattern of repetition. He suspected that "The Grapes of Wrath," with its grim narrative about a family of inarticulate farmworkers who travel from Oklahoma to California in search of relief from poverty only to find worse, would be dismissed by these critics as the fulfillment of their prophecies. He was even more convinced as he approached the completion of the manuscript that the reading public would reject it. Times were getting markedly better for most of the country, he reasoned, and all literary indicators pointed to a rebirth of optimistic and inspirational literature.

Steinbeck finished "The Grapes of Wrath" in October 1938 and, after making a few revisions in the typescript, sent it to Pat Covici with the altogether serious warning that he should plan on printing only a small number of copies. Covici, Guinzburg and Best were highly impressed by the novel. But they felt that some of its language and imagery needed toning down and that its ending was both literarily weak and sexually offensive.[24]

In December, Elizabeth Otis arrived in California with the

typescript and a commission from Covici to persuade John to make the suggested changes. Steinbeck agreed to a few minor alterations, but refused to budge on the questions of language and the book's ending. As an aftereffect of his long and exhausting stint of writing, and possibly of his tension over his deteriorating relationship with Carol, he had been laid low by a severe attack of lumbar back pain shortly after sending the finished typescript to New York. Confined to bed, he was in no mood to entertain the idea of doing any more major work on the novel. He believed in the correctness of his approach and cared little if it offended or caused the book to be a failure.

Viking accepted John's insistence on keeping the integrity of the language but continued to nag him by wire and mail about the book's ending. When he refused to soften its sexual overtones, the editors asked him to at least prepare the reader for it by bringing the dying man into the story earlier so that he would not be a total stranger to the girl who offers him her breast. Steinbeck remained obdurate, writing to Covici in January 1939, "I am sorry but I cannot change that ending. . . . If there is a symbol, it is a survival symbol not a love symbol, it must be an accident, it must be a stranger, it must be quick. To build this stranger into the structure of the book would be to warp the whole meaning. . . . The fact that the Joads don't know him, don't care about him, have no ties to him — that is the emphasis. The giving of the breast has no more sentiment than the giving of a piece of bread."[25]

In the same letter, Steinbeck sternly rebuked Viking's requests for other changes. The implication was that he would put up with no more nitpicking. He had never been more sure of the integrity and artistic rightness of a book than he was, by then, of "The Grapes of Wrath." "I tried to write this book the way lives are being lived," he said, "not the way books are written."

Steinbeck also argued with Covici over John's wish to

have the complete lyrics of "The Battle Hymn of the Republic" printed in the book's endpapers. Covici intended to print only the stanza of the hymn that contained the "grapes of wrath" phrase, but John insisted on the entire hymn. *The Grapes of Wrath* was published in accordance with John's demands in March of 1939. Dedicated to Carol and to Tom Collins, the labor-camp manager from Bakersfield, the book's endpapers carried the complete "Battle Hymn of the Republic."

The novel took the country by storm. Despite Steinbeck's warning, Viking came out with a large first printing and even at that was hard put to satisfy the national demand for it after a month. It quickly hit the top of the best-seller list and would remain among the nation's ten best-selling books well into the following year.

The reviews were numerous and mixed. The book was treated not just as a literary work but as a political event as well; interest in it rapidly leaped beyond the book-review pages of newspapers and magazines to their political columns and editorial pages. Many respected reviewers who dealt primarily with its literary worth criticized it as meretriciously sentimental and false. Others praised it without reservation, claiming that Steinbeck had achieved a perfect union of form and substance and, as a result, was the most powerful and accomplished American novelist alive. The political and sociological commentary on the book was similarly divided. There were those who contended that in his hard-bitten but sympathetic portrayal of the Joad family, Steinbeck had unfairly "loaded the dice" against the villains of the book — the farmers and corrupt government bureaucracies — and that in reality people like the Joads were, because of their ignorance and illiteracy, just as responsible for their tragic plight as the establishment that exploited them. Others saw the Joads as proof of the evils of the American system and roundly applauded Steinbeck's portrayal of them as victims of a greedy and unfeeling society.

More reflective and less hysterical analyses of *The Grapes of Wrath* were to come later, but at the time of its publication few critics were able to approach its literary and political merits with any depth of insight. It mattered little anyway, since public reaction to the book was largely so favorable. Most people were captivated by Steinbeck's sonorous descriptive prose, his eerily accurate dialogue, his poignant scenes, his authoritative philosophical perceptions and his incisive images and symbols.

To achieve all this, Steinbeck had written what were essentially two distinct books — one a pulsating, idiomatic human drama, the other a more abstract sociological treatise — and had interwoven the two into a harmonious whole. His principal story, the tale of the Joads in their trek west from Oklahoma to California and their pathetic struggles there, was punctuated by what Steinbeck called "interchapters" in which he angrily philosophized about the human impulses and motivations that created the conditions that existed in California. These brief interludes disturbed many reviewers, who contended that they were preachy, patronizing of the reader's intelligence, and disruptive of the flow of the story.

On the contrary, they were an inventive device on Steinbeck's part to blunt the political criticism he expected to receive. He had feared critics would claim that the travails of the Joad family were unique and were not a true representation of the conditions affecting California's migrant-labor force. In the interchapters, he was able to show that the Joads, rather than being the exception, were the rule. Nor did the interchapters disrupt the flow of the action. Although they occasionally contained an excess of moral fervor, they were for the most part concise, and managed to neatly frame the issues inherent in the Joads' misfortune and to give their characters a nobility they might otherwise not have had. Through the interchapters, Steinbeck was able to integrate the different thematic and philosophical concepts he had been pursuing for so long into a unified whole, and at the same time to present a more balanced picture of the situation in California.

Many readers initially took his portrayal of the Joads as a one-sided peroration against the establishment and an expressly implied cry for revolution of the type the Communists were trying to achieve. A more careful reading of the inter-chapters revealed that Steinbeck was impelled by a desire for reform, not revolution. Moreover, he *did* recognize the responsibility the Joads had to bear for their own plight. For someone who was as critical of the simple black-and-white approach to solving problems as Steinbeck was — particularly as represented by organized religion, the business establishment, the government with its welfare programs, and the Communists — it would have been inconsistent of him to place the entire onus for the farm laborers' tragedy on these institutions. The laborers themselves bore some of the responsibility, and Steinbeck's ultimate point in the book was that proper reform could never be achieved unless they, as well as the establishment that exploited them, educated themselves to the necessity of human cooperation. Much of their plight derived from their own superstitions, myths and prejudices.

The most frequently and severely criticized aspect of the novel was, as anticipated by Viking Press, its ending. Many critics agreed with Clifton Fadiman, who wrote in *The New Yorker* that "the ending is the tawdriest kind of fake symbolism." To many ordinary readers, its symbolism — the offering of the woman's breast to the dying stranger — was gripping. But the fact that Steinbeck ended the book there left them puzzled and disappointed. Having become so emotionally involved in the Joads, or in the surviving remnants of the family, readers felt that Steinbeck had denied them a resolution of the story. In other words, what was to become of the family?

Steinbeck refused to say. And yet the artistic whole of the novel was skillfully completed by his refusal, for symbolically the story ended at precisely the right place. His point that the education of the Joads was as necessary to reform as the education of the villainous elements was symbolically hammered home in the breast incident. It was Ma Joad, the leader of the family, who suggested that her daughter nourish the dying man from her milk-swollen breast after her child was born dead. By having her do so, Steinbeck indicated that the Joads had indeed experienced an important enlightenment as a result of their sufferings. At the beginning of the book Steinbeck had presented the Joads as a family that primitively perceived itself, in all its superstitions and prejudices, as special and self-important. Throughout the narrative of their forced migration westward and their experiences in California, he subtly wove in incidents designed to reflect their awakening awareness of the fact that their survival depended on their willingness to shed their selfish insularity and become integrated into the much larger human family of which all people are a part. The final scene of the book symbolized the completion of their education. By not letting her postpartum milk dry up, but offering it to the dying man, Ma Joad's daughter, Rose of Sharon, and the matriarchal Ma herself, completed the education Steinbeck set out to make the family undergo. This final scene did not leave the story incomplete. Rather, it logically concluded the story Steinbeck had set out to tell about the Joads. Their enlightenment was complete. What was to happen to them or, more to the point, to the thousands of real-life people they represented, depended now on the ability of the rest of society to undergo a similar enlightenment.[26]

✳ ✳ ✳ ✳ CHAPTER TWENTY-ONE

Despite the critical discussion over its deeper merits, The *Grapes of* W*rath* established Steinbeck in the public's mind as one of the country's most important serious novelists, a writer capable of achieving the highest aspiration of literature: the creation of art.

Art in literature is a rare thing when one considers all the fiction that has made its way into print over the centuries. Its achievement implies extraordinary powers on the part of its creator. First, the writer must have a vision that is more sharply perceptive and cohesive than the ordinary person's. What's more, it must be a vision that compels others to assent to its power. Second, the writer must have the sensibility and craft to transform his vision, and the narrative materials through which he elects to embody it, into a finished product that needs only to be experienced to be understood. Through the synergy that exists between the thoughts, feelings, actions and logic of the writer's characters, and the thoughts, feelings, actions and logic of the reader, art occurs. In the end the artist is the writer who elevates and transforms the reader's vision.

We have seen that Steinbeck consciously set out in his career to be not just a writer but an artist. His early novels were deliberate attempts to achieve art through the successful fusion of thought (philosophical and thematic idea) and craft (literary technique). His successive works increasingly approached this achievement, and in *Of Mice and Men*, the novel that immediately preceded *The Grapes of Wrath*, he came closest to accomplishing the fusion of form and content, idea and technique, that constitutes literary art. In *The Grapes of Wrath*, he achieved the complete fusion.

Strangely enough, for a man who was so conscious of his artistic purpose, Steinbeck doubted that he had in fact achieved art in the Joad novel. Its popular success pleased him immensely, of course, but this was because of his writer's ego, his hunger to be read widely, and not his artistic ambition. Indeed, although he had worked hard and inspiredly to incorporate the totality of his philosophical convictions in the book — his phalanx theory — he felt that he had failed to make it clear. The book did have a unified vision, to be sure, but it was not really the one he had set out to convey. Instead, the writing of the book — or better, the actions of the characters following their own logic — had itself transformed Steinbeck's vision. He had originally thought that his phalanx conceptions were too complex to be reflected with clarity in a single novel. Now he suspected that the novel form was too complex for his philosophical theory, that in fact it reduced the theory to only a minor component in the much larger explanation and understanding of human behavior.

On a spiritual or ideational level, then, Steinbeck was dissatisfied with *The Grapes of Wrath*. He sensed that he had achieved art, but he knew that in so doing he had rendered his phalanx theory inoperative. There was much more to human behavior, both individual and group, than such a tidy philosophical notion could account for. Steinbeck had learned as much of philosophy as of art in the process of writing the Joad novel. And although he would never discard his phalanx ideas, he could no longer depend on them as the philosophical motive of his literary striving. He had to go beyond them to a more basic world view.

A large part of his changing perspective was due to Ed Ricketts. Ricketts himself had proceeded through an evolution of thought during the time Steinbeck was living in Los Gatos. His ideas had become more rigidly scientific vis-à-vis his own work and, as a consequence, in regard to nonscientific matters. He and Steinbeck had remained in close contact after John's move to Los Gatos, but because of the lack of the almost daily contact and discussion they had enjoyed before, John had not kept up with him. He was disappointed but not surprised to learn that Ricketts took exception to *The Grapes of Wrath*. Not that Ricketts thought it was a bad novel. But he did criticize its tone and viewpoint as not being detached enough. It was overly moral, he claimed, "teleological" and therefore redolent of the very impulses of religion, government and the business world which John had attacked in his story.[27] Ricketts had come to view teleological approaches to life as useless because they concerned themselves with what should be, could be or might be instead of with what actually "is." As far as he was concerned, the preoccupation with teleological thinking — the need to find a purpose and explanation for everything — was society's principal problem because it led to the destructive compulsion to make things in nature conform to a society's conceptions of what they ought to be, which in turn led to war, injustice, inequality and so on. Infinitely better and more useful, said Ricketts, was "nonteleological" thinking. If man merely concerned himself with the observable and verifiable "what is" of life, and allowed his thoughts and actions to be governed by this reality rather than by the unnatural imperatives of the teleological "what ought to be," he would be much better able to create a sane and integrated society.

Ricketts's was the purely scientific view juxtaposed with the traditional religious and moral view of man. He chided

Steinbeck for giving *The Grapes of Wrath* a teleological character in his attempt to recommend one moral condition of
society over another. At the same time, he was able to com-
mend John for at least achieving a nonteleological distance in
certain aspects of the novel — in his detached examination of
the Joads, for instance, and his minimally colored descriptions
of the forces and cycles of nature that helped to create the
conditions that brought about the strife between the opposing
sides in *The Grapes of Wrath*.

What Ricketts was saying was that John had made some
progress toward establishing a purely nonteleological approach
to his art, and that if he could rid his vision altogether of
teleology he would create an even more powerful art. Steinbeck
was not, as it may appear, a slave to Ricketts's philosophy. But
he was powerfully susceptible to his friend's rapidly evolving
ideas, particularly as they related to his own. With the sense
of philosophical loss he experienced as a result of *The Grapes
of Wrath*, he once again turned to Ricketts for enlightenment.
That was the beginning of a radically new and, in the end,
disappointing phase of his artistic life.

As we have seen, while Steinbeck was in the process of
writing *The Grapes of Wrath*, he predicted that once finished
with it he would have exhausted his capacity to write novels
and would need to find some other form in which to express
himself. His prediction was fulfilled, at least spiritually, after
the book appeared. In the fall of 1939 he wrote to Duke
Sheffield: "I must make a new start. I've worked the novel
as I know it as far as I can take it. I never did think much of
it — a clumsy vehicle at best. And I don't know the form of the
new but I know there *is* a new which will be adequate and
shaped by the new thinking. Anyway, there is the picture of
my confusion."[28]

The "new thinking" to which Steinbeck referred was the
nonteleological theory of Ed Ricketts. He quickly became convinced of the virtue of Ricketts's ideas and resolved not to write

again until he had mastered them himself. But the new thinking was not the only thing on his mind.

Local reaction to *The Grapes of Wrath,* particularly on the part of the farm organizations and their members, was unrelentingly vicious. The Steinbecks received at their Los Gatos house hundreds of crank letters and not a few death threats. Although John shrugged them off, Carol was terrified. Her terror was made more acute by sightseers who penetrated the grounds of the ranch and ogled the house from a distance. Her fears and John's refusal to be intimidated deepened the tensions between them. Steinbeck later claimed that a local sheriff's deputy had warned him that there was a plot afoot among some angry farmers to avenge *The Grapes of Wrath* by entrapping Steinbeck in rape charges.

Steinbeck continued to suffer from a painful back, but he and Carol traveled to Hollywood during the spring so that he could consult on the filming of *Of Mice and Men.* Steinbeck found himself a celebrity upon his arrival. Not only was *Of Mice and Men* about to go before the cameras under the direction of Lewis Milestone, but *The Grapes of Wrath* had also been sold to Hollywood. A screenplay was being prepared by Nunnally Johnson for filming at the Twentieth Century Fox studios.

Steinbeck's first extended Hollywood experience was pivotal for him. Up to then he had scoffed at the movie industry as a medium for serious writing and had adamantly declined to participate in it, despite screenwriting offers he had received at salaries reaching as high as five thousand dollars a week. Upon his first "official" visit to Hollywood, however, he met many of the powers of the industry — directors, writers, stars — and was impressed not only by their celebrity but by their earnestness. He was also diverted by their attentions to him. His prejudices underwent a rapid change. Although he continued to distrust the industry's ability to make meaningful and faithful motion pictures out of his two major works, he held his final judgment in abeyance.

During their stay in Hollywood, John and Carol had a nasty argument based, apparently, on Carol's jealousy of the attention John was getting. Steinbeck abruptly moved out of their hotel and into an apartment. Carol returned to Los Gatos. On his own now, John began to see a good deal of his childhood friends from Salinas, Max and Jack Wagner. Both were still struggling to establish themselves in the movie business and were suitably impressed by John's tales of his conferences and socializing with some of the industry's biggest names.

Midway through his stay, Steinbeck suffered another attack of paralyzing back pain and was forced to confine himself to his bed in the apartment. Max and Jack Wagner tended to his needs, and one evening Max brought around a woman friend to meet the illustrious writer. The young woman, Gwendolyn Conger, was an attractive aspiring actress-singer. Confused and depressed over his growing troubles with Carol, Steinbeck fell immediately in love with her, although he kept his feelings to himself. She thereafter joined Wagner in his nightly ministrations of his bedridden friend. When Steinbeck was well enough to move about, the three of them were seen together around Hollywood and Beverly Hills. Friends assumed that Gwen Conger was with Max Wagner and that John was merely a tag-along third party. That was exactly the way Steinbeck wanted it to appear. He would soon be returning to Los Gatos and Carol, and did not want to make any rash or premature moves. Indeed, he could not even be sure that Gwen felt toward him the way he felt toward her. Only her occasional lingering glances hinted that she might.

Steinbeck limped back to the ranch in Los Gatos in June of 1939. He found Carol still edgy and unhappy, but he managed a reconciliation. They spent most of the summer at the cottage in Pacific Grove, and it was during this time that Steinbeck fell under the spell of Ed Ricketts's nonteleological theories. In fact he not only fell under their spell, but resolved to reorganize his own literary ambition in accordance with them.

The Pacific Biological Laboratories corporation was, as

usual, skating on thin financial ice under the quixotic business leadership of Ed Ricketts, its sole owner. Steinbeck spent many hours during the summer at the lab, assisting Ricketts in his work, absorbing more of his scientific theories as applied to literature, and trying to help his friend and mentor sort out his financial affairs. Two projects Ricketts hoped soon to undertake were a specimen-cataloging expedition through the coastal waters of Northern California and a second such trip into the Gulf of California, which separates Mexico's Baja California peninsula from that country's mainland. Flirting with bankruptcy, however, he was unable to afford to charter a boat for the extended periods required. Steinbeck stepped into the breach.

John's earnings had mushroomed enormously in 1939, so much so that his federal income tax payment for that year would be in excess of forty thousand dollars. He offered to buy half the stock in the Pacific Biological Laboratories corporation in order to save Ricketts from bankruptcy and give him the operating capital he needed to make his expeditions. Aside from the stock, which in effect would make him Ricketts's business partner, he asked for one other condition: that he accompany Ricketts on the expeditions. It was his idea not only to work on the principal purpose of the ventures — specimen-collecting and cataloging — but to write a nonfiction book about the expeditions. He had come to believe that a book about a scientific voyage, written in a literary form but from a scientific view, would help him to acquire the discipline and craft he needed to progress to the "new" method of writing he sought in the wake of *The Grapes of Wrath*.

Ed Ricketts agreed and the financial arrangements were completed in the fall of 1939. He and Steinbeck thereupon began to plan their trips. With Carol back in Los Gatos, John continued to spend most of his time at the lab in Monterey, trying to soak up as much knowledge about invertebrates and the methods of marine biology as he could. As he studied, he found that "I have no education. I have to go back to school in a way. . . . I bought half the stock in Ed's lab which gives me equipment, a teacher, a library to work in."[29] And writing a few months later of his studies at the Cannery Row laboratory, he said to Duke Sheffield, "I like the discipline. I've grown more and more dissatisfied with my [writing] and this will help it, I hope. Besides, it will drop me out of this damnable popularity, for, while it will be a good book, there won't be a hell of a lot of people who will want it. I'm very sick of this prominence business."[30]

The book to which he referred was the proposed journal of his and Ricketts's voyage to Baja California. They had decided to do their initial collecting along the northern California coast by working from the shore in a small boat and using a truck to cart their catch back to Monterey. But the waters of the Gulf of California were accessible only by sea. For that more extended expedition, they arranged to charter a seventy-six-foot fishing boat with a crew of three.

In December of 1939 John took a brief interlude from his preparations to return with Carol to Hollywood to view screenings of the motion-picture versions of *The Grapes of Wrath* and *Of Mice and Men*. Steinbeck was genuinely pleased with both. He thought the film of *The Grapes of Wrath* was even more powerful than his book, and claimed that Lewis Milestone had bestowed a lyric quality on *Of Mice and Men* that gave it greater appeal than the play.

During the trip, Steinbeck managed to work in a visit with Gwen Conger without Carol's knowledge. He braved telling her of his feelings, and was surprised to hear her profess love for him. Her declaration confused him even as it elated him. He slunk guiltily back to Carol, but could not dismiss Gwen from his mind.

He cemented a number of other friendships in Hollywood, as well. One was with Henry Fonda, the star of *The Grapes of Wrath*, whom he had insisted Darryl F. Zanuck cast as Tom Joad instead of the actor Zanuck wanted, Tyrone Power. Although Fonda was forced to sign an oppressive seven-year contract with Twentieth Century Fox to get Zanuck to give him the part, he was eternally grateful to Steinbeck. The two men were much alike in temperament — shy, hypercritical and stubborn — and they formed a fellowship that lasted for the rest of Steinbeck's life.

Another friendship he established was with Spencer Tracy. Tracy wanted to make a movie of *The Red Pony*. Steinbeck, who had received a hundred thousand dollars for the movie rights to *The Grapes of Wrath*, agreed, but only on the condition that all the picture's proceeds be assigned to children's charities, particularly to those that covered victims of infantile paralysis. Tracy was happy to go along, since his own son had been crippled by polio.

It would not be accurate to say that Steinbeck was starstruck by Hollywood. Most of the celebrities he met were as impressed by him as he was by them. Yet he admired in many the special qualities that had brought about their celebrity. And he began to seriously reevaluate his prejudices against writing directly for movies.

The Grapes of Wrath opened later in December to stunning nationwide reviews. It was followed shortly, in January 1940, by *Of Mice and Men* which, although not as generously acclaimed, also found a large audience, primarily because of the passion for Steinbeck that gripped the country.

John and Carol, in the meantime, had returned to Monterey and Los Gatos. Later in January Steinbeck announced to his wife that he and Ricketts would depart on a two-month boat voyage to the Gulf of California or, as it was known in Mexico, the Sea of Cortez. According to friends, Carol, although pleased with John's success and the money it was bringing them, was by now deeply distrustful, resentful and jealous of the time John was spending away from Los Gatos. She was uncomfortable in the company of the celebrities he seemed to be cultivating in Hollywood — several had visited them at the ranch, including Charlie Chaplin and his wife Paulette Goddard — and resented the intellectual companionship he sought in Ed Ricketts. Nor could she understand his need to produce a new style of writing. In her view he had found the formula for literary success. His tampering with it, or abandoning it, threatened to topple the structure of financial security he had built for her. She demanded to be taken along on the voyage. She would not let him run away from a shaky marriage. If he wouldn't work to restore it at home, then she would do so at sea.

John, despite his powerfully amorous feelings for Gwen Conger in Hollywood, was amenable to the idea of trying to put his marriage back on sound footing. He did not argue with Carol's demand, therefore, particularly because he was aware that no one in his family had ever gone through a divorce — an action Carol may have previously threatened in moments of pique. With Ed Ricketts's agreement, then, in March the three embarked from Monterey on a voyage to the Sea of Cortez in a chartered purse seiner called "Western Flyer."

✳ ✳ ✳ ✳ CHAPTER TWENTY-TWO

The trip went without any jarring incidents between John and Carol. But it did little to repair their relationship. Indeed, although the cruise was in many respects idyllic, removing them all from their landward concerns, six weeks of living in each other's pockets further deteriorated Steinbeck's affection for his wife. Exposed as he had been to the general admiration of Hollywood and to the specific attentions of the softly beauteous Gwen Conger, he had begun to view Carol in a swiftly changing light. By the time they returned from Mexico at the end of April, he was barely able to tolerate her. And yet his guilt over his feelings forced him to maintain the front that their marriage had been restored.

Much of Steinbeck's time on the voyage was spent in discussion with Ricketts over scientific and philosophical issues, most of them centering on the concept of nonteleological approaches to life and literature. John made copious notes of their discussion, and as the book he had projected formed in his mind, he realized that it would be improper for him to write it without crediting most of its ideas to Ricketts. Consequently he proposed that it carry a dual authorship. Although he would do most of the actual writing, he would give his friend and mentor co-billing as its author. As soon as he landed and was settled back in Los Gatos, he commenced outlining the book. He would call the manuscript "Sea of Cortez: A Leisurely Journal of Travel and Research." When he sent it to Covici at Viking Press a year later, he would attribute its authorship to John Steinbeck *and* Edward F. Ricketts, Jr.

On his return to California, Steinbeck learned that *The Grapes of Wrath* had won the Pulitzer Prize in fiction for 1939. And he discovered something even more momentous. During his voyage, Eleanor Roosevelt, wife of the President of the United States, had come to California to inspect the migrant-labor camps. Following her visit, she was quoted in the press as saying she had read *The Grapes of Wrath* and found that it provided a depressingly accurate depiction of the conditions in the camps. Steinbeck immediately wrote her a letter of appreciation in which he said that because of her endorsement, the doubters of his book would be forced to stop calling him a liar. Thus began a series of contacts with the White House that would soon culminate in a personal meeting between Steinbeck and President Roosevelt.

Steinbeck returned from his Mexican expedition to find the country preoccupied by the war in Europe. He had thought seldom about the events in Europe prior to the voyage, but when he got back to Los Gatos the country's preoccupation became his. He was particularly alarmed by the military advances of Nazi Germany on the European and African continents and, because of his own German heritage, was ashamed of it. When France fell in June, he could no longer suppress his anxiety. On a trip to Washington to visit his Uncle Joe Hamilton, then working for the WPA, he wrote a letter to President Roosevelt requesting an interview. What he had in mind was to propose a scheme, based on an idea of Ed Ricketts's, to counter the effects of the powerful and efficient German propaganda machine.

John had not remained long at the ranch after his and

Carol's return from the Mexican expedition. During his stay in Hollywood the previous December, he had tentatively agreed to write the narrative screenplay for a documentary film on the poor but proud peons of a remote village in Mexico confronted by the introduction of modern medicine. On the Sea of Cortez expedition, the *Western Flyer* had put in at various ports along the Mexican coast and John had witnessed the extent to which the German government was using Mexico to disseminate its Nazi propaganda throughout the Americas. He traveled to Mexico City in May to join the movie company that was forming there to film the documentary and saw further evidence of the vastness and seriousness of the German propaganda effort. It was this that compelled him, on his trip to Washington in June, to try to get an audience with President Roosevelt. He believed that Roosevelt should be warned of Germany's obvious designs on the Western Hemisphere.

Roosevelt saw Steinbeck and listened to him outline a plan that called for the movie and radio industries to be mobilized to subvert the Nazi propaganda machine and to develop a mass resistance to German intentions in Central and South America. Steinbeck offered to drop everything else he was doing and organize the mobilization himself. Roosevelt expressed gratitude for Steinbeck's concern but failed to act on his proposal. Nevertheless, Steinbeck's first venture into the halls of high power gave him a sense of political self-importance that he would cultivate with increasing gusto in the months and years to come.

He returned to Los Gatos in early July and spent the rest of the summer there, interspersing his stay with visits to Pacific Grove to consult with Ed Ricketts on the book he was intermittently writing about their voyage. One of Ricketts's other visitors was Dr. Melvyn Knisely, chairman of the anatomy department at the University of Chicago. Ricketts introduced Steinbeck to Knisely, and the two developed a quick friendship based on their similar anxieties about the German threat to international peace. When John explained the plan he had brought to Roosevelt, Knisely mentioned an idea of his own. The idea was for the United States to scatter great sums of counterfeit German money throughout the world so as to undermine the value of the deutsche mark and weaken Germany's economic grip on Europe. Steinbeck thought the idea exemplary and once again sought an appointment with Roosevelt. The audience was granted in September. Once more Steinbeck traveled to Washington, this time with Knisely, and presented the plan. He later claimed that the President was enthusiastic about it but was dissuaded by Henry Morgenthau, the secretary of the treasury. In any event, it was never adopted. Steinbeck did not realize that Roosevelt had been giving him his time only to humor his wife Eleanor, who had become an advocate of Steinbeck the author.

Although the vast majority of the population of the United States was complacent about the government's position on the hostilities in Europe late in 1940, war fever had broken out among the country's intelligentsia. Steinbeck had caught the fever,[31] and when he returned to Mexico in October to work on the actual filming of the village documentary, it intensified. Several of the people connected with the production were Jewish, and from them he heard tales and rumors of the anti-Jewish measures that were being implemented in Europe by the Nazis. From the film's director he received an education in the entire history of anti-Jewish pogroms in Europe — a history of which he had been unaware. He experienced deepening embarrassment about his own German heritage, and his views about Jews underwent a rapid, sympathetic change.

John had hoped to obtain for his friend Max Wagner the job of narrator on the Mexican documentary, but the producers deemed it necessary to engage a star for the narration in order to sell the movie. By then Steinbeck had confessed his love for Gwen Conger to Wagner and had commissioned him to "look after her" on his behalf until he could sort out his relationship with Carol. He continued to press the producers to hire Wagner, but they continued to hold out for someone who was better known. Steinbeck left Mexico at the conclusion of filming in November and stopped in Hollywood to personally press his case for Max. He renewed what had by now become his affair with Gwen, but was still unable to procure the narrator's job for Wagner. He finally agreed to Spencer Tracy. But he returned to Los Gatos and Carol laden with tense remorse over his affair and his failure to procure for Wagner, who was bothered by heart problems and a drinking habit, the career break he so desperately needed.

By the beginning of 1941, John's affair with Gwen had begun to dominate his life. He had devised a mail and telephone subterfuge so that he could communicate with her from the ranch without Carol's knowledge, and he was in almost daily touch with Gwen through December and into early January of 1941. To him, Gwen was, as he said to Max Wagner, "everything Carol isn't." Where Carol was cold, possessive, dependent and excruciatingly orderly, Gwen was warm, giving, free spirited and adventurous. Where Carol's attention to John was dour, almost matronly, Gwen's was cheery and girlish. Besides, Carol had already taken on the look of middle age, whereas Gwen exuded youth and sexuality from face to shapely leg. Approaching the age of forty, still nagged by a chronically aching back that robbed him of the mobility and grace of his youth, and conscious of the way both the years and his physical pain were exaggerating his already uncomely features, Steinbeck had reason to be grateful that he had found Gwen.

He returned to Hollywood in mid-January to wrap up his writing work on *The Forgotten Village,* the title given to the Mexican film.[32] Back at the ranch a week later he and Carol, who was enduring a severe case of flu, had another furious dispute. John went to Pacific Grove to begin writing the final draft of the "Sea of Cortez" book. He was motivated to finish it as quickly as possible because both Pat Covici and Elizabeth Otis in New York had reported that the sales of his previous books had fallen off, and they were anxious for something new. John assured them that "Sea of Cortez" wouldn't sell — it would be too heady and philosophical for readers who expected another "story" — but he would write it anyway. In the meantime, Covici had arranged for Viking Press to publish a book of photographs from the filming of *The Forgotten Village* with captions by Steinbeck. John had at first objected, saying that the book was nothing more than a promotional stunt for the movie. But then he agreed, in the hope that the book would guarantee the success of the film.

Steinbeck engineered a truce with Carol at the beginning of February and persuaded her to go to Hawaii on her own for two months to recover her health and reflect on their marriage. While she was away he mixed his work on the "Sea of Cortez" manuscript in Pacific Grove with brief trips to Hollywood to see Gwen and to discuss the filming of *The Red Pony* and *Tortilla Flat*, which had been purchased by MGM. Writing on "Sea of Cortez" went slowly. Steinbeck was trying to distill all of his and Ricketts's complex notions about nonteleological thinking into an intelligible theory and then illustrate it by writing the book in a nonteleological manner — that is, as a piece of scientific observation and reporting. It was the toughest book he had ever set out to write, and as he struggled with its conceptual complexity he grew gloomier and more frustrated. The Gwen-Carol conflict remained a constant distraction.

When Carol returned from Hawaii at the beginning of April, she seemed revitalized and changed. It was obvious to John that she had used the time to take stock of her own problems, had consciously worked on repairing whatever defects she had been able to identify in herself, and had come back with optimism and hope in her heart of salvaging their marriage. She even suggested that they sell the ranch, since John got little joy out of it and was much happier in Pacific Grove and Los Angeles.

Carol's generosity, and her blithe assumption that life

could go on as if nothing had happened, merely sharpened Steinbeck's antagonism toward her. Yet because he knew that she was operating from an ignorance of what was really in his heart, he pitied her as well. The loyalty he felt he owed her he could not make materialize, which expanded his guilt. Finally, in a rush of remorse, he told her of his affair with Gwen Conger.

Steinbeck was so astonished by her reaction to the news that he was at a loss as to what to do next. Instead of the histrionics he expected, Carol took his confession with calm and announced that she would not let him go. There followed a month of nerve-racking indecision while John continued to try to write "Sea of Cortez." When he couldn't, Ed Ricketts took up some of the burden and thus became Steinbeck's coauthor in fact as well as fiction. Finally John left Carol in the Eleventh Street cottage and purchased another small house nearby. He began to see Gwen again. And then he was sure. He told Carol he wanted a divorce.

Carol was now beginning to feel the humiliation of her situation. She nevertheless refused John's request. Believing that he would get over his "infatuation" and would profoundly regret the breakup of their marriage, she traveled to New York to enlist the help of Pascal Covici and Elizabeth Otis in getting John to "come to his senses." Covici and Otis felt as loyal to Carol as they did to John, but neither wished to be thrust into the middle of the marital dispute. When it became clear to Carol that John was obdurate in his desire for divorce, and when she learned that Gwen had moved into John's new Pacific Grove house, she decided to remain in New York. She was still sure John would tire of Gwen, but she could not return to Monterey while her rival lived openly with her husband.

Carol's departure and Gwen's arrival relaxed tensions enough to allow Steinbeck to plunge back into his work on "Sea of Cortez." He wrote for long stretches during the days and spent the nights introducing Gwen to his life and friends on the Monterey Peninsula. He finished "Sea of Cortez" at the end of June, and a month later, after making revisions with Ed Ricketts, sent the final typescript to Viking Press. Almost immediately he began to think about what he would do for his next fiction work. He had consulted with Toby Street on what his hoped-for divorce would cost him. He learned that in order to shed Carol, given her obstinacy, he would probably have to buy himself out of the marriage with all the money he had. Whatever he wrote next, it would have to be for money, not love. He put the Los Gatos ranch up for sale and was dismayed to discover that there were no buyers at the price he wanted. When he lowered the price there was still little interest.

There was no doubt of it as summer turned to fall: John and Gwen were deeply in love with one another and wanted to get married and have children. Steinbeck commissioned Toby Street to persuade Carol, who was still in New York, to enter into divorce proceedings, and then to act as the lawyer for both of them in arriving at a financial settlement. John began to lose his remorse over Carol. Instead he developed a healthy abhorrence of her and rechanneled his anxieties into keeping the impatient Gwen content.

In his travels about Monterey during the summer of 1941, John became involved in a number of speculative conversations with people who were concerned about what would happen to the town if the United States entered the war. With a great show of knowledgeable authority, he contended that Germany was in the process of establishing a large Bund south of the border so that when war broke out, the Nazis could gain control of Mexico and use it as a staging area to invade the Gulf and West coasts of America. Many agreed with him (there was little common concern at the time over a direct Japanese threat to the U.S.), and out of the discussions an idea planted itself in Steinbeck's mind for his next work: a story of a coastal town like Monterey invaded by a foreign enemy. As the idea grew, his attention shifted to the method he would use. Anticipating the need to write something that would make as much money as possible, he thought back to *Of Mice and Men,* his novel-cum-play, which had been a source of income from two simultaneous media, book and stage production. By September, he had decided to write the invasion story in the same form — a novel that could be simultaneously performed as a play.

As he worked into the summer on the new novel, he learned that his film *The Forgotten Village* was running into censorship problems due to some of its graphic scenes of Mexican village life. John had invested a good deal of thought and writing emotion in the project and had even applied a generous dose of his and Ricketts's nonteleological theory to the screenplay in an attempt to revolutionize documentary-film methods. Up to then the standard method of the sociological documentary had been to examine large masses of people and their interaction with events. Steinbeck felt that the method was ineffective because viewers, like readers, tended not to be affected by mass phenomena. The effect of five thousand people killed by an earthquake was invariably less on the average person than that of a single person killed in an automobile accident. So in putting together his screenplay for the film, he had focused on a single impoverished village family. He believed that by seeing what happened to the family, and identifying with it, audiences would be better able to empathize with the social tragedy of the entire society of Mexican villagers. The technique had worked in the fictional *The Grapes of Wrath.* Steinbeck and his collaborators believed that it would have similar power in a nonfiction movie.

Because of its censorship problems, the film had been blocked from release during the summer of 1941. In September, in the company of Gwen Conger, Steinbeck traveled back to Washington to enlist Eleanor Roosevelt's help in getting *The Forgotten Village* cleared. She agreed to take up his cause. From there, he and Gwen went to New York so that he could do some further work on the problem. He also wanted to introduce Gwen to Pat Covici and the people at the McIntosh and Otis agency.

His arrival in New York brought a burst of unpleasant publicity. Gossip columnists took note of the fact that while he was traveling with Gwen, his wife Carol had been seen around town on her own. Steinbeck refused to comment on the matter, but Carol gave a few interviews in which she admitted that her husband had left her for another woman. She claimed that she was in New York "to fight for my man." She told the *New York World-Telegram* that she expected John to give up his paramour and return to her. To all observing eyes it was apparent that he had no intention of doing so. Steinbeck finally announced that he would remain in New York to work on his new play in novel form. The resultant public laundering of their marital problems so embarrassed Carol that she fled New York and returned to California. Shortly thereafter, through the offices of Toby Street, she agreed to begin negotiations leading to divorce.

Steinbeck was equally irked by the publicity. Seeking to protect Gwen from being pestered by newspaper reporters and photographers, he arranged for them to retreat to the country estate of Burgess Meredith, about forty miles north of New York in Rockland County. The two settled in at the Meredith place and John began to write the play-novel about the foreign invasion of a fictional coastal town and its effects on the natives and invaders alike. The play was to be a political statement — a warning to America about the war that Steinbeck believed was inevitable. Writing out of his Teutonic shame, he decided to make the invaders Germans so as to give the United States a taste of what would happen if the country did not abandon its complacency and face the reality of Nazi intentions.

With the manuscript half done in mid-November and most of the marital publicity having died down, John and Gwen moved back into the city and took up residence at a small, out-of-the-way hotel recommended to them by Henry Fonda. During his trip to Washington two months earlier on the censorship matter, John had agreed to write radio scripts for a small federal agency just formed by the Roosevelt administration to condition the country to the prospects of war. The administrators of the agency, which would grow into the Office of War Information, wanted Steinbeck in Washington. But he managed to postpone his commitment there on the ground that finishing his book-play was more important to getting Americans to understand the need to stem the Nazi tide than were radio broadcasts.

Steinbeck had settled on a title for the play-novel: "The Moon Is Down." In a literal sense it referred to the dark-of-night conditions under which the German invaders materialized in the town that was the locus of the action. Symbolically it was meant by Steinbeck to represent the extinguishing of moral illumination and enlightenment wherever Nazi Germany spread its iron tendrils. He tried to refrain from preaching in the work. Instead he applied to his characters and action the techniques of *The Grapes of Wrath* and *The Forgotten Village*. He shaped the town and townspeople of "The Moon Is Down" to function as a microcosm of the country as a whole so that audiences and readers would recognize that what transpired in his fictional seaport could happen anywhere in America. Despite his efforts to keep from blatantly moralizing — to counter the temptation, he wrote the manuscript with a view to further incorporating his nonteleological theories into this technique — it was a preachily cautionary tale. His moralistic impulses clashed constantly with his nonteleological ones throughout the writing. The "what might be" and "what ought to be" of the political impulses that motivated him engaged in a continual struggle with the "what is" of his new nonteleological imperative. As a result, when he finished "The Moon Is Down" in late November, he was profoundly dissatisfied with it. The scene and the mood were finely crafted, but the characters were mechanical and symbolically fleshless. The imbalance was a reflection of his failure to resolve the artistic conflict within himself. He had set out after *The Grapes of Wrath* to write in a new form. His resolve had not successfully filtered through *Sea of Cortez* and *The Forgotten Village,* neither of them being representative of his real artistic impulse to fiction. With "The Moon Is Down" being his first attempt at fiction after *The Grapes of Wrath,* he had fallen back into the old form. Although he had infused it with his new vision, to his disappointment it hadn't worked.

The euphoria of his relationship with Gwyn[33] and his urgency to publish another popular book may well have clouded his critical judgment, however, for he immediately delivered the manuscript to Pat Covici and made sure that Annie Laurie Williams circulated it among theatrical producers for a stage production. *Sea of Cortez* had recently been published, and although the initial reviews were thoughtful and for the most part favorable, commercial interest in the Steinbeck-Ricketts treatise on nonteleological theory appeared to be scant.

In early December, while John awaited reaction from Covici and others to the manuscript of "The Moon Is Down," the Japanese attacked Pearl Harbor and the nation went to war. Steinbeck's theme in "The Moon Is Down" seemed ever more urgent.

❋ ❋ ❋ ❋ CHAPTER TWENTY-THREE

Immediately after Pearl Harbor, the Roosevelt administra-
tion instituted a program whereby thousands of Japanese-
American families, most of them living on the West Coast,
were rounded up and herded into detention camps as security
risks. The action provoked a hue and cry from civil-liberties
advocates. Except for wondering about the fate of the Japanese
gardener he and Carol had employed at the Los Gatos ranch,
Steinbeck, in New York, was curiously quiet about it.[34]

Theatrical producer Herman Shumlin had taken an option on the play version of "The Moon Is Down" while Steinbeck was still writing it during the late months of 1941. But
when it was finished he did not care for its politics and decided
not to stage it. Another producer, Oscar Serlin, acquired the
rights and hired the politically active Lee Strasberg to direct.
Strasberg, a founder of the Group Theater, which had gained
fame for its staging of leftist dramas by playwrights such as
Clifford Odets, worked with Steinbeck through January and
February of 1942 on the playscript. The Viking Press at the
same time prepared to publish the work as a short novel.

Steinbeck in the meantime awaited the call from Washington to undertake what he hoped would be an important mission in the war effort. Having just turned forty, he was not yet eligible for the draft and, with his back problems, would probably never be. His few flying lessons and boat journeys having been his only experience with the machinery of war, he had little to recommend him for a direct officer's commission in any of the military services. He nevertheless hoped to be given an assignment in intelligence work. Toward this end he seized on another idea given to him by Ed Ricketts.

Ricketts had reminded John, shortly after Pearl Harbor, that the files of their Monterey laboratory contained a number of prewar international biological journals in which Japanese marine scientists, reporting on their studies of marine life in the waters of the Japanese-occupied islands of the Western Pacific, had inadvertently supplied a great amount of useful data concerning the undersea terrain surrounding the islands. Since charts, soundings and other information about these waters were unavailable to the United States and other Allied nations, Ricketts thought that they would be of important intelligence value to the U.S. Navy as it planned its Pacific war campaigns. Steinbeck agreed and made a concerted effort to bring the existence of the reports to the attention of the government, hoping in the bargain to secure, finally, a job for himself. Naval Intelligence showed a brief but passing interest, and the hoped-for summons from Washington remained unforthcoming.

The Moon Is Down was published as a book by Viking in February and was an immediate success, outselling even *The Grapes of Wrath* during its first few weeks in print. By March, when it became clear to Steinbeck that the government was not as anxious to have him as he thought it should be, he and Gwyn moved to a rented house in a pretty, residential enclave called Snedens Landing on the shore of the Hudson River, twenty miles north of New York. *The Moon Is Down* opened as a play in April. Although poorly received by the critics, most of whom found it hackneyed and naive in its characters, murky in its theme, and trite in its patriotism, the play enjoyed popular approval and would run to packed houses for several months.

Steinbeck's cash flow continued to be favorable, but he knew that it would not remain so for long. Toby Street had sent him a list of Carol's financial demands, which called for him to settle a large amount of money on her in exchange for the divorce, and also to give her half interest in all the future proceeds from the books he had written. John, anxious to be free of her so that he could marry Gwyn, reluctantly consented.

July finally brought Steinbeck a war assignment — not up to his expectations, but an assignment nevertheless. He was appointed a "special civilian consultant" to the Army Air Corps. His job was to go to Hollywood and write a movie script that would glorify the Air Corps' role in the war and help the War Department extract increased appropriations from Congress to expand the corps' strategic bombing capability. He was promised that once he finished the motion picture, he would be commissioned as an officer into the Air Corps uniformed intelligence branch.

John and Gwyn left Snedens Landing for Los Angeles in September. They arrived to find the movie industry on a solid war footing. Dozens of pictures were being slapped together under government auspices to glorify and propagandize America's military activities. Hollywood was awash in popular writers operating under the same commission as Steinbeck. He found the cynicism of most of them repugnant. Having long tried to warn the country of the Axis menace, he had put aside his exceptions to the inequalities in the American system of capitalistic democracy and given full rein to his patriotic impulses. Steinbeck renewed some old acquaintances, but for the most part he and Gwyn socialized little after they settled into another rented house in Van Nuys. John spent the fall writing his assigned script and consulting on the filming of the movie, which was to be called "Bombs Away: The Story of a Bomber Team."

When his work was finished in December, John waited for the order that would send him back to Washington to take up his duties in Air Corps intelligence. While he waited, he received a call from Darryl Zanuck at Twentieth Century Fox asking him to write the screenplay for a picture that the U.S. Maritime Commission had requested the studio to make about the merchant marine. The merchant marine had suffered monumental losses transporting military cargoes to England and Russia and was, in the government's eyes, badly in need of a morale booster. Such a movie might provide it, and the studio had assigned no less a director than Alfred Hitchcock to direct the film. All that was needed was an original and quickly-put-together screenplay.

Steinbeck agreed to the request, contingent on his being called to his intelligence duties after he had finished, and in January 1943 he commenced meetings with Hitchcock to work out a story. Hitchcock had more than a passing interest in the project. It was partly due to the exploits of the American merchant marine that England, his native country, had been able to stave off the Nazi evil. He wanted to make not only a war-morale movie but, like Steinbeck, a picture that would enshrine the courage and determination of mankind in resisting fascist aggression. As a consequence, the two applied themselves to the project with fervid devotion.

The result was *Lifeboat*, a movie that was to become a minor classic of Hollywood filmmaking. In conceiving and writing the script, Steinbeck returned to the symbolic and allegorical forms he had abandoned after *In Dubious Battle*. His lifeboat and its quarrelsome passengers were meant to represent a world adrift, but he presented them to the viewer with the nonteleological detachment of a museum curator. Indeed, the *Lifeboat* script was the closest Steinbeck ever came to successfully applying his nonteleological ideas to a work of fiction. This was undoubtedly due to the fact of his collaboration with Hitchcock — a master at maintaining a disinterested distance from the characters of his films — and due to impressions the movie version of *The Grapes of Wrath* had had on him. Steinbeck realized that in the film medium, the camera was the story's narrator. In showing the audience exactly what it wanted the viewer to see, it made whatever it focused on, whether in the foreground or background, larger than life. In riveting the viewer's attention to the objects it selected, it imposed a point of view on him that was much more immediate and urgent than the descriptive words of a novel.[35]

After finishing the *Lifeboat* script in February, John and Gwyn returned to New York. Steinbeck, frustrated by the failure of the Air Corps to put him to work as promised and still champing to be involved in the war, approached several New York newspapers with a proposal that they send him overseas as a war correspondent. The *New York Herald Tribune* agreed to the idea, and he spent much of the next month getting clearances from the War Department. In the meantime, Toby Street informed him from Monterey that Carol's divorce action had been taken up by the court and would be acted upon any day. John and Gwyn thereupon began to make definite plans to be married.

The divorce came through at the end of March. In anticipation of it, John and Gwyn traveled to New Orleans, where they were married in the house of a friend, Lyle Saxon. On their return to New York, John's delight was increased when he learned that the War Department had finally accredited him as a war correspondent for the *Herald Tribune*. He hoped to leave for London immediately, but it was June before he was able to work through the red tape and obtain a travel priority.

Steinbeck's marriage to Gwyn, although it was to last for four years, was for all practical purposes over at its very beginning. Gwyn had suffered John's transient life without complaint during the previous two years. But upon their marriage she expected them to settle down into a home in New York so that she could establish the comfortable and secure life Steinbeck had promised her. He had, of course, already experienced the transformation of his first wife from an apparently happy-go-lucky single girl into a domestically focused housewife, but had convinced himself that Gwyn's desire for the trappings of home and hearth was different. Gwyn for her part could not understand John's desire to leave her immediately for the war zone when he was under no obligation to do so. As soon as they were married, she began to press him to abandon his war-correspondent plans and remain in New York. He testily dismissed her entreaties, and they spent most of April and May wrangling over his forthcoming trip. When he finally had to make it clear to her that his writing had priority over all other things, she angrily predicted that if that were the case, their marriage would be short-lived. It was with a sense of bitter foreboding, then, that Steinbeck boarded a troopship for London in June of 1943. Gwyn remained in the New York City apartment they had rented on their return from Hollywood. To mollify her, John promised that he would stay abroad no longer than a few months, and that when he returned they would settle down permanently in New York. Gwyn had grown to love the city. John was unsure of his ability to work there, but found its life and people increasingly agreeable.

Steinbeck arrived in London at the beginning of July and for the rest of the month acclimated himself to England, sending off dispatches to the *Herald Tribune* about the British war effort and the rapidly expanding presence of American forces there. He tried to locate his sister Mary's husband, William Dekker, who was a combat officer in the Fifth Army and was thought still to be in England. He also had a reunion with Max Wagner, who was serving as an enlisted man with the American army. And he did some casual historical research on the fabled lands that were said to be the setting of Arthurian tales he had grown up on. While in Hollywood the previous winter, he had engaged in long talks with several prominent filmmakers about the Arthurian legends and had further developed the theory, first explained to him by Edith Mirrielees, that the "western" of American literature and movies was rooted in the very same impulses that created the knightly legends of medieval England. Nineteenth-century American cowboy culture was similar if not identical to the culture of the medieval Arthurian Round Table in its moral outlines, Steinbeck had proposed. He would like someday to write a western movie script that would draw on the theory. While he was in England rummaging about in the Round Table lore, he also reinforced his ambition to one day "translate" the *Morte d'Arthur* of his childhood from its archaic English into the modern American idiom.

August brought Steinbeck to the heat of North Africa to cover the aftermath of the American-British invasion of that continent. While there he learned that his brother-in-law, Bill Dekker, had been reported missing in action after the Fifth Army's invasion of Sicily. In September he finally got to see some of the combat action he had been craving to cover — almost too much. He took part, with a number of other correspondents, in the invasion of the Italian mainland at Salerno, and on the fourteenth was trapped with an army unit in a terrifying German mortar and cannon barrage. His need to experience the war had indeed been fulfilled.

By November Steinbeck was back in New York and suffering the effects of his Italian experience, in blackouts and blinding headaches. Gwyn was astonished to see the extent to which he had aged. Between his constantly nagging back and his head episodes — later diagnosed as the result of burst eardrums suffered in Italy — he was in almost constant pain. His already craggy face was more deeply creased, and his hair and mustache had thinned and started turning gray.

Coming back by boat to New York, Steinbeck could well say, as he did in a letter to a friend, that he had "done the things I had to do and I don't think any inner compulsion will make me do them again." It was time to return to his real work, the writing of fiction, and during the voyage home he had begun to outline a novel. The idea for his new project did not come out of the blue. The critical failure of *The Moon Is Down* had provoked Steinbeck, over a period of time, into a reexamination of the novel-play. Most of the critics agreed that the primary reason for the work's failure derived from the fact that Steinbeck had gone far out of his own experience for his material. The leader of the German force that invaded the town of the story had been singled out for particularly harsh criticism as a character whose shallowness and falsity were symptomatic of the entire work's. Initially, Steinbeck had rejected the critics' insights, blaming whatever weaknesses the work had on his having written it so rapidly and under the disruptive conditions occasioned by the newspaper publicity over his failed marriage. Reflecting later on it in Europe, though, he grudgingly conceded that the critics might have been right. During his hair-raising experience in the Italian offensive, he had vowed to return to writing what he knew best if he only survived the battles that raged around him. On the way home he decided to honor the vow, ignoring speculation in New York that he would return bent on writing a war novel.

Moreover, during Pat Covici's visit with Steinbeck in Pacific Grove shortly after the publication of *Tortilla Flat*, John had taken his editor to see the book's locale and had also shown him around Monterey's Cannery Row. Ever since, Covici had urged him to write a novel in the style of *Tortilla Flat* about Cannery Row. Ed Ricketts had made similar suggestions, insisting that John could effectively use the milieu of the noisy, colorful Monterey waterfront to further refine his nonteleological writing techniques. The inhabitants of Cannery Row could serve as specimens for Steinbeck's scientifically shaped literary experiments to further isolate and examine the qualities in man that make him different from other animals.

The idea for a novel about Cannery Row had thus been

gestating in Steinbeck's mind for a number of years. On the boat back from the war he had begun to plan the work. Settling into an apartment on the far East Side of New York with Gwyn, he wrote sporadically on the book, his headaches and blackouts seriously impeding his progress. So too did his concern about Gwyn. He had come home to a loving reception by her and during the first few nights had unknowingly conceived a child. But as 1943 became 1944, with winter sitting heavily on New York and his head and back pains weighing even more heavily on his spirit, her resentment at his absence and at his seeming disinclination, now that he was back, to set up house resurfaced. Steinbeck also suffered an intensifying spiritual melancholy over his experiences in the war zone and the disappearance in combat of his brother-in-law, Bill Dekker. Coupled with his attempts to launch the "Cannery Row" novel, it caused him to fall into days-long bouts of depression which had the effect of shutting Gwyn and her mundane social and domestic ambitions out of his life. January began between them on a tempestuous note. Gwyn, who had been a liberal social drinker for as long as John had known her, took refuge from the hurt and disappointment she felt in an increase of alcohol. Steinbeck, himself an occasionally heavy drinker, followed suit.

Matters brightened somewhat during a long trip to Mexico in February and March. John's affection for Mexico and Mexican culture had now become ritualized. He hoped that a sojourn there would not only shake him of his depression but also revitalize his and Gwyn's relationship. While there, he renewed acquaintances with a number of Mexican movie people who had been involved in *The Forgotten Village*. Conversations led to a proposal that he write another screenplay to be filmed in Mexico. One idea he had was based on a folktale he had heard during his voyage with Ed Ricketts four years before and had written about in *Sea of Cortez*. The legend was about a boy from an Indian fishing family near La Paz who finds a massive pearl. Dreaming of the fortune that awaits him, he goes to sell it only to have the buyers try to cheat him. When he refuses to sell, others try to steal it by beating and torturing him. The boy soon realizes that instead of providing him with the fortune that would free him from the drudgery of his life, the pearl has enslaved him. To become free again, he hurls it back into the sea. The tale was to serve as the seed from which "The Pearl" would grow.

Steinbeck left Mexico in April after concluding an agreement with his friends to write the picture for an otherwise all-Mexican production later in the year. When he and Gwyn arrived in New York, they learned officially what they had already concluded: that Gwyn was pregnant and would have the child around the end of July or beginning of August. The news gave them both a renewed spirit of optimism about their marriage. John settled down to spend the summer on his "Cannery Row" novel and the two gave up drinking, Gwyn because of her pregnancy and John for moral support.

The next few months passed uneventfully, although as time went on and John got into his book, the strain crept back into their marriage. It was an underlying tension, much of it due to the return of Steinbeck's alternating black moods and incommunicativeness, some to Gwyn's by-now compulsive, middle-class preoccupations with domesticity and the prospect of having a child.

The baby, a red-haired boy, was born August 2, 1944. They named him Thom. The unusual name was arrived at, according to some, because of Gwyn's interest in numerology. Shortly after the birth, John persuaded Gwyn to move back to California. In writing the "Cannery Row" novel, thematically the most ambitious of his works so far, he had grown distracted by New York and felt cut off from his material. California would be a much better place to raise Thom, he argued, promising Gwyn a house of her own in Monterey. Gwyn was unenthusiastic about living in Monterey, a town she cared little for. She preferred the Los Angeles area, where she had friends.

John was beginning to think seriously about another

novel that had been growing in the back of his mind for some time, however. It was the big novel about the Monterey Peninsula and the Salinas Valley, one that would incorporate and synthesize all that he knew, that would be the climax of his writing life (which others already thought *The Grapes of Wrath* to have been) that would possibly even be his masterpiece. He was a long way from writing it yet. He would have to carry out extensive on-the-scene historical research, and he convinced Gwyn that only by resettling in Monterey would he be able to do his research and at the same time recapture his feel for the region.

In September John finished the "Cannery Row" manuscript, which he had decided to entitle by that name, and handed it over to Covici at Viking Press. In October, Gwyn flew to California with the baby. Driving a secondhand station wagon purchased for the purpose of carrying household goods, John followed by road.

❄ ❄ ❄ ❄ ❄ ❄ ❄ ❄ ❄ *Part Three*

❋ ❋ ❋ ❋ CHAPTER TWENTY-FOUR

Upon his arrival in Monterey, John learned that a property he had long admired was for sale, and he immediately bought it. Four blocks from the waterfront, it consisted of an old Mexican-style house surrounded by an extensive garden and an adobe-brick wall that he thought would afford them the privacy he needed. Gwyn liked it and busied herself with redecorating plans. She and John moved in with their infant son in November.

While Gwyn continued to work indoors, John spent a great deal of his time sprucing up the landscape. And, of course, he took pains to revive his personal relationship with Ed Ricketts. The "Cannery Row" novel he had just finished was in a way an homage to Ricketts. Its main character, Doc, was intimately drawn from Ricketts, and the book's fundamental story was based on the camaraderie that Ricketts had with many of the real-life characters of Monterey's fish-cannery and fishing-pier district. In writing the novel, John had endeavored to follow a strict nonteleological method in examining the lives of a group of largely inept, uneducated but ambitious characters; he had used the principal technique of *The Grapes of Wrath* — main chapters, which carried the basic narrative along, laced with "interchapters" meant to punctuate the action with Steinbeck's "scientific" observations on the characters — to tell the story.

The literal story of the novel focused on the efforts of a group of poor Cannery Row characters to throw a party in honor of their friend Doc, the owner of a biological laboratory. By relating the various machinations they undertook to organize and pay for the party, and by showing with humor and compassion the ways in which they themselves consistently thwarted their goal, Steinbeck constructed a dense allegory about the folly of misplaced human ambition. In this case the ambition was the achievement of respectability, a theme he had tackled with less artfulness twelve years before in *The Pastures of Heaven* and had focused on in several of his later short stories. And while depicting the striving for respectability and conformity as that which undermines the creative potential of mankind, Steinbeck made the "Doc" of his novel a symbol of all he found desirable in man. In his view Ed Ricketts, by his very lack of the spurious social ambitions Steinbeck deplored, was able to live a much more creative and fulfilling life than those who sought security and respectability. Through the character of Doc, Steinbeck in the end forged his novel as a tribute to men such as Ed Ricketts.

But on a deeper psychological level, the book was an effort to revitalize his own faltering striving for uniqueness. Since the success of *The Grapes of Wrath*, Steinbeck had felt a growing dismay over his own entrapment in the symbols of security and respectability. He had left Carol precisely because of her sudden preoccupation with these symbols, but now found himself even more involved in them as a result of Gwyn. In the "frog-hunt" chapters of the novel, which would soon become famous, Steinbeck alluded to his feelings about his

life. Mack and his fellow Cannery Row inhabitants travel up
the Carmel River to hunt for frogs, hoping to sell them to Doc's
laboratory and use the proceeds to pay for the party they are
secretly planning for him. Their hunt is interrupted by a land-
owner, "the captain," who, after some debate, is enticed by
Mack to invite them to his house.

The captain, a respectable but bored and unhappy man
attached only to a sick dog, is obviously Steinbeck himself. He
indirectly complains about his wife, who's not home much.

> The boys stood in the kitchen and gathered quick impressions.
> It was obvious that the wife was away — the opened cans, the
> frying pan with lace from fried eggs still sticking to it, the
> crumbs on the kitchen table, the open box of shotgun shells on
> the bread box all shrieked of the lack of a woman, while the
> white curtains and the papers on the dish shelves and the too-
> small towels on the rack told them a woman had been there.
> And they were unconsciously glad she wasn't there. The kind
> of woman who put paper on shelves and had little towels like
> that instinctively distrusted Mack and the boys. Such women
> knew that they were the worst threats to a home, for they
> offered ease and thought and companionship as opposed to
> neatness, order, and properness. They were very glad she was
> away.[36]

Later, after Mack and his cohorts include the captain
in their drunken frog hunt, he is so grateful for the fun that
he tells them not to worry about having accidentally set fire to
his wife's curtains.

> He felt it was an honor to have them burn his house clear
> down, if they wanted to. "My wife is a wonderful woman," he
> said in a kind of peroration. "Most wonderful woman. Ought
> to of been a man. If she was a man I wouldn' of married her."
> He laughed a long time over that and repeated it three or
> four times and resolved to remember it so he could tell it to
> a lot of other people. He filled a jug with whiskey and gave
> it to Mack. He wanted to go live with them. . . .[37]

Finally, the captain falls into a drunken sleep and the Cannery Row revelers leave. As they do, Mack says, "I got to thinkin' about his wife comin' back and it gave me the shivers. . . . From the way things are pannin' out, it looks like Doc is a pretty lucky guy."

Mack's allusion to Doc is not meant exactly as a comparison to the captain, but it can easily be taken as such. Ed Ricketts is Doc and Steinbeck is the captain. Doc is a thoughtful but free spirit, whereas the captain is loaded down by the trappings of landowning respectability and a contentious, domestically obsessed wife. In the comparison Ed Ricketts is lucky, and Steinbeck, by implication, unlucky. Although the derogatory "wife" references (and these are only a few of many in the book) were primarily meant to depict his relationship with Carol Henning Steinbeck, they were also applicable to the shape his relationship with Gwyn Conger Steinbeck had taken. If anything, she was proving even more demanding in her thirst for security and conformity than Carol had. Her compulsion had turned into what John viewed as an obsession, once their child was born and they had moved into the new house in Monterey. When he gave Ed Ricketts galleys of the Cannery Row novel to read, the perceptive Ricketts easily recognized the agony of disillusionment his friend was going through. He and John had several private talks about the problem of Gwyn, who had expressed hostility toward Ricketts once she saw how much John admired and depended on him. Ricketts, predicting the inevitable outcome, counseled John to end the marriage early instead of allowing it to drag out as he had with Carol. Steinbeck was tempted. But having released some of his frustration on the subject in the writing of "Cannery Row," and feeling both an intense responsibility for and attachment to his four-month-old son, he vowed to continue to try to make the union work.

Cannery Row was published at the beginning of 1945 to great popular acclaim, although most reviewers judged it as a case of Steinbeck's repeating himself to ill effect. During January and February John worked on the filmscript of his Mexican story, tinkered about house and garden, and sought to maintain a semblance of harmony in his relationship with Gwyn despite her increasing preoccupation with unreliable decorating contractors and baby nurses. His problem with Gwyn was exacerbated by the fact that *Cannery Row* was taken by many in Monterey as another of Steinbeck's insults to the city. As a result, Mrs. Steinbeck was received in many places with a cold shoulder and a deliberately uncooperative attitude. Steinbeck even found that a number of old friends had begun to speak uncharitably about him.

In April he went to Mexico — first to Mexico City and then to Cuernavaca — to participate in the making of the movie from his script, which he called "The Pearl." Gwyn and Thom later joined him and they remained there through July. While working on the filming of "The Pearl," he was approached with a proposition to write another all-Mexican movie about the life of the Mexican social revolutionary Emiliano Zapata. He agreed in principle, but demanded assurances that there would be no government interference or censorship — Zapata, although dead, was still a figure of great controversy in Mexico.

Also during his long Mexican sojourn, he revived an earlier idea for a new novel. Toward the end of his stay, as he grew bored with the filming of "The Pearl," he began to sketch it out, first as a screenplay, then as a book. It would be an expanded version of *Lifeboat,* but without the interfering emendations of Alfred Hitchcock. About a busload of Mexicans and tourists making their way from one town to another, the story would provide a fertile garden, he thought, for an allegory about the distastefully changing society of America. Many critics had dismissed *Cannery Row* as a harmless, unimportant diversion on Steinbeck's part. According to his own later claims, that was all he had set out to write — a pleasant antidote to his unpleasant war experience.[38] But now he ached to come back with a significant book, a book as important as *The Grapes of Wrath*, but one that would establish him not just as a social critic but as a visionary — a writer capable of affecting not only a segment of American society but the society as a whole. He called the nascent novel "The Wayward Bus."

When the Steinbecks returned to Monterey at the end of July they found the general community attitude toward them even cooler than before. The stay in Mexico had once more had a salutary effect on John and Gwyn's relationship that carried over for a few months after their return. In October, after Gwyn had once more become pregnant, their relations again deteriorated. Gwyn suffered considerably during the beginning stages of the pregnancy and grew increasingly resentful of John's preoccupation with "The Wayward Bus" and his long visits with Ed Ricketts. She also became bored with the house and carried every insult she experienced or imagined at the hands of Montereyans back to John. By November her complaints over the disorder and disharmony of her life had become a litany and she pleaded for a return to New York, or at least to Los Angeles. Steinbeck, still willing to mollify her, finally agreed. In December he sold the Monterey house and the three of them moved back to New York. There they bought and renovated adjoining old brownstones on East Seventy-eighth Street, a rather dismal side street between noisy Lexington and Third Avenues. As far as Steinbeck was concerned, he was finished with California and its narrow provincialism for good. He began to see New York in a different light than before. Suddenly it was attractive — "truly the great city of the world . . . unique" — and he resolved that he would make it his permanent home. Not a little of his resolve derived from his rapidly growing fascination with the important, wealthy and celebrated people who made up the constantly energized society of East Side New York, and from the self-esteem he felt at their acceptance of him as one of them.

He, Gwyn and their son moved into their house in March

of 1946, but John's darkening mood over his marriage failed to improve. At Gwyn's insistence he was relegated to a writing workroom in the basement of the house, surrounded by cement walls and exposed pipes. He accepted her dictates without protest, still trying, with a second child on the way, to keep their marriage together. The more he tried, the more contempt Gwyn showed for him.

Much of Steinbeck's depression over his marriage was mixed and confused with a growing anxiety about his writing powers. It was difficult for him to tell where one worry left off and the other began, or if in fact they were interrelated, the one shaping the other. All he knew was that in almost six years he had written little of consequence. Since *The Grapes of Wrath* he had done only two works of literary fiction — *The Moon Is Down* and *Cannery Row* — and both had been manhandled (probably justly so, he had begun to believe) by the critics. He had been able to rationalize his lack of quality productivity by blaming it on the war and his diversion into movies.

But now he was eager to restore himself to a place of critical acclaim. His efforts so far in the writing of the "Wayward Bus" novel had been dissatisfying, however. He had started out in Mexico with a clear and incisive perception of what he wanted to do in the book. Once started, though, it had gone along only in fits and starts. He could again attribute this to his last few unhappy months in California and the move back to New York. Yet now there was no more room for rationalization. Once settled into his basement studio, he had to face the cold reality of writing and sustaining his vision. And it wasn't working out as he had originally conceived it. He pressed on nevertheless during the spring of 1946, using the task of solving the "Wayward Bus" problems as a shelter from his marital dissatisfaction. Neither the book nor the marriage came any easier, despite his efforts.

A second son was born to Gwyn on June 12, 1946, and the boy's arrival served to lighten Steinbeck's gloom for a while.

Gwyn brightened as well, and after a series of long talks the two worked out what they hoped was a formula for compatibility. They celebrated their resolve with a trip together to Denmark and Sweden in the fall, leaving Thom and their new son, named John Steinbeck IV, behind in the care of a nursemaid. Away from home, and with John not writing, their relationship had always seemed to prosper. They realized that it was only when they were surrounded by domestic concerns that it veered back toward disintegration. They returned from Scandinavia in November with an agreement to use this knowledge to improve their relations.

Steinbeck's good intentions were fated to fail, however. Before leaving for Scandinavia, he had struggled to the end of a first draft of "The Wayward Bus" and had left the needed revision of it for his return, thinking that a few weeks away from the manuscript would sharpen his faculties enough to quickly whip it into shape. But when he returned and read it through he was dismayed by the extent of the work it needed. He realized that he hadn't even come close to fulfilling his original intention. Instead of committing himself to a laborious rewrite of the book, still without any certainty of improving it (for perhaps the original idea was defective), he decided to shelve it.

Pat Covici wouldn't hear of it. Almost anything that Steinbeck wrote now — certainly fiction — was bound to have a large sale. He prevailed upon John to publish the book as it was. Steinbeck, probably for the first time in his literary life, succumbed wholly to expediency. In reluctantly acceding to Covici's wishes, though, he suffered an attack of private remorse which, coupled with his intensified anxiety over his writing skills, immediately cast a new pall of gloom over his life at home.

Covici was not disappointed in his commercial expectations for *The Wayward Bus,* as the novel's title remained when Viking Press published it in February of 1947. Advance sales were far beyond those of anything Steinbeck had previously published, and even the initial superficial reviews were for the most part favorable. Steinbeck, much to his surprise, was back on top of the popular literary heap again. Although he distrusted the reception *The Wayward Bus* received, it somewhat soothed his guilt at having permitted its publication in what to him was an unrealized and defective form. It did little, however, to ease his worry over his writing skills.

Except for Covici and Elizabeth Otis, no one knew of Steinbeck's dismay. He himself kept up a front, and when more thoughtful critics began to take *The Wayward Bus* apart, a few months after its publication, as being another failed and even meretricious effort, he was properly indignant. His indignation was not deeply felt, however. As he later admitted in a letter to Roland Dickey, director of the University of New Mexico Press, which had published a critical review of his works,[39] "A few of the critics saw through *The Wayward Bus* and they were right. It was a paste-up job and I should never have let it go out the way it did."

His chagrin notwithstanding, Steinbeck was happy to accept an assignment from the *New York Herald Tribune*, on the basis of his revived celebrity, to go to Russia during the summer and write a series of reports on the Soviet Union. After the publication of *The Wayward Bus*, he had begun to think even more seriously about the "big" California novel that had been in the back of his mind for so long. He viewed it in terms of being the ultimate test of his ability to still write an important novel. But the closer he came to formulating it, the more reluctant he was to embark upon it. Like an aging athlete grown conscious of his diminished strength, he was afraid to put his skills to the test. Instead he welcomed less challenging writing ventures. He used the *Herald Tribune* offer to postpone having to face what he was certain was the reality of his staled literary power.

During the spring, in preparation for his journey to the

Soviet Union, which he would make with famed war photographer Robert Capa, Steinbeck immersed himself in Russian history and Marxist-Leninist theory. One day he absently leaned against a wrought-iron railing on a small outdoor balcony at the rear of the second floor of his Seventy-eighth Street house. The railing had been removed a short time before to facilitate the moving of a piano into the house. It had been sloppily replaced by workmen and, when he leaned against it, gave way. He tumbled into the courtyard below, shattering a knee. The injury required hospitalization and resulted in a postponement of his Russian trip. When he did set out in July, first visiting Paris with Gwyn, he required a cane to get about. Gwyn returned to New York while he embarked from Paris with Capa for Russia. When he returned to New York in October, he was immediately aware of a sharp difference in Gwyn's attitude toward him. It was an indifference — toward his ideas, his insights, his talk. At first he couldn't figure it out. But it made him uneasy. Gwyn had even grown indifferent to the children. And she had taken up drinking in a serious way again.

What Steinbeck didn't know was that while he was gone — and even before, while he was in the hospital with his damaged knee — Gwyn had been involved in an extramarital affair with a man several years younger than herself. The man had "jilted" her a few days before John's return from Russia. This was the reason she was drinking so heavily. Although unaware of the situation, Steinbeck himself took to drinking more heavily. In between bouts of unhappy drunkenness and arguing with Gwyn over her own drinking, he produced his Russian articles for the *Herald Tribune*. The articles were laden with portentous political aperçus and gained Steinbeck somewhat of a reputation as a savant in foreign affairs — a reputation he was pleased to cultivate. As one of the few Americans to have visited repressive, hostile, postwar Russia, his impressions quickly gained currency in American academic and political circles. For the first time in a long while he felt that he had something important to say and was being listened to.

It was a change from his wartime days when he had been so eager to share his schemes for waging war only to be ignored or rebuffed. The *Herald Tribune* articles, which would be published in book form the following year under the title *A Russian Journal,* were the start of a new life for Steinbeck, a life in which he would put political observation and activism before his continuing but uncertain literary ambitions.

Despite his sudden political prominence, he still pondered his confrontation with the long-postponed test of his insecure literary powers. He faced the test with increasing trepidation at the beginning of 1948. The film *The Pearl* had been released while he was in Russia and a book version had also been published, but neither had enhanced his critical reputation. On his return from Russia, then, he was met not only by his wife's troubling behavior but by a fresh onslaught of negative critical opinion about his capacities as a writer. Some critics even suggested that he was living on his *Grapes of Wrath* eminence and was betraying the public with more recent jury-rigged performances. Would Steinbeck ever write another book worthy of his past? went the question. Could he?

John resolved to do so. And the subject he chose was the "big" novel he had been reserving. He was at once enthusiastic to get to it and fearful. Enthusiasm finally conquered fear at the beginning of 1948. He left Gwyn and his sons in New York to return to Salinas and Monterey to conduct the research he had intended to do two years before. The novel would be his monumental work about the Salinas Valley. In fact "Salinas Valley" is what he decided to call it as he prepared to immerse himself in it.

Gwyn did not take kindly to his almost-three-month stay in California. Still drinking regularly — indeed, on the verge of becoming an alcoholic — she was plainly bored with John and let him know it in no uncertain terms. John, a man who usually struck out with high vindictiveness at insults and other types of offensive behavior directed at himself, was extraordinarily patient with her when he returned to New York.

Although he could see the breakup of their marriage coming, he held on to the slim hope that what Gwyn was going through was merely a stage, perhaps even a temporary illness, and that she would soon get hold of herself if for no other reason than the children's sake.

Steinbeck had himself to blame for much of his trouble with Gwyn. It was true that after their marriage she had suddenly manifested an unexpected desire for a comfortable, secure life. But John himself had undergone a change. As he gradually discovered that people of achievement — whether in government, show business or the literary world — admired his work and accepted, even sought, his company and conversation, he was able to shed most of his outward shyness. He had gained an expanding measure of confidence in himself as a social being and actively began to seek the approval of his peers. As he did so, his social as well as literary celebrity enlarged and his circle of friendships rapidly widened. He consciously began to shape his character and personality to sustain the at once sagacious and witty persona he had presented in his books, and this led to a degree of personal pomposity and overbearingness that Gwyn found increasingly infuriating. It was John's very shyness and introspectiveness — his social helplessness, in a sense — that had attracted her to him in the first place. Now he was neither shy not introspective, at least on the outside. Instead he was expansive, garrulous and imperious. Since these new characteristics were practiced and recently acquired and did not come naturally to him, they had the effect of blurring her original image of him. In her view he had changed enormously over the previous five years. And the change was intolerable, mainly because he no longer took her seriously. He treated her merely as the mother of his children and reserved the sharing of his thoughts and emotions for his friends. When he did deign to talk to her, it was usually in terms of criticizing her shortcomings and demanding that *she* change.

What Gwyn didn't know, or couldn't perceive, was that John was acting as he did as a way of insulating himself from his increasingly nagging anxiety about himself as a writer. Symptomatic of the anxiety was his inability to get started on the Salinas novel — "What I have been practicing to write all my life," as he said to a friend at the time. He continued to postpone it even after his research trip to California. He took to insisting that more extensive research was necessary to sharpen his memory and solidify his material for this most important of all his writing endeavors to date. Yet what he wanted to write about in the novel was basically what he had lived and experienced of central California during his youth. The experience and memory of the valley were as much a part of him as his ungainly features. Why did he need to conduct extensive research, unless the invented imperative of research was an easy excuse for not having to face the actual writing task?

On his return to New York in April, Steinbeck had further reason to postpone the start of the Salinas novel. His balcony accident of the year before had inflamed a varicose-vein condition with which he had lived for some time. Back in New York, he went into the hospital to have it remedied surgically. Then, shortly after John's release from the hospital, Ed Ricketts died in Monterey after his car was struck by a Southern Pacific Railroad train at a grade crossing. Ricketts's death devastated Steinbeck in two ways. He had not only lost his most valued friend, but his philosophical and literary mentor as well. He quickly realized that most if not all of the best work he had done derived from the force of Ricketts's inspiration and mental discipline. He had consulted closely with the biologist on the planning of the Salinas novel during his recent stay in Monterey. To Steinbeck, he was "the greatest man I have known and the best teacher." When he returned from the funeral, John seriously doubted his ability to continue with his plans for the novel.

And, of course, there remained the disturbing distraction

of Gwyn. John had taken a room at New York's Bedford Hotel in order to escape the oppressive atmosphere of the Seventy-eighth Street house. As he wrote to Toby Street in May, shortly after Ricketts's funeral, "I've got trouble coming and bad trouble." What had happened was that Gwyn, out of some perverse sense of spite, and in a drunken state, had cheered the news of Ricketts's death, declaring that John would no longer have his friend to lean on. She accused him of having been a parasite on Ricketts's mind and having appropriated Ricketts's ideas as his own. "Now your public will see you as you really are," she is said to have hissed at John in inexplicable fury, or words to that effect. "Without him you are nothing. You will now be the failure you were before you met him, and I don't want to be married to a failure!"

John made a brief, agonized trip to Mexico in June on his own to confer about the Zapata movie, which seemed to be taking financial shape. When he returned to New York, Gwyn had packed up the children and left for Los Angeles to stay with her family. A few weeks later John received a letter from her lawyer demanding a divorce and a huge financial settlement. He meekly agreed, glad to have her weight off his shoulders but despondent at the prospect of losing his sons. In August he signed a separation agreement preparatory to a Nevada divorce. Then, disgusted with New York, he packed up his few remaining belongings and moved back to the little family cottage in Pacific Grove.

✳ ✳ ✳ ✳ ✳ CHAPTER TWENTY-FIVE

It was another deeply melancholic time for Steinbeck. Shattered by the spitefulness and ruthlessness of Gwyn's sudden actions, unable to write, he nervously settled down once again at Pacific Grove and allowed himself to plunge into a long period of self-pity and almost hermitlike inactivity. Gwyn obtained her divorce at the end of October, along with a large portion of John's financial resources. All he ended up with was the right to have his children visit him for a month each summer. His bitterness was sharpened by his conviction that he was the blameless victim in the marital disaster. And being back in Pacific Grove, without Ed Ricketts to nurture his creativity, he suffered a profound sense of déjà vu; it was as though his life were starting over again. But it was a life without promise — or even anticipation.

He went to Hollywood during the first week of November 1948 to check on the filming of *The Red Pony,* and then traveled on to Mexico with Elia Kazan, "Zapata's" screen director, to scout locations. He had originally gotten to know Kazan through Lee Strasberg, who had directed the stage version of *The Moon Is Down*, and his actress-wife Paula. The Zapata film project had not been able to make its way financially as an all-Mexican venture, and Steinbeck had brought the proposal to Kazan. Like Strasberg, Kazan was a proponent of the Stanislavski method of acting, then coming into vogue, and a veteran of the Group Theater. A founder two years earlier of the Actors Studio, he had enjoyed several recent film and stage successes and had practically been given carte blanche by Hollywood on future movie projects. Steinbeck liked the diminutive, fiercely intelligent Greek, and Kazan liked him. When John brought the "Zapata" idea to him, he quickly agreed to present it to several Hollywood studios as a directorial project for him. Twentieth Century Fox thereupon commissioned him to make the film from Steinbeck's screenplay.

John, his mind elsewhere, was able to accomplish little on the Mexican trip and returned in a black mood to Pacific Grove in mid-November. Mildred Lyman, a member of the McIntosh and Otis staff, had visited him in Pacific Grove prior to his trip to Mexico and was distressed by what she saw. "He is deeply disturbed and frightened about his work," she wrote back to the New York office. ". . . The fact that so much time has elapsed without his accomplishing anything to speak of worries him a great deal. He has a defense mechanism which is constantly in action and it is hard to get behind that. . . . He is in a strange mood and has very peculiar ideas of women these days. . . . I presume he will come out of it but my only hope is that it will not be too late as far as his work is concerned."[40]

Steinbeck's "peculiar ideas of women" revolved about his deepening conviction, once the immediate shock of Gwyn's divorce action had worn off, that he had been had by her. He projected his growing contempt of her onto women in general and deliberately went off on a binge of fornication with every willing woman he could find on the Monterey Peninsula, often coldly insisting on paying for his pleasure. After a while, he narrowed his abhorrence to American women. "Part man, part politician," he wrote to a friend, "they have the minds of whores and the vaginas of Presbyterians. They are trained by their mothers in a contempt for men. . . . The American girl makes a servant of her husband and then finds him contemptible for being a servant. American married life is the doormat to the whorehouse. Eventually they will succeed in creating a race of homosexuals."[41]

During this time Steinbeck worked haphazardly at his "Zapata" script. But then, on November 23, 1948, he learned that he had been elected to membership in the exclusive American Academy of Arts and Letters. In line with his changed image of himself, he had begun to appreciate honors and prizes, much in contrast to his pre-forties days, and this was a significant one. It also had the effect of nudging him out of his spiritual anomie and turning his attention back to the task of disciplined, purposeful writing. His election he viewed as something that came to artists and writers whose productive careers had been adjudged as having come to an end. Although he had had fears about this with respect to himself, the academy's action whipped him into a determination to prove it untrue. He therefore hastened to finish the "Zapata" screenplay so that he could finally get to the long-postponed Salinas book.

Steinbeck started out of the doldrums at the beginning of 1949. "I'm getting the old ecstasies back sometimes," he wrote in January to Pat Covici. "It is a pleasure to write again. . . . I was getting deeply worried thinking my will power was gone." And in February: ". . . another year and the first one I haven't dreaded for a long time. I just finished my day's work. . . . As always when I am working I am gay. I'm terribly gay. . . . I don't know what has happened but the dams are burst. Work is pouring out of me. I guess maybe I am over the illness."[42]

The "work" was the Salinas Valley novel. He had rid

himself of the ghost of Ed Ricketts, had managed to submerge his hurt and anger over Gwyn, had finished the "Zapata" script and given it to Elia Kazan for revision suggestions, and had set out to write the Salinas novel under his own discipline and on the wings of his inspiration alone. His resolve intensified after a brief trip to New York to see his sons. He would no longer be writing for Ed Ricketts's approval. But he had to write the Salinas novel for someone. He settled on Thom and John IV. He would write it for them so that they would one day know their father and learn of their paternal heritage. He returned to Pacific Grove and attacked the novel with heightened zeal. He worked diligently on it well into the summer, when his concentration was diverted by the arrival of Thom and John IV for their first stay under the visitation provisions of his divorce.

His sons, however, were not the only people to ruffle his concentration at this time. On his last trip to Los Angeles, he had met Ann Sothern, the Hollywood actress. He took a liking to her and had invited her to spend the Memorial Day weekend, at the end of May, in Carmel. She accepted the invitation on the condition that she be permitted to bring along a friend. The friend was Elaine Anderson Scott, the wife of the actor Zachary Scott. Steinbeck readily assented.

Despite his current views on American women and his vocal resolve never again to become attached to one, he promptly fell in love with Elaine Scott. An attractive, husky-voiced blonde from Texas, she was thirty-four to John's forty-seven. She was also, presumably, happily married to Zachary Scott, and the mother of a daughter. Notwithstanding all this, Steinbeck did little to conceal his infatuation with her. By the second day of their visit he was audaciously flirting with her. She surprised him my responding in kind. Soon he learned that her twelve-year-old marriage to Scott, whom she had met when both were drama students at the University of Texas, was not all that happy. Two weeks later he drove to Los Angeles for further script conferences with Kazan on the "Zapata" film. Elaine Scott was apparently agreeable to John's suggestion of an assignation at his hotel, and thereafter the two carried on an intensifying romance. At the beginning it was conducted mostly at a distance. John had to spend the rest of the summer in Pacific Grove with his sons, while Elaine was constrained to conceal the affair from husband, daughter and friends. As he had with Gwyn Conger nine years before, John established a secret channel of communication with Elaine, code names and all, through Max and Jack Wagner. Being in love again, according to a missive he sent to Elaine at the time, was "like the crazy time of children. . . ."

Their relationship was cemented late in July when Elaine, accompanied by Joan Crawford, who acted as her cover, again visited Monterey. John and Elaine agreed that as soon as she could get out of her marriage to Zachary Scott they would marry. She had to be careful, though. Should her husband learn of her romance with Steinbeck prematurely, she might have difficulty retaining custody of her daughter. Despite the fact that he had often held forth in high moral tones about sexual fidelity and conjugal honor, Steinbeck felt few qualms about cuckolding Zachary Scott.

The romance brought him to a dead stop in the writing of the Salinas novel. After returning his sons to Gwyn in September, he went back to rewriting the "Zapata" script while he waited for Elaine to find the opportune moment to ask Zachary Scott for a divorce. The moment came in early November. Unfortunately, Elaine was forced to confess her relationship with John, which threatened to complicate and delay the hoped-for divorce. It did.

During the early years of her marriage to Scott, while he was struggling to build an acting career in New York, Elaine had established a career of her own as a production assistant and later as a stage manager for the illustrious Theatre Guild, which produced several new plays every year. An outgoing woman, she was vitally involved in the theater and knew well hundreds of important theater and movie figures. During the early stages of their romance, John had mentioned his ambition to write once again for the Broadway stage in a combined novel-play form. He claimed to have recognized the faults of his last venture, *The Moon Is Down,* and thought he could still duplicate his earlier success with *Of Mice and Men.* Elaine, always interested in being involved in new plays, encouraged him. Out of their discussions came ideas for a number of play-novels. After he finished his "Zapata" rewrite, John began to develop one of them — in a way as a tribute to his love for Elaine. His idea was based on the theme of the ancient poem *Everyman,* and his intention was to resolve the eternal transcendentalist paradox: that man must be both self-fulfilling and selfless at the same time. Since Ed Ricketts's death, Steinbeck had gradually weakened in his intellectual commitment to his phalanx theories and to the nonteleological approach to literature. In *Everyman* he saw a way out of the transcendentalist dilemma — that by working to realize one's individual potential, one serves not only oneself but mankind as well. He resolved to state this idea in the new play-novel Elaine encouraged him to write. As it took shape in the form of an allegory during the last weeks of 1949, he gave it the title "In the Forests of the Night."

As a result of her estrangement from Zachary Scott, Elaine had moved, with John's blessing, to New York with her daughter Waverly. John closed up the Pacific Grove cottage and followed at the end of November, taking a small apartment in East Fifty-second Street. Elaine soon made him a busy participant in the New York theatrical and social whirl, and he grew to like it even more than he had when he had lived with Gwyn. He explained the main reason for his new enthusiasm in a letter to his friend Bo Beskow, the Swedish portrait painter: "I am not as shy and frightened as I was. I realize now what did it. Both of my wives were somehow in competition with me so that I was ashamed of being noticed. I am not a bit ashamed now. Elaine is on *my* side, not against me. The result is that I am more relaxed than I have ever been."[34]

During the spring of 1950, Steinbeck socialized extensively in Elaine's company while he finished the "Everyman" work, wrote a brief memoir of his friendship with Ed Ricketts for a new edition of *The Sea of Cortez,* and dabbed at the put-aside Salinas novel. Still unable to get into the latter with renewed concentration, he began another play-novel after completing "In the Forests of the Night."

For the summer he and Elaine rented a house in the familiar surroundings of Rockland County and took his sons — now six and four — there for their annual visit. The theatrical team of Richard Rodgers and Oscar Hammerstein, aside from being the creators of memorable musical shows, also engaged in producing and had arranged to stage the play version of "In the Forests of the Night." They urged John to change the title to "Burning Bright." Steinbeck agreed and spent much of his writing time during the summer preparing the acting script. He also conferred with Elia Kazan on last-minute changes in the "Zapata" script, which was about to go into production as *Viva Zapata!* with Marlon Brando starring in the title role. John was enormously proud of the script and confident of the film's success. He was equally confident that "Burning Bright" would be a Broadway hit under the Rodgers and Hammerstein banner.

He was correct on the first score. The popularity of the movie, however, had more to do with Brando's idiosyncratic acting style and Kazan's bravura camera work than it did with the screenplay. Although about Mexicans in Mexico, the movie nevertheless had a recognizable amount of Steinbeck's sensibility and personal experience in it. One of the principal supporting characters, an American journalist who tracks Zapata in his revolutionary crusade through the Mexican back country, could have been Steinbeck himself fifteen years earlier following the revolutionaries and migrant farmworkers who populated *In Dubious Battle, Their Blood Is Strong* and *The Grapes of Wrath*.

On the second score he was to be bitterly disappointed. *Burning Bright* was taken to Boston in early October for try-outs and John was soon summoned to make extensive fixes. It opened in New York two weeks later to disastrous reviews and closed shortly thereafter. Steinbeck lashed back at the critics in an article in the *Saturday Review of Literature* entitled "Critics, Critics, Burning Bright."[44] In it he publicly vented his long-stored distaste for reviewers, although he readily admitted privately that *Burning Bright* "was not a good play. It was a hell of a good piece of writing but . . . it just did not play." He had no one else to blame. "I had the best possible production, the best direction. . . . And the producers are the finest people I have ever met."[45] A few years later he would confess to a college professor that the play was too abstract and filled with blatant preaching. "The audience was always a step ahead of it." Indeed, the play version of *Burning Bright* was awkward and self-conscious in the extreme in its writing, its theme confused and without conviction. Had one been aware of the personal demons Steinbeck was wrestling with vis-à-vis the future of his writing powers, one would have perceived the work as a manifestation of that struggle. And one might have guessed that Steinbeck was on the verge of losing it. When published as a short novel, *Burning Bright* was again dismissed.

The pleasurable experience of castigating the fraternity of critics in the *Saturday Review* was like that of a man enjoying a party before having to face up to the harsh realities of the next morning. Once *Burning Bright* was behind him, he dropped the second play-novel he had been toying with and returned his attention to the prospect of proceeding with the Salinas novel. The prospect dismayed him even that much more. Yet driven by the inspiration of his feelings for Elaine —

he expected their marriage to take place at the end of December; he was in the process of buying a townhouse for them in East Seventy-second Street, and he would soon run out of money if he didn't produce a commercial book — he went back to daily work on the novel. He was still agonizingly tentative in his approach to it, however.

Elaine's divorce from Zachary Scott became final December 1, 1950, and she and John were married on the twenty-eighth at the home of Harold Guinzburg of Viking Press, with Pat Covici serving as best man. John had no misgivings about marrying again except for wry ones. He was more than ever convinced that in Elaine he had found the "real" woman he had been deprived of in his previous marriages. "Not like American women," he boasted about her. "She doesn't want to be a man."

After a wedding trip to Bermuda, John and Elaine moved into the Seventy-second Street house with Elaine's daughter Waverly. John by now was determined that New York would be his permanent home and had abandoned all thoughts of returning to California for any reason save visits. His sons still lived with their mother in the Seventy-eighth Street house and he was able to see them regularly.

Steinbeck had been talking for a long time to Elaine of his big novel about the Salinas Valley. Most of what he had accomplished on it thus far, however, had been little more than sketching and note taking. When they moved into the Seventy-second Street house it was in the process of being redecorated. Elaine quickly established a pleasant working room for John overlooking the street and urged him to get on with the novel. On February twelfth, using the right-hand pages of a large, clothbound ledger, he began writing, setting aside his previous false beginnings and starting all over again. By now its eventual form had taken a general shape in his mind. It was to be a family saga set in Salinas, with his own family and his own California experience the basis of the story's material. He began with his grandfather, Samuel Hamilton.

Steinbeck was of two minds and two moods as he began "The Salinas Valley," as he continued to call it. On the one hand he felt comfortable, even optimistic about the book's ultimate virtues, because he was returning to the old-fashioned kind of storytelling that had produced his best and most admired work. And he would be writing out of his own direct experience in the bargain. On the other hand he wondered whether he would be able to sustain reader interest in a story based on his family. It was his desire to trace a history of human struggle against nature and portray the contribution of the hardiness of the human spirit to survival and betterment. The theme would be embodied in a barely fictionalized history of the Hamilton family after its arrival in California from Ireland at the time of the Civil War. As he had grown older and various forebears had passed away, John had developed a reverence for the family that verged on the romantic and idealized. He realized that his view was retrospective, however, and that in fact his forebears had been far more prosaic than heroic in their values and aspirations. Could he transform this rather ordinary group of real-life people into the larger-than-life characters that superior fiction demanded? Had he still had faith in his writing powers, he would have had no doubt of his ability to do so. As it was . . .

As he prepared to begin writing, he struck on an idea that might help him nourish his failing confidence and overcome the complex of craft problems posed by the novel. It was not exactly a new idea, since in previous manuscripts he had jotted notes to himself on such matters as character motivation, plot continuity, interior logic and speech patterns. But now he decided to carry out the practice in a more deliberate and organized way. Hence, while writing the novel proper on the right-hand pages of his ledger, he reserved the left-hand pages for an ongoing commentary about the work's progress. It would be like the log of a ship's voyage. And since his log would be more disciplined and compelling if addressed to someone, he chose Pat Covici to be the recipient of his notations. When he was ready to hand the finished manuscript to Covici, he would also give him the log so that the editor might better appreciate the dynamics of the novel. Moreover, it would be a long, slow novel in the writing. Daily entries about its progress would provide John with the discipline and impetus to keep at it and not shrink from it when the going got tough, as he knew it was bound to.

Steinbeck worked with disciplined regularity at the book through the spring of 1951 in his town-house study, writing almost daily for five or six hours and entertaining or being entertained with Elaine at night. By April he knew that the Hamilton family saga was not sufficient to his thematic goal. But instead of letting it throw him, he created a second family and endeavored to fuse its rather dark and harrowing history with the brighter one of the Hamiltons. As he worked, he felt a growing surge of the power and intensity he feared he had lost. That, coupled with his enjoyment of Elaine and their life together, made him happier and more vigorously outgoing than he had ever been. In June he and Elaine moved to a rented house on the island of Nantucket for the summer, bringing Thom and John IV, now nicknamed "Catbird," with them.

Steinbeck continued on the book without a break. Once under way, the story took on a strong biblical character as the saga of the second family, the Trasks, gained precedence over that of John's original protagonists, the Hamiltons. Although the book was still rooted in the Salinas area, John decided on a new title as a result. Referring to the opening verses of chapter four of Genesis, he renamed it "East of Eden."

The summer idyll of isolated work and rest was marred only by the increasingly errant behavior of the two Steinbeck boys. Their father saw in their often disruptive deportment the symptoms of a discontent that he had long hoped to help them avoid. The disparity between their lives with their mother Gwyn, who had grown sharply indifferent to their problems while cultivating her own social life, and their lives with their father, who was attentive and alternately indulgent and stern, had become a source of psychic confusion to them. Elaine, who was having her own problems with Waverly, tried her best to respond positively to John's sons but found their conduct as troublesome as her daughter's. She was from the old school of child rearing and made demands on the two boys that more often than not only heightened their rebelliousness. At first John backed her up. But as the summer wore on he increasingly withdrew from the situation, leaving it to Elaine to deal with the boys and occasionally chiding her for what he claimed were her excessive disciplinary demands. Tension over the behavior of his sons and her daughter would become a lasting source of dispute and distraction between them during the coming years. Happily for both, the disputes would be counterbalanced by their enduring love and companionship. It was true; John had finally found a woman who met his hopes and expectations. He would remain devoted to her for the rest of his life, as she would to him.

The Steinbecks returned to New York in September, and John, nearing the end of "East of Eden," intensified his labors. He finished the first draft in November. At a quarter of a million words, it was the longest work of fiction he had ever written. The time span of the story ran from the Civil War to the end of World War I. So enthusiastic was he over what he had accomplished, and so sure was he that he had realized his artistic intention in the novel, that he began to plan a sequel, which would continue the story to the present. As he wrote to Bo Beskow upon finishing, he had put into the novel "all the things I have ever wanted to write all my life. This is 'the book.' If it is not good, I have fooled myself all the time. . . . Having done this I can do anything I want. Always I had this book waiting to be written."[46]

Steinbeck spent the next two months on manuscript revisions. Despite Pat Covici's enthusiasm, the first draft received an avalanche of what John viewed as nit-picking criticisms on the part of the editorial staff at Viking Press. Much of it, nevertheless, was justified. Steinbeck had buried and lost a good tight story in the sprawl of his novel. Many at Viking who read the manuscript recommended large-scale cuts and changes to bring economy and unity to the book. John would have none of it. It was as if he equated the rambling character of the manuscript with the complexity and density he believed he had endowed it with. "East of Eden" was to be his magnum opus, and he forbade anyone to tamper with it.

He handed in his final revised draft in March of 1952. Then he and Elaine embarked on a six-month trip to Europe, which he had promised her at the time of their marriage. To help underwrite the trip, John had made a deal with *Collier's* magazine to write about it. And he had arranged for Elaine to be his photographer.

❋ ❋ ❋ ❋ ❋ CHAPTER TWENTY-SIX

A*lthough not his last book,* East of Eden *was the climax* of Steinbeck's artistic life, and a sad climax it was indeed. The book was published in the early fall of 1952 while he and Elaine were still in Europe. Although it did well commercially, Viking Press promoted it as John's masterwork and the serious critics proceeded to treat it with rough condescension. The consensus was that John had clearly reached the end of the creative road and was a writer whose value lay only in the books of his long-distant past. The best that could be said about it was that it was a noble allegory that didn't work. The reason was that Steinbeck, although he continued to write effectively evocative physical description, had lost his talent for characterization. In the members of the Trask family and other characters, he had created papier-mâché figures whose souls lacked life and whose actions lacked logic and believability.[47]

Steinbeck was at first not overly concerned by the critics' reactions. He believed that he had written a controversial book and had armored himself against negative critical comment.

It was only as he cast about for an idea for his next effort that his artistic demons began to haunt him again. What if the critics were right, he thought, and he *had* reached the end of the road? Had they now perceived what he had long suspected?

The critical reception *East of Eden* received quickly discouraged him from following up with its sequel, for he simply could not risk working so exhaustively again for so little critical reward. During his European trip he had been given the idea of turning Henrik Ibsen's play *The Vikings* into a movie to be made in Sweden with Ingrid Bergman. After his return, he worked briefly at this before abandoning it. Then the composer Frank Loesser, whom John had met through Elaine, suggested that they collaborate in turning *Cannery Row* into a Broadway musical.

The notion appealed to Steinbeck, largely due to his ever-widening admiration for the social and creative life of theater people. Also instrumental in his decision to proceed was money. The commercial success of *East of Eden* would keep him solvent for a while, but his new life-style had placed increasing financial demands on him. If *Cannery Row* were successful as a stage musical, it might well become a perpetual annuity as a movie property.

He and Loesser went to work on the project in November of 1952. Soon it became apparent that an adaptation straight from the book would not be feasible — what was needed for a Broadway musical, after all, was a love story. Steinbeck thereupon invented a new tale based on the character of *Cannery Row*'s Doc and shaped the story around his efforts to win a woman — a prostitute well beneath his intellect.

As he and Loesser proceeded with their collaboration into the spring of 1953, Steinbeck decided to convert his new "Doc" story into a novel rather than wait for it to materialize in musical form. He was feeling bitter at the negative reaction in Salinas, Monterey and Pacific Grove to *East of Eden* and decided in the bargain to use the new book to ridicule what he saw as the provincial and pious hypocrisy of the region. He finished the book in November and realized that it was a decided departure for him. Wrting to an old acquaintance at the time, he said, "I've just finished another book on the [Cannery] Row. It is a continuation concerned not with what did happen but with what might have happened to Ed and didn't. I don't seem to be able to get over his death. But this will be the last piece about him."[48]

By writing another story using Ed Ricketts as his principal character, John was clearly hoping to exorcise the dead biologist's residual influence on his literary life. And by writing not about "what did happen" but about "what might have happened," he intended to complete his abandonment of Ricketts's nonteleological theories. He had started to shed them in *Burning Bright* and had continued the process in *East of Eden,* which was criticized for its tendentiously moralistic tone. He was out to prove that he could write good literature without Ed Ricketts looking over his shoulder and guiding him.

Steinbeck entitled his new Cannery Row novel *Sweet Thursday,* and when it came out in 1954 it was roundly denounced as a cheap effort to capitalize on the popularity of the original. More perceptive critics saw in its almost childishly satirical style an artistic petulance and discontent that further reflected Steinbeck's loss of confidence in himself — indeed, the actual loss of his ability. John answered the critics by saying that the book was an experiment with a new technique, but few took him seriously. His talents were clearly in decline and only a work of his former brilliance and cogency could save his reputation. In reality, John was confused and hurt by the reaction. He believed that he had written a poignant story of two characters, opposite in every way, who preferred to endure the emptiness of being together rather than the loneliness of having no one to be with.

Frank Loesser had broken off his collaboration with John, and Rodgers and Hammerstein had taken over the composing chores for the *Sweet Thursday* musical, which they entitled *Pipe Dream*. The show finally reached Broadway at the end of the following year and was received with even more disdain than the novel. By that time Steinbeck was aware of its inadequacies. He had desperately wanted *Pipe Dream* to be a success, but when he saw it in its out-of-town tryouts in New Haven he despaired of its prospects. "We are," he said to Oscar Hammerstein, "in grave danger of mediocrity."

The show closed quickly. All in all, the *Sweet Thursday–Pipe Dream* combination served Steinbeck poorly.

During his six-month *Collier's* trip to Europe, John had gotten himself involved in some heated literary and political exchanges, particularly when traveling through Italy. He had been surprised to learn how much of the European literary pulse was powered by political thought and action, and he was at once fascinated and repelled by the rising influence of the Communist movement in the governments of Italy and France. When he returned in September of 1952, he considered himself more expert than ever on European political affairs. His subsequent articles for *Collier's* reinforced that view, both in his mind and the minds of others. He volunteered to do some writing for the presidential campaign of Adlai Stevenson, who was running on the Democratic ticket against Dwight D. Eisenhower to succeed Harry Truman in the White House. After Stevenson's loss in November, the two quickly became friends. Stevenson promised that he would most likely run again four years later and asked Steinbeck to be ready to help him on matters relating to European affairs in a more significant way then. John took the request seriously and began to immerse himself in the study of recent European history and politics.

After handing in the final manuscript of *Sweet Thursday* at the beginning of 1954, John began planning another long trip to Europe with a view to settling for a time in Paris, which had become Elaine's favorite spot. Their first stop would be in Spain. It was a measure of the changes John had gone through that he remarked, when discussing the forthcoming trip, that "I feel an affinity there. Mexico is a kind of fake Spain." He had gotten California, Mexico, his past, out of his system and had begun to take a peculiarly "New York" view of life. It is quite likely that a major reason for the failure of *Sweet Thursday* was that he wrote it from this viewpoint. In losing his California sensibility — which many who knew him at the time say he did not so much lose as deliberately discard — he lost his sense of place and character that had once made it possible for him to write original and powerful fiction. The disturbingly manufactured characters and action of *East of Eden*, and the even more artificially executed characters and action of *Sweet Thursday*, were indicators of Steinbeck's having lost touch with the material that had formed his art. That he had lost his touch became an ever-increasing source of anxiety to him after *Sweet Thursday* was published. But in all his self-questioning efforts to find it again, he was never able to correlate his loss of touch with his having lost touch. He was happy with Elaine, happy in New York, and happy with the rapidly expanding social and political breadth of his life. His only unhappiness was with his clearly fading power to compellingly draw his readers into his narratives. He would never have thought, however, to trace the problem to his altered life and his more sophisticated outlook. He could only say in passing that "maybe it's impossible for a happy man to be a good writer."

John and Elaine spent most of 1954 in Europe, living for four months in a sumptuous house that they leased in Paris. Steinbeck continued to widen what was now his international social circle. Except for a weekly article for the French newspaper *Le Figaro Litteraire* while in Paris, he wrote little and thought even less about another major and original fiction project. He continued to worry, however, about his future. A letter to Elizabeth Otis from London in September reflected his concern. In it he blamed the style and technique he had developed over the years for his inability to write anything new and worthwhile. He wanted to change his approach to themes and narrative, he said, but his writing style had become so set that it wouldn't allow him to do so. "I want to dump my technique, to tear it right down to the ground and to start all over. I have been thinking of this a lot. I think I have one answer but I have not developed it enough to put it down yet."[49]

Another letter of the same time to Elia Kazan also spoke of his agony. "A whole revolution is going on in me. I talk and talk [about his writing worries] and I don't know whether or not it means anything. I do nothing except short pieces. Good thing. I'm not ready to start yet. . . . It's hard to throw over thirty years work but necessary if the work has pooped out."[50]

When the Steinbecks arrived back in New York at the end of the year, he still did not have the "one answer." John sporadically experimented with a new novel but soon gave it up in frustration. Most of his spare time he spent in renovating a house he and Elaine had purchased near the quaint fishing village of Sag Harbor, toward the eastern end of Long Island. They had briefly rented a house in Sag Harbor three years earlier. The village, vaguely reminiscent of the Monterey–Pacific Grove area of his youth, had appealed to John. When he and Elaine decided to acquire a permanent weekend and summer home outside of New York after their return from Europe, they looked for and found one in Sag Harbor. The house would become an increasingly important part of his life. There are some among his friends who claim that John bought it because he believed the seaside ambience of Sag Harbor would enable him to recapture his fugitive writing powers.

For a while he was sure that it had. After the stage failure of *Pipe Dream* he and Elaine took a vacation in the Caribbean. On their return they moved more or less permanently into the Sag Harbor house. John, still trying to find the "answer" he had alluded to a year and a half before, concluded that he could do so only by experimenting with a new type of fiction. Hence he began to write what he called a "practice novel." He soon became serious about it, however, and during the spring of 1956 worked hard at styling it into the new form he had been seeking. The novel became, and was published a year later as, *The Short Reign of Pippin IV, A Fabrication*. Based on an amalgam of French history that John had picked up during his long stay in Paris, it wove a whimsical fable about a man, Pippin, who declines the opportunity to ascend to the throne of France rather than compromise his principles by failing to tell his people the hard truths they must hear. The tale was in a way a celebratory one for Steinbeck. What he was celebrating was his rejection of the bitterly cynical view of man with which he had started out his writing career in *Cup of Gold*. He no longer believed that the nature of the world and society made it necessary for man to be stripped of his ideals and illusions as he passed from childhood into adulthood. Instead, man was capable of imposing his ideals on the world and retaining the integrity of his principles; it was up to the world to recognize, and benefit from, the noble individual's actions in refusing to compromise.

This was the new theme Steinbeck had been "talking and talking about" and the one for whose expression he had been seeking a new form. The historical narrative had another almost equally important significance for him, however — an intensely current political one. Adlai Stevenson was preparing to mount a second challenge to Eisenhower by once again winning the Democratic presidential nomination. Steinbeck's secondary motive in writing *The Short Reign of Pippin IV*, perhaps even his primary inspiration, was as an homage to Stevenson, for whom as both a friend and political figure Steinbeck had developed an unbounded admiration. The character of Pippin was Adlai Stevenson in historical disguise, as well as, by association, Steinbeck himself. John's kinship to Stevenson was based on his view of the soon-to-be presidential candidate as a man of sterling integrity struggling valiantly and thoughtfully to transform the world from its irrational nuclear-tinged bellicosity into a place of international cooperation and peacefulness. With his own internationalism and political consciousness on the rise, Steinbeck had in his own way committed himself to the same ideal. In order to sustain the validity of the ideal, he had to write a novel affirming man's ability to fulfill his own ideals.

So sharply did John's political concern intensify during the writing of the Pippin book that he decided he must play an active role in the forthcoming presidential campaign. As a result, he sought and received an assignment to cover that summer's presidential conventions for the *Louisville Courier-Journal* and its syndicate. He had met and become friendly with Mark Ethridge, the publisher of the *Courier-Journal*, during his last trip to Europe. Ethridge and his editor in chief, James Pope, were more than delighted at John's offer to report his conventional impressions.

John rushed to finish the Pippin novel prior to embarking on his convention coverage in Chicago and San Francisco in July and August. He was further diverted by preparations being made by Elaine for the wedding of her daughter Waverly, now eighteen. The wedding was to be a lavish and expensive social affair in New York, and John had disturbingly mixed feelings about the virtues of such ostentation. He winced in advance at the criticisms that were bound to be aimed at him. How was he to explain why the author of *The Grapes of Wrath*, the defender of the oppressed, the champion of democratic causes (there were many who still thought of him as a crypto-communist), had consented to sponsor or participate in such upper-crust debauchery?

That Steinbeck mused over the question reflected his continuing concern about his life and work. Had one known of his thoughts, one might have surmised that his writing of the Pippin novel was not so much an effort to express a revised artistic vision as to rationalize the turn his life had taken, along with his corresponding view of the world. In achieving financial security, in aspiring to wide social and political personal acceptance and achieving it, in settling comfortably into the sophisticated and often artificial living environment that was New York — all things that he had formerly professed little interest in — he had betrayed his own fiery artistic principles. The original fire had been reduced to barely glowing embers. As in a self-fulfilling prophecy, the world had forced him, like the Henry Morgan of his first book, to compromise his youthful ideals in order to live comfortably in it. But he was unable to accept the fact that he had unwittingly sold out, that the world had humbled him. Instead he turned his vision of the world around. It was now possible to live in the world and still retain the ideals and hopes of childhood. He wrote *The Short Reign of Pippin IV* to confirm this. In itself it was a childlike self-delusion.

❀ ❀ ❀ ❀ CHAPTER TWENTY-SEVEN

For all practical purposes, the productive creative life of John Steinbeck ended with his Pippin novel. When it was published in 1957 the critics marked it not as an affirmation of Steinbeck's new if slightly suspect optimism, but as the final signal flag of his decline, the denouement of his career. He was not surprised.

He was fifty-five at the time, and his life would go on for another eleven active, varied and superficially contented years. But his interior discontent would continue to build. Coupled with a succession of physical maladies, including a series of light heart attacks, it would turn him into a prematurely petulant old man.

Knowing that *The Short Reign of Pippin IV* was a weak book, and having lost some of his emotional commitment to its subtheme once Adlai Stevenson was so roundly rejected by the electorate in November 1956, Steinbeck made plans to get out of the country again. As a solace for his Pippin failure (for he still needed to work), he decided to fulfill his

long-sustained desire to produce a modern version of the
Arthurian Round Table tales. Once committed, he pursued
the project with an ardor that bordered on obsession. He
spent a good part of the next three years in England and
Europe with Elaine, and a great deal of his money, on archival
and field research into the Arthurian period — this despite the
discouragement of Pascal Covici, who felt that John was wasting
his time on a completely uncommercial publishing venture.
Robert Wallsten, who knew John intimately at the time, opines
that Steinbeck's extended involvement in the project was his
way of circumventing his loss of confidence in his writing
powers. Steinbeck himself defended his absorption in the
project by claiming that "it might teach me to write again,
and what a good and necessary thing that would be." But even
King Arthur defeated him. By 1960 he had abandoned the
venture in midwriting and was telling Elizabeth Otis that he
was truly beginning to feel "that my time is over and . . . I
should bow out."

He didn't, of course. He was still sure he had something
to say, if only he could find a way to say it. Most of what he
wanted to impart was political in nature — a comment on what
he viewed, after three years of steady travel and living abroad,
as the moral corruption of an America made complacent by the
Eisenhower administration, which he had learned to despise
with growing intensity. To him Eisenhower was a symbol
of all that was wrong with America. "How can I teach my boys
the value and beauty of language and thus communication," he
wrote to Dag Hammarskjöld, with whom he had become
friendly, "when the President himself reads Westerns exclusively and cannot put together a simple English sentence."

Out of these and similar feelings, Steinbeck seized on the
idea of writing another novel. In 1958, between stays in England on his Malory research, he had started a novel on a topical
subject in the hope that it would counterbalance his extensive
historical delvings into Arthurian times. He failed to complete

it. What little he did do was in the form of an experiment in the technical use of time. Retaining his interest in the experiment, he decided to continue it in the new novel, setting the story in time that was contemporaneous, to the very day, with the time at which he wrote. For his material he went back to a short story he had written a number of years before, which had been published in *The Atlantic Monthly*. Entitled "How Mr. Hogan Robbed a Bank," it was a brief, wry entertaining tale, told in a detached journalistic style, about how a simple grocery-store clerk plans and carries out a bank robbery. The story was an almost perfect realization of the narrative effectiveness of the Ricketts-Steinbeck theory of nonteleological writing. John was no longer much interested in the non-teleological approach, however. What interested him was the cryptic point he had tried to make by the story — that American society tends to corrupt even the most virtuous and God-fearing of men. He wanted to depict this syndrome in more detail, to at once explore and satirize the reasons behind it. He thus conceived of transforming the short story into a novel about the struggle between virtue and corruptibility. He began writing early in 1960 and worked on the book with an urgency fueled by a mild but alarming stroke he had suffered a short time before. He called it "The Winter of Our Discontent," and as he progressed, his initial enthusiasm about its worth became diluted by deepening doubts.

While Steinbeck was recovering from his stroke late in 1959, Adlai Stevenson suggested that it might be a good thing for him, when he was on his feet again, to make a tour of the country and write a book about his impressions. John had been downgrading the United States to Stevenson. The former presidential aspirant had argued that his friend's derogatory views were unjustified. Stevenson assured John that a tour of the country would prove him right. Stevenson spoke from experience, for twice during the previous eight years he had made such circuits in quest of the presidency.

The attractiveness of the idea grew in Steinbeck's mind during the spring of 1960 as he worked on "The Winter of Our Discontent," particularly the prospect of writing a politically oriented nonfiction book. The idea was well received by Pat Covici, Elizabeth Otis and others he tested it on. During the summer he procured a camper-truck and commenced to outfit and stock it. He raced to finish "The Winter of Our Discontent," but in his haste he cut it off before he could properly complete it. After making some further quick revisions in August, he handed it over to Covici with the remark that he cared little whether it was published or not. His mind was now fully occupied by the adventure ahead.

With his only companion his and Elaine's French poodle, which they had acquired in France eight years before and named Charley, Steinbeck set out on his tour in September. He drove to Maine, then crossed the northern states to the West Coast. From California he went to Texas, then traversed the South and returned home in time to accept an invitation to attend the inauguration of John F. Kennedy in January of 1961. Along the way he kept a log of his trip in the form of letters to his wife. Upon his return, as he prepared to write his book, his cynicism about America was considerably muted.

The accession of Kennedy to the White House buoyed Steinbeck's spirits, not only because of the political promise he perceived in the new administration but because Kennedy had appointed his friend Stevenson as ambassador to the United Nations. John was not offended on Stevenson's behalf that he did not get the job he had hoped for — secretary of state. With Stevenson in New York, Steinbeck would have easy access to him and might even contribute a few ideas to the new administration, through him, on foreign policy. John was now in the country's political mainstream and relished the prospects before him.

After the inauguration, he and Elaine vacationed for a few weeks in Barbados. While there, John mulled over his book, which he planned to call "Travels with Charley in Search of America." Because of the political potentialities he envisioned for himself, he was intent on making the work not just a piece of entertaining reading but a book of political and social wisdom. He wanted it to have an impact not only on the general public, but on the government as well.

On their return to New York from the Caribbean, the Steinbecks discovered that his two sons, now teenagers and boarding school students, had been thrown out of their house by Gwyn. John and Elaine took them in and thereafter the two boys lived with them between stints at several boarding schools. This served as a serious complication in Steinbeck's life, for now he had to become a full-time father. Close to sixty, he was ill prepared and ill equipped for the task. As a result, Elaine bore most of the burden of reordering the boys' confused lives.

The Winter of Our Discontent was published in June to what had by then become the usual dreary reviews. Steinbeck had few expectations for the book and was dismayed — bemused is perhaps a better word — only by the rancor with which it was attacked. It was a trifling work and a sloppy one in the bargain, he realized. He remotely wondered why such a minor effort should draw such heavy fire.

The experience did convince him, however, that unless some miracle occurred he was finished with fiction. Politics and nonfiction (reporting) were now the order of the day. He settled down at Sag Harbor to write "Travels with Charley."

After finishing the book in August, Steinbeck, Elaine, the two boys and a tutor embarked on what John planned as a trip around the world.[51] One of the purposes of the trip was to give Thom and John IV a chance to remove themselves from their continuing personal miseries. The journey began peacefully enough in England in September, but it came to an unhappily aborted end in Greece in June of 1962. They all returned to New York and installed themselves again for the summer at Sag Harbor. Tension remained high between John and Elaine over the boys.

John's discontent with his domestic situation was somewhat eased by the fact that *Travels with Charley* had been published to generally kind if puzzled reviews (some publications reviewed it as a travelogue). The book got a tremendous boost financially though, as did Steinbeck spiritually, when in October it was announced from Sweden that he had been awarded the 1962 Nobel Prize for Literature. Only five other Americans had won the prize before him — Sinclair Lewis, Eugene O'Neill, Pearl Buck, William Faulkner and Ernest Hemingway. Although he had scoffed at the meaning and significance of the prize in earlier years, describing it as the equivalent of a writer's funeral service, he was enormously proud to receive it. While before he had viewed it as marking the effective end of a writer's career and had therefore feared it, he was now aware of and had grudgingly accepted the fact that his own artistic productivity had long ago ended. He joked about the prize and the ceremonies surrounding its formal award as being an elaborate wristwatch of the kind given at company retirement dinners. But he took it with deep seriousness and spent weeks laboring over the writing of his acceptance speech, according to Robert Wallsten.

The speech, which he delivered at the Nobel ceremonies in Stockholm in December, was Steinbeck's valedictory. It was at once thoughtful and properly humble in its conception, graceful in its vernacular, and moralistic in its message — a microcosmic amalgam of Steinbeck's lifework. There was nothing more for him to say.

John Steinbeck lived the rest of his life doing battle with politics, whether at home or while traveling, and with his own failing bodily mechanisms. *Travels with Charley* and the Nobel Prize gave him the political cachet he had long sought. After John Kennedy's death he became an unabashed admirer and confidant of Lyndon Johnson, glorying in his invitations to spend evenings at the White House and taking on unofficial speech-writing jobs for the President. His devotion to Johnson and his inherent patriotism made him a vocal apologist of Johnson's Vietnam military escalations. Only a trip to Vietnam in 1967 to write reports on the war for the Long Island paper *Newsday*, and contemporaneous debates with his sons, who had joined the antiwar movement, would eventually disillusion him.

His disillusion, when it came, would kill his spirit. The America of his fast-aging years was no longer an America he could comprehend. In August 1967, after his return from Indochina, he wrote to Elizabeth Otis that "I have nothing I can or want to communicate — a dry-as-dust, worked out feeling."

While in Vietnam his chronic back condition was severely aggravated. In November he submitted to a delicate spinal-fusion operation that kept him bedridden into February of 1968. In the spring he and Elaine moved back to Sag Harbor so that he could recuperate. At the end of May, feeling useless, he had another slight stroke. In July, he suffered a series of heart attacks and was rushed to a New York hospital. He was released after a while and returned to Sag Harbor, remaining there into the fall while Elaine tried to nurse him back to health. Probably the last letter he wrote was an unfinished one to Elizabeth Otis. Apologizing for the fact that he had written nothing for so long, he said that "my fingers have avoided the pencil as though it were an old and poisoned tool. . . ."

The Steinbecks had sold their Seventy-second Street house and taken an apartment in a high-rise building a few doors away. John Steinbeck died there of a massive heart attack on December 20, 1968. His death came at five-thirty of a wintry afternoon. He was sixty-six years old.

❊ ❊ ❊ ❊ ❊ ❊ ❊ ❊ ❊ AFTERWORD

The reader might wonder what has happened to the various people and places, most important to John Steinbeck, whose fates I have not mentioned in the text.

Carol, his first wife, now an elderly woman, eventually remarried; today she continues to live in California.

Gwyndolyn Conger Steinbeck, John's second wife and the mother of his two sons, died recently in Denver, Colorado. She was an alcoholic at the time of her death.

Thom and John IV, when last heard of, were living in Colorado. John IV wrote a book about coming of age in the Vietnam War years. Called *In Touch*, it was published by Knopf in 1969.

Elizabeth Otis is now a retired literary agent but still looks after Steinbeck's literary estate. She lives outside of New York.

Mavis McIntosh is dead, as is Annie Laurie Williams.

Pascal Covici is dead.

Elaine Steinbeck continues to live in the New York City apartment that she shared with her husband at the time of his death, as well as at the house in Sag Harbor.

Steinbeck's two older sisters, Elizabeth and Esther, have survived him; they live in California.

His sister Mary died several years before he did.

The house in which Steinbeck grew up in Salinas is now a restaurant.

The cottage in Pacific Grove he bequeathed to Elaine Steinbeck.

THE WORKS OF JOHN STEINBECK

NONFICTION (*continued*)

A Russian Journal (*with pictures by Robert Capa*)
The Log from the Sea of Cortez
Once There Was a War
Travels with Charley in Search
  of America
America and Americans
Journal of a Novel: *The* East of
  Eden *Letters*

PLAYS,
A DOCUMENTARY,
AND A SCREENPLAY

Of Mice and Men
The Moon Is Down
The Forgotten Village
Viva Zapata!

❀ ❀ ❀ ❀ ❀ ❀ ❀ ❀ ❀ ❀ ❀ ❀ NOTES

1. Nelson Valjean eventually did write a biography of sorts. Entitled *John Steinbeck: The Errant Knight*, it was published in 1975 by Chronicle Books of San Francisco. The title refers to Steinbeck's career-long preoccupation with the ancient fable of King Arthur and the knights of the Round Table. Valjean's book is more a romanticized account of Steinbeck's early years in California than a full-scale biography.

2. Elaine Steinbeck and Robert Wallsten, eds., *Steinbeck: A Life in Letters* (New York: Viking Press, 1975). Penguin Books (paper), 1976. The book is cited on a number of occasions in this work. Hereafter it is referred to as *Steinbeck: Letters*.

3. *Journal of a Novel: The East of Eden Letters* was published by Viking Press in 1969, a year after Steinbeck's death. It was compiled, however, during 1951 when Steinbeck was writing *East of Eden*. A compendium of daily letters to his editor and diarylike observations centering on the progress of his work on *East of Eden*, the posthumously published journal, which he called a "log," was billed as a memorial to Steinbeck.

4. John Steinbeck, *The Acts of King Arthur and His Noble Knights*, from the Winchester Manuscripts of Thomas Malory and Other Sources, ed. Chase Horton (New York: Farrar, Straus & Giroux, 1976). From the introduction.

5. *Ibid.*

6. In 1912 automobiles were still few and far between in Salinas. Almost every family of means had its own horses and carriages, and many of those without means would still get around on horseback. John's father maintained a brace of handsome carriage horses at a neighborhood stable, and they were the Steinbecks' primary mode of transportation.

7. John Steinbeck, *Travels with Charley in Search of America* (New York: Viking Press, 1962).

8. Valjean, *Errant Knight*, p. 40.

9. A year or so later, when he was a full-time but starving author, Steinbeck would mention in a letter to one of his Den of Pegasus friends that he had decided to alter the symbol of the flying horse to one of a winged pig with its feet firmly rooted to the ground. "I find that I am more Pigasus than Pegasus," he lamented, "a lumbering soul but trying to fly." To another he remarked that his new symbol aptly summed up the progress of his career: "Not enough wingspread but plenty of intention." Indeed, Steinbeck became so fond of the pig symbol that he used it throughout his life as an ironic talisman.

10. *Steinbeck: Letters*, p. 7.

11. John Steinbeck, "The Making of a New Yorker," *New York Times Magazine*, 1 February 1953.

12. Valjean, *Errant Knight*, p. 102.

13. Note the identicality of La Santa Roja's characterization of Morgan in the novel with Steinbeck's description of his feelings about the book in his letter to Duke Sheffield in early 1928, just after he finished the manuscript, quoted on page 121.

14. *Steinbeck: Letters*, p. 18.

15. *Ibid.*, p. 30.

16. *Ibid.*, p. 39.

17. *Ibid.*, p. 106.

18. Steinbeck's younger sister, then Mrs. Mary Dekker, had two children. On visits to Salinas during Olive Steinbeck's illness, the Dekker children had driven their uncle to distraction with their rambunctiousness.

19. Covici, Friede was trying to acquire the publishing rights to this and *The Pastures of Heaven*, with a view to reissuing them.

20. Of such misunderstandings are personal feuds born. Based on his 1936 misreading, Steinbeck railed against Mary McCarthy and her writing talents whenever he could for the rest of his life. I once witnessed a loud encounter between Steinbeck and Mary McCarthy's brother, the actor Kevin McCarthy in the early 1960s. It was evident that Steinbeck still had little use for Mary McCarthy.

21. John Steinbeck, *Of Mice and Men*, in *The Portable Steinbeck*, ed. Pascal Covici, Jr. (New York: Viking Press, 1971), pp. 227–228.

22. Wallace Ford as George the itinerant ranch hand, Broderick Crawford as his dim-witted sidekick Lennie, and Claire Luce as the pivotal woman character known only as "Curley's Wife" were the three actors chosen for the leading roles.

23. The suit was eventually dismissed.

24. Steinbeck ended the novel suddenly with a scene in which one of the Joad girls, after undergoing a stillbirth, feeds a starved and dying man, a stranger, from her breast. The symbolism is powerful, but it is arbitrary in relation to the prior narrative. Viking Press felt that Steinbeck would be overly criticized for engaging in gratuitous sexual sensationalism.

25. *Steinbeck: Letters*, p. 178.

26. The question of Steinbeck's motivation in ending *The Grapes of Wrath* as abruptly as he did remains open to interpretation. It was reported by members of his family after his death that he had on several occasions admitted to having ended the novel at the point that he did because his back agonies prevented him from writing any further.

27. Teleology is the study of evidence that points to the existence of a coordinated, creative design in nature; it presumes that the existence of everything can be explained in terms of a divine or other higher purpose.

28. *Steinbeck: Letters*, p. 194.

29. *Ibid.*, p. 193.

30. *Ibid.*, p. 197.

31. In August, in anticipation of his being needed to serve during the coming war, Steinbeck began to take flying lessons at the airfield in nearby Palo Alto. Many of the friends he had made in Hollywood were doing the same thing at the Burbank airport.

32. Spencer Tracy would be blocked by Metro-Goldwyn-Mayer, the studio to which he was under contract, from doing the narration on *The Forgotten Village*. Another actor, Burgess Meredith, eventually got the job.

33. From the very beginning of their relationship, Steinbeck had playfully called Gwendolyn Conger "Gwyndolyn" in celebration of his love for the Knights of the Round Table sagas. In moments of passion he would tell her that she was the holy grail he had been searching for and was truly a damsel of legendary character. To honor the game, she began at this time to spell her name in Arthurian fashion as Gwyndolyn, and immediately became known as Gwyn. This has been Gwyn's version of recent years. Others who knew the couple at the time, however, claim that she changed the spelling of her name after visiting a numerologist, and that it had nothing to do with John's love of the Arthurian legends.

34. He once hinted that he had been personally asked by Mrs. Roosevelt, if not to support the Japanese roundup, at least not to speak out against it. The implication was that he complied because he thought he might receive an important post in the war effort. *Steinbeck: Letters.*

35. *Lifeboat* would not be released for almost a year. Unknown to John, Hitchcock would hire a succession of other writers to doctor the script and lighten the uncompromising bleakness of the story. Steinbeck would be angered by the changes when he saw the movie a year later and would fire off letters of protest to MGM, demanding that his name be removed from the credits as the author.

36. John Steinbeck, *Cannery Row* (New York: Viking Press, 1945), chapter 15.

37. *Ibid.*

38. Steinbeck often explained that he had written *Cannery Row* as a way of diverting himself from the oppressiveness of World War II. It is more likely that he wrote it, as I have suggested, out of his residual anger at Carol and his expanding realization that he was in for the same problems with his second wife. Whatever the reason, the novel has proved to be one of Steinbeck's three or four most literarily accomplished in its fusion of storytelling and meaning.

39. E. W. Tedlock, Jr. and C. V. Wicker, eds., *Steinbeck and His Critics: A Record of Twenty-five Years* (Albuquerque: University of New Mexico Press, 1957).

40. *Steinbeck: Letters,* p. 339.

41. *Ibid.,* p. 343.

42. *Ibid.,* p. 349.

43. *Ibid.,* p. 400.

44. John Steinbeck, "Critics, Critics, Burning Bright," *Saturday Review of Literature,* 11 November 1950, pp. 20–21.

45. *Steinbeck: Letters,* p. 414.

46. *Ibid.,* p. 431.

47. The public refused to go along. It took the book seriously, at least as literary entertainment of a significant sort. A later movie based on the book, made by Elia Kazan and starring yet another immensely magnetic actor, James Dean, swelled the public's appreciation of Steinbeck. The novel is today treated as somewhat of a classic and is studied intently in high school and college literature courses. Kazan managed to get Steinbeck a twenty-five-percent participation in the movie's profits. All in all, *East of Eden* proved to be a major financial boon to its author.

48. *Steinbeck: Letters,* p. 474.

49. *Ibid.,* p. 497.

50. *Ibid.,* p. 496.

51. The tutor was a recent Columbia University graduate by the name of Terrence McNally. An aspiring playwright, he had been admitted to the playwrights' group at the Actors Studio, which was run by Elia Kazan's wife, Molly. She recommended McNally to the Steinbecks.

INDEX